How to Live with an Idiot

Clueless Creatures and the

People Who Love Them

By

John Hoover

CAREER
PRESS
Franklin Lakes, NJ

HOW TO LIVE WITH AN IDIOT
EDITED AND TYPESET BY KRISTEN PARKES
Cover design by Lu Rossman/Digi Dog Design
Printed in the U.S.A. by Book-mart Press

ComposiTeam is a registered trademark of Valenti & Hoover, LLC

To order this title, please call toll-free 1-800-CAREER-1 (NJ and Canada: 201-848-0310) to order using VISA or MasterCard, or for further information on books from Career Press.

CAREER
PRESS

The Career Press, Inc., 3 Tice Road, PO Box 687,
Franklin Lakes, NJ 07417
www.careerpress.com

Library of Congress Cataloging-in-Publication Data

Hoover, John, 1952-
    How to live with an idiot : clueless creatures and the people who love them / by John Hoover.
        p. cm.
    Includes index.
    ISBN 1-56414-770-3 (paper)
    1. Interpersonal relations. I. Title.

HM1111.H67 2005
302—dc22

2004054470

To my mother, Ruth Schultz Hoover, whose brilliant editorial prowess delights my publisher. She loves a recovering idiot son as only a mother and his Higher Power can.

Thanks, Mom.

Acknowledgments

I once again credit my publisher, Ron Fry and his staff, for having the courage to step outside the box—and twist the lens—on the zany world of idiots at work and play. My sister, Ann Graziano, worked tirelessly to keep me editorially honest. She also reminded me constantly that this book isn't intended to help recovering idiots like me. It's intended to help the rest of the world learn to grin and bear recovering idiots like me. Dr. Beth Hoover Langhorst, also my sister, lent expert psychological advice and gently reminded me that whatever mental health credentials I had before will be forever suspect after this book is released. My Career Press editors, Michael Lewis and Kristen Parkes, are ultimately responsible for the lucid content, yet wish to disavow any suggestion they might agree in principle with anything I've written.

Contents

Introduction

If you're buying *How to Live with an Idiot* to throw across the room at your spouse, significant other, sibling, child, parent, friend, coffee-counter clerk, coworker, boss, or anyone else you've determined is too clueless for words, please, close the book, put it back on the shelf (face out, if you don't mind), and back away slowly. I don't want to be the author of the first literary assault weapon. If you're hoping to discover a way to live with the significant idiots in your life in a more tolerant and forgiving atmosphere, proceed to the cash register.

Reading this book may help you accomplish one or more of the following:

⇨ You could emerge with a kinder, gentler attitude
   toward clueless creatures.

⇨ Your kinder, gentler attitude could give the clueless
   creature(s) in your life incentive and tacit permission
   to become *less* clueless.

⇨ You could discover that you're a clueless creature who
   shouldn't be pointing fingers (oops).

⇨ Your new attitude could make you serenely unaffected
   by cluelessness, no matter where it comes from.

Many people tell me that living with idiots is frustrating because clueless creatures don't *get it*. Idiots haven't a clue, I'm told, as to what makes their partners happy. This brings two questions to mind. Do we know what makes our significant idiots happy? (I mean, *really* know?) Does our happiness depend on them? (I mean, *really* depend on them?) Relationships are difficult. Nothing in this book will make them easy.

People have been trying to find a way to change the *other* people in relationships for as long as eccentric inventors have been trying to invent the perpetual-motion machine. No progress to report on either, as far as I know. We can't take other people's medicine for them. I wish we *could* take the pills, swallow the syrup, do the exercises, join a group, and go to therapy to make *them* treat *us* the way we want to be treated. But, we can't. Not directly, anyway.

You can take the pills, swallow the syrup, do the exercises, join a group, go to therapy, and make *yourself* feel better. When you feel better, everything feels better. Not perfect, but *better*. The more okay you feel about who you are, the more okay you are with who everybody else is.

It sounds simple. It is and it's not. *How to Live with an Idiot* is about emotionally enabling yourself to feel good in relationships; particularly relationships that haven't turned out the way you had hoped. The folks on the other side of those relationships will need to decide what they're going to do and how they want to feel. When you start to change, your spouse, significant other, siblings, children, parents, friends, auto mechanics, coworkers, bosses, or whomever, might like it. They might not. You must decide if—for you—it's worth stirring the pot.

A friend of mine described the popularity of *How to Work for an Idiot: Survive and Thrive Without Killing Your Boss* (Career Press, 2003) by saying, "We all like our medicine to taste good." This pithy observation presumes that we feel the need to take medicine in the first place. To this day, despite an avalanche of pop psychology and mood-management medications, a psychologist's ability to change a lightbulb still depends on the lightbulb's willingness to change.

The response from *How to Work for an Idiot* readers who *got it* and reported positive changes in their sense of purpose, perspective, fulfillment, and satisfaction at work indicates there are a lot of lightbulbs out there willing, and eager, to change. One woman, who spotted the book in the Feltrinelli bookstore in Rome, wrote to tell me she read it twice in the first 48 hours after her purchase and had become a "...less harassed radiologist since reading your book." She closed her e-mail with, "complimenti."

How many arguably clueless authors such as myself get a "complimenti"? At last, my 12-step program for recovering idiots is beginning to pay international dividends. While Señora radiologist might have appreciated the sugar coating on my medicine, I get a sense that she was sufficiently motivated to improve her working conditions— sugar-coated or not.

The greater the motivation, the more discomfort people will endure to achieve a positive outcome. How willing and eager are *you* to change? This medicine is intentionally light-hearted, but proven to work, if taken properly. It seems every advertised diet pill or supplement disclaims, "This product works best when combined with a change in eating habits and exercise." Duh. Any effort to live a rewarding life despite idiot-ism requires a change in habits and attitude, as well as persistence and infinite patience.

Nobody said hard work can't be fun and rewarding. How badly do you want to be a "less harassed" spouse, significant other, sibling, child, parent, friend, coffee-counter clerk, coworker, boss, or person at-large? This could be your opportunity. Enjoy the medicine.

PART I

GETTING TO KNOW YOUR IDIOT

Chapter 1

Idiots Exposed

"MY NAME IS JOHN. I'M AN IDIOT." That's how I introduce myself at recovery meetings in the basement of the Methodist church on Thursday nights. I'm not just a garden-variety idiot, I'm a *recovering* idiot. I've admitted my powerlessness, that my life has become unmanageable, and it will take a Power greater than me to overcome my cluelessness.

We wanted to call our recovery group Idiots Anonymous out of respect for the life-transforming potential of traditional 12-step programs. However, our idiotic antics make us anything *but* anonymous. Other people seem to be aware of our idiotic thoughts and actions long before we realize there's anything wrong. So, we decided to call ourselves Idiots Exposed, or IE for short.

Because I'm your tour guide for this excursion into the workings of the idiot mind, I'll give you a peek inside my own mind. Our mantra at IE is "Once an idiot, always an idiot." We recovering idiots never dare to think we're cured, completely out of the woods, or somehow immune to the destructive potential of our idio-t-syncracies.

At any given moment on any given day we have the ability to think right thoughts and do right things. However, as idiots, it's within our essential natures to think and do dumb things without receiving mental, on-screen error messages. Such is the nature of cluelessness. Our special talent for thinking we're doing smart things when the negative consequences of doing dumb things are obvious to even a water buffalo is part of what makes us idiots. As recovering idiots, we know we're only one thought away from a relapse. It's sobering.

Many people find the word "idiot" offensive. It's a term of endearment only to those of us who find inspiration in the strength and honesty of our fellow recovering idiots. Yet, for so many to bristle and recoil at the mere mention of the word, it must touch a nerve. Methinks they protest a bit much. But that would be judging on my part, a recovery no-no.

The Open Hand

When tempted to commit a recovery no-no, I've learned to take a moment, close my eyes, open my hand, release the thought, and let it go. There's a difference between *releasing* something and *letting it go*. A sleight-of-hand trick newcomers to recovery pick up is to release a troubling thought, then snatch it back before it gets out of reach. It's frightening to say "good-bye" to dumb thinking and behaviors that have become near and dear to us over the years.

Only later in the recovery process, after much practice, can we truly release a self-destructive or *get even* thought. As jittery and palm-perspiring as it can make us, we will nevertheless develop the ability to serenely watch it float away and dissipate. I made up a song for just such occasions (sung to the holiday melody "Let It Snow!"):

> Oh, judging won't make folks like you.
> In fact, they might despise you.
> Give yourself a chance to grow,
> Let it go, let it go, let it go.

Humor: It's Not Just for Breakfast Anymore

I sing similar verses so often, on every topic from anger to denial, I need only skip to the "Let it go, let it go, let it go," for full effect. Seem trivial? There's nothing trivial about humor when you're troubled or frustrated. If you're not frustrated, then you'll appreciate the frolic. Open your hand. Let it go. Poof. If you started laughing when you read the title of this book, the stage is set to have some fun and, at the same time, do personal fine-tuning as you deal with the significant idiot(s) in your life, be they your spouse, civil partner, children, parents, in-laws, friends, clients, bosses, coworkers, or all of the above.

Sigmund Freud said that laughter is a release of energy. I'll go further and say that laughter releases toxic gases, which, if not released, become increasingly combustible until downright ugly things begin to happen. George Bernard Shaw wrote: "Life does not cease to be funny when someone dies, as it does not cease to be serious when people laugh."

The humor therapy movement, inspired by former *Saturday Review* editor Norman Cousins in his book *Anatomy of an Illness as Perceived by the Patient* (Bantam, 1991) makes a compelling case for the importance of laughter in the healing process. If worrying and fretting can make us physically ill, I believe laughter will contribute to emotional and physical healing. Laughing itself does not heal cancer any more than laughing in an idiot's face will engender a more congenial and copacetic relationship.

Although it's not easy to learn to laugh if you've had little to laugh about, laughter nonetheless brings a fresh perspective. The chicken vs. egg, "You're an idiot," "No, you're an idiot," discussion suggests that laughter might be as much an *indicator* of a healthy perspective as it is the *cause* of a healthy perspective. Generous amounts of laughter are essential to a healthy, hopeful lifestyle—*as long as the first laugh is at our own expense.*

Laughing at my own idio-t-syncracies is the same as saying, "I mean you no harm. Can't we all just get along?" The same holds true in relationships with significant idiots, parents, siblings, children, friends, coworkers, bosses, and in-laws. By humor, I'm not talking about gratuitous and pointless comedic comments such as, "I have dental floss and I'm not afraid to use it." Finding humor in the human condition is the cure for much of what ails us. Finding humor in the suffering of others is not healthy, unless *they* fictionalize and dramatize their suffering for the purpose of tickling our funny bones, like the Three Stooges, in which case they are giving us the gift of laughter. I don't recall a time when I didn't feel that humor was a high calling.

If no smile comes to your face when you see the title *How to Live with an Idiot*, I will worry. "Idiot" is a term often born and expressed in anger, but saying it aloud has a certain cleansing effect, especially when it is part of a personal confession. Sometimes it takes getting a little riled to launch a search for solutions. I've found that people who laugh at the word "idiot" and gladly apply it to their own circumstances are most open to solutions.

Humorless people too often allow toxic gasses to compound until immense pressure blows the lid off the container. In social, family, and romantic relationships, we often think open or covert hostility will bring about a satisfactory solution. But how often do we think of giving the healing power of humor a chance?

People with perfect partners probably won't purchase *How to Live with an Idiot*. But their perfect partners might give them a copy as a self-deprecating gesture of good faith and humor. How cute and clever would it be for a significant idiot to imitate the perfect partner by giving this book as a gift? A healthy sense of humor is a characteristic of a well-balanced human being. We recovering idiots try to exercise our funny bones every chance we get. It's part of the healing.

Looking Ahead

We idiots, recovering or not, have limited random access memories. This explains, in part, why we lack consciousness about how our words and deeds affect other people. So, we make lists that can, like the 12 steps and traditions we follow, bring a sense of order to our otherwise chaotic lives.

As you've already figured out, I'm setting the stage by introducing you to the world of relationships through the eyes of an idiot. It's a perspective that might surprise you, but don't be alarmed if the view from here begins to look vaguely familiar. There is an *inner idiot* in all of us. Sometimes it's small and insignificant. Sometimes it's huge and funny-looking. Sometimes it's docile, and sometimes ferocious. Sometimes it remains hidden in the far reaches of our psyches. Sometimes it's up-front and in our faces.

We're all probably closer to understanding and empathizing with our significant idiots than we realize. As we become more familiar with what the world looks like through the eyes of idiots, living with one or more of them becomes easier. (Just because I'm a recovering idiot doesn't mean I don't have to deal with other idiots in my life.) As you get in touch with your inner idiot and apply the recovery principles of Idiots Exposed, one or more of the following things will happen:

1. You will change your outlook and expectations of the idiots in your life.

2. Your significant idiot will respond positively to the new you with agreeable attitudes and behaviors.

3. Your significant idiot will respond negatively to the new you with disagreeable attitudes and behaviors.

4. Your changed outlook and expectations will render the idiot's disagreeable attitudes and behaviors powerless to upset you.

If all you do is number one, life will be much more pleasant. If number two happens, sing hallelujah! If numbers one and four happen, you'll probably never notice or care much if number three happens at all. The caveat I mentioned in the introduction bears repeating: This book doesn't contain secret methods and techniques for changing the idiots in your life. It's about reinventing *yourself*, and thereby making you immune to the frustrations of their idio-t-syncracies. As we say in the Methodist church basement on Thursday nights, "It's not them, it's me." If the idiots change as a result of what you do, it's the hand of your Higher Power at work, not you.

Here's my disclaimer: people should be so lucky. If you can manage to get someone else to change in a positive way without first changing your own habits and attitudes, you should rush down to the 7-Eleven and buy a lottery ticket because it's your lucky day. It can happen. I won't say it can't. Some people win the lottery. But the odds are more in your favor if you go about it the old-fashioned way.

Investing in our own personal growth virtually guarantees a jackpot, if we're willing to stick with it long enough. Even if we entice our significant idiot(s) to the edge of the healing waters, somebody has to step in first. Ideally, all would step in together. But waiting for our significant idiots to take the leap before we do only holds back our progress. Haven't we waited long enough? It's time to get wet *now*.

The road to serenity in idiot city begins in Chapter 3 with an introduction to Dr. John's six categories of humanity. Each of us operates out of one or more of the six categories. This new context takes the conversation beyond simple idiot-ism in a hurry. Fret not. These are not clinical categories. This book, after all, is called *How to Live with an Idiot*. The medicine is intended to be as good-tasting as possible, while still containing active ingredients.

I've chosen to use animals to represent certain characteristics in some cases, so have a lint roller handy. Attributing human attitudes and behaviors to animals and other natural phenomena makes the attitudes and behaviors feel less threatening. A warm, fuzzy truth is just as true as the cold, hard truth, so that's why our furry friends get into the act.

In the chapters ahead, taking a fresh peek at the world through the eyes of an idiot, each of the six categories will be examined in the context of seven (deadly) relational sins. Granted, every reader can probably name a multitude of relational sins I don't have on my list. Seven is sort of a biblical number. Besides, why should I have more sins to deal with than Stephen R. Covey has habits of highly success- ful people?

Each relational sin is paired with a relational *solution*. I'd never take anything away without offering something better to take its place. This is my displacement theory. Good things (solutions) dislodge bad things (sins) because they can't occupy the same space at the same time. It's as simple as that. Every chapter contains at least two sec- tions called "Keys to living with an idiot."

Keys to living with an idiot

⇨ **Practice patience.** You will recognize idiotic behavior in oth- ers before they do—if they do at all. Frustration is usually self-induced. Take a deep breath, count to 10, and wait it out. Open your hands and sing, "Let it go, let it go, let it go." Idiots usually know not what they do. Is intervening worth it? Will your frustration change anything except your own blood pressure? Unless it's important enough to teach a pig to sing, let it go.

⇨ **Anticipate.** Forewarned is forearmed. Significant idiots are never far from an annoying blunder. Anticipation avoids knee- jerk reactions. At the first sign, try suggesting alternative behavior or take the softer Socratic approach and say, "Re- member what happened the last time you (fill in the blank)." Anticipating can merely be a way to protect yourself. If the idiot has a habit of lighting the gas burner on the stove with a match rather than fixing the pilot light, you can save your own eyebrows with the duck-and-cover maneuver.

⇨ **Calm yourself.** If the title of this book brought a laugh, or even a smirk, there is hope. If not, you may be experiencing pre-traumatic stress disorder anticipating your significant idiot's next blunder. You can sit quietly, turn up the corners of your mouth in the Buddha smile, and hold the smile while you breathe. Your diaphragm should expand with each breath. Think "Idiot," "Idiot," "Idiot," with each exhale. Smiling like Buddha and exhaling the idiots from your life, you should be smiling for real at about the 12th "Idiot."

The Initial Argument

"This is nonsense, John," says Shirley, my fictitious alter ego.

I'm not Shirley's therapist, even fictitiously. We're both regulars at Idiots Exposed, and engage each other in the typical post-meeting chat on the sidewalk outside the Methodist church. As IE buddies, we have granted each other *permission to speak freely.*

"What do you find so difficult to swallow?" I ask, implying that the sugar coating on my medicine isn't sweet enough.

"I didn't cause my (fill in the blank with spouse's, parents', in-laws', siblings', or significant other's) misery," she shoots back. "And I can't fix them."

"I couldn't agree more," I say. "Why would I, of all people, suggest you're responsible for another person's feelings?"

"Because my significant idiot is making my life miserable," Shirley explains. "And I already know you're going to tell me that my happiness is my responsibility."

"No more entries please," I say. "We have a winner."

"So, I'm right?"

"No," I reply. "I mean, yes *and* no. You're half right, but you can't have it both ways."

"Which part can't I have?"

"The part about them being the cause of your unhappiness."

"Well," she says indignantly. "They are."

"Break this down with me," I invite with calm deliberateness. I've been stuck in this wicket before. "If you refuse to claim responsibility for their unhappiness, which I agree you shouldn't, how can you pin responsibility for *your* unhappiness on *them*? Hmmmm?"

"Simple," Shirley retorts. "I'm right and they're wrong."

"You're in quicksand here," I warn. "Stop wiggling so hard."

"Hold on, John," she warns, raising her index finger for emphasis. "If they would just think, say, and do what I tell them to think, say, and do, my unhappiness would be over in a minute. Theirs would be, too."

"It must be very frustrating when others refuse to acknowledge that you know better," I sympathize with all due sarcasm. But it's too late. Shirley can't hear me. She's disappeared beneath the quicksand. The conversation is over. I tried to warn her, but she clung to her belief that the solution to another's unhappiness was the same as whatever would end hers. She clutched her belief all the way down to wherever quicksand goes down to.

Looking in the Mirror and Saying, "Glad I don't look like that."

Even if my example is too on the nose, shouldn't we all be glad we're not like Shirley? We are more sensible than to think we actually have that kind of power over others. Aren't we? I admit it would be *nice* if significant idiots lived according to our rules, but trying to pull that off by coercion, manipulation, and/or edict would only end in frustration and resentment—*our* frustration and resentment.

It wasn't too long ago that I believed similar idiot-isms. I would have denied having a hidden agenda all the way to the bottom of the quicksand pit. And I nearly did. I can appreciate the ire with which some readers will respond when I suggest the only hope for their happiness and serenity is to shoulder the responsibility for change and to exercise tolerance and empathy in relationships. Put another way, if you and I are going to feel any better about our relationships, it won't be because somebody else changed.

It would be great if your partner, parents, children, pets, bosses, and bowling buddies suddenly became obsessed with shouldering responsibility for their part in a healthy relationship. But what's the chance of that? Suppose the God of your understanding decides to issue an omnipotent order that causes your significant idiot to be radically transformed before your very eyes. If you don't do the things to become a changed creature—ready, willing, and able to accept and reciprocate respect, friendship, and love—the almighty gesture will be wasted. Here's some good news: even if the significant idiot in your life remains oblivious to your transformation, you'll still feel better about yourself and your relationships.

If Idiots Didn't Exist, Would We Create Them?

Not every significant other is an idiot and not every idiot is a significant other. Idiots come in many forms and many sizes. Just because I'm letting you examine the brain of a recovering idiot doesn't mean your significant idiot is going to look or act like me. Remember, the essential characteristic of idiot-ism is cluelessness. In most cases, cluelessness is more of an annoyance and aggravation than a genuine threat to health and well-being. But it can strike without warning in devastating ways.

Automobile accidents caused by applying make-up in traffic, dialing a cellular telephone in traffic, or reaching into the backseat to rummage through a briefcase for a phone number while using cruise control will all cause temporary lapses in crucial awareness. Such lapses into idiot-ism might only last a moment. But if timed perfectly, suspending consciousness about the consequences can change lives forever.

Otherwise innocuous idiots can be dangerous—especially temporary idiots. Otherwise reasonable people occasionally believe they can get away with something "just this once." I suspect you bought this book because you feel as if you're saddled with an eternal idiot. Perhaps someone bought this book for you because he or she feels you are saddled with an eternal idiot. Or your significant idiot bought you a copy as a clumsy-yet-endearing way of apologizing and making amends for the grief you've suffered at his or her hands. Regardless of how you got your hands on this book, I'll go out on a limb here and guess that you probably don't feel your idiot problems are short term.

Good thinking. Whatever is causing cluelessness in your significant idiot didn't happen overnight. The attitude adaptations required to live a happier and more fulfilling life with this nincompoop will also take time, especially if you're a nincompoop, too. Get used to it. From here on in, what applies to the idiots in front of you applies to the idiot inside of you. You mustn't start by misdiagnosing your parents, children, friends, spouse, significant other, boss, best friend, in-laws, or whoever is playing the role of primary idiot in your life.

Leaping Into Reality

Although not much inspires significant idiots, and significant idiots do little to inspire others, an idiot is an idiot only relative to your expectations. Some might not be idiots at all. Some might find the idiot's clueless behavior adorable, even entertaining. Others might find it disgusting and irritating. The latter represents the primary audience for this book. Like so many other things in life, it's all relative—not only the cluelessness, but how you feel about it, and how you choose to respond to it.

A thinking disorder you might not even be aware of can turn reason inside out. Your perception of reality can be distorted over time and you run the risk of misinterpreting what you're dealing with. For example, pouring water on a grease fire is not a good idea. It only spreads the grease and the fire. Smothering the flames is the proper technique. Save the water for a wood or paper fire.

Accepting reality as it truly is, and thereby properly diagnosing the type of fire, is the only effective way to determine how to suppress it. Yet it is human nature to fight for your unique and often inaccurate interpretations of reality instead of using the best techniques to fight fires that singe your sensibilities. Sometimes the prospect of opening your eyes is frightening, often to the point of sabotaging any effort to embark on a liberating journey of personal growth, healing, and recovery. In other words, people resist change.

Childhood flashback: Remember when you and some friends decided to take that first terrifying leap off the high dive? You climbed the ladder, imagining yourself heroically diving, piercing the surface of the water, with the others looking on in admiration. Then you looked down. If you were the one who summoned the courage to go first, you experienced the grip of fear almost to the point of blacking out as you leapt off the edge. The squeezing sensation of fear was instantly followed by a rush of mind-clearing terror as you had no choice but to accept reality. You were in midair. No going back.

Once irrevocably committed to the act, the fear that resides mostly in your imagination, where you can embellish it, steep it, bring it to a boil, and turn it into a catastrophe, vanishes. Imagined fear can't exist in the same space as real fear. Falling through the atmosphere, you're well aware of a potentially painful moment ahead. But instead of ruminations of catastrophe in your imagination, your survival instincts are engaged. You focus like a laser on doing whatever can be done in that moment to bring about a happy ending.

All of this happens in a matter of seconds that feel like a lifetime because of the adrenaline turbo boost to the brain. In a splash, there is a sudden temperature change and the diving bird becomes a fish. What a remarkably adaptive creature you are. Even the most clueless among us might notice the droplets of water bounding skyward in contrasting motion to the swoosh of bubbles you drag under the surface.

As quickly as it started, it's over. Relief and confidence replace fear and terror. Bobbing back up to the surface, you are a veteran high-diver motioning to more timid first-timers saying, "Come on. Jump. There's nothing to it." Back on the platform, high above the water, the others hesitate, even though a trusted person affirms that the leap is not only survivable, but there is relief and exhilaration following the experience. I've played both roles in my life; the bold one or the timid and hesitant one, depending on the degree to which I allowed fear to hold me in its icy grip.

You must accept reality when contemplating improvement in personal relationships and, more fundamentally, when accepting that a relationship needs to be or can be improved. How desperately do you want to feel better? How many friends who have found greater happiness and fulfillment after taking the leap will it take to convince you to take the plunge? How much evidence do you need before you accept change can lead to a happier and more fulfilling life—idiots or no idiots?

When I'm faced with the daunting task of accepting a realistic (not defensive) assessment of relational strife and my role in it, I invoke the principles of idiot recovery and say to the other person, "You might be right," instead of automatically becoming defensive and argumentative. That simple statement leaves the door open instead of slamming it shut. That's what learning to live with an idiot is all about; creating opportunities filled with positive possibilities for you, and for the significant idiot in your life.

Keys to living with an idiot

⇨ **Learn to laugh.** Not at other people's expense or as a form of self-abuse. Healthy laughter is a hedge against taking things too seriously. Laughing at your own absurdities is like being the first off the high dive. You prove to yourself and your significant other that life is ultimately harmless. If self-deprecating humor feels alien, if you've never laughed at yourself, it's time to start practicing. If you're too bound up in anger and resentment to yuk it up once in a while, there's relief waiting on the other side of the punch line. Learning to laugh at your own idio-t-syncracies is a process you'll explore throughout this book.

⇨ **Learn to leap.** Like learning to laugh, learning to leap is a start. Making a conscious choice to venture into unfamiliar territory can be extremely intimidating and must be undertaken intentionally and intelligently to avoid placing yourself in greater turmoil. This medicine can be yucky, at least at first. But confessions to self and others plus reality checks are key to unlocking the answers you always hoped you'd find. The answers may not look the way you thought they would. Your perceptions of relationships and the roles you play can be distorted. Pray for clarity.

⇨ **Meet and greet your inner idiot.** Not the idiot you originally intended to beat over the head with this book, but your inner idiot; the part of you that resonates in synchronous simpatico with the idiots in others. First, you must locate the rascal and make a positive ID, and then the chase begins. This tricky character, who has managed to avoid detection to this point, will run even faster now, in a serpentine pattern. None of the aforementioned self-deprecating laughter or boldness will be genuine (and thereby helpful) until you admit and accept your role in whatever is bothering you.

Chapter Summary

This is a book about living with the significant idiot in your life, as told from the idiot's point of view. Even as an enlightened, recovering idiot, my essential cluelessness is like a torn fish net. Much slips through. Take it in stride. Keep it in perspective. Humor is your friend. You must learn to use it in healthy ways.

Try to find a way to laugh at the sometimes misguided ways things are handled. There isn't much humor in a perfect relationship. See how lucky you are? "Honey," she said. "We might not be the perfect couple. But we're always good for a laugh." When we're close to perfection, just smile contentedly and breathe a big sigh of relief. But if you're like me, there's a barrel of laughs hiding behind the bucket of tears we tend to cry when things don't go our way.

Do not cling to assumptions (like Shirley did) and let them pull you down when you can open yourself to new ideas. Be willing to refurbish old ones. Practice patience. Give yourself a break from the craziness that living with an idiot can become. You can anticipate behavior you know is likely to be repeated. It will save you the trouble of being surprised and disappointed all over again. You can test yourself to keep track of where you've been and whether you're making strides in living a healthier existence with the significant idiot in your life.

Laugh, leap, and meet your inner idiot. Once you begin to make laughter a conscious and intentional part of your daily routine, it becomes easier to keep a more realistic perspective. With a more practical and less catastrophic outlook, you will start to take risks you've never taken before. Venturing into uncharted waters is never a stroll on the beach, but it will become easier.

As you more confidently step into healing waters, you-know-who might do a cannonball right behind you. It will be childlike, noisy, and you'll end up drenched, but at least your idiot is in the water. If you connect with that wee, small part of yourself that would also like to do a cannonball, the pressure begins to ease between you and the significant idiot in your life.

To-do list:

☑ Practice patience.

☑ Anticipate.

☑ Calm yourself.

☑ Learn to laugh.

☑ Learn to leap.

☑ Meet and greet your inner idiot.

Chapter 2

Through the Eyes
of an Idiot

PERHAPS IT'S BEST TO THINK OF ME as an example of before, during, and after—unconscious idiot-ism became conscious idiot-ism followed by a lot of healthy new behaviors. Idiot recovery runs on a big loop. When learning how to live with an idiot, the loop starts with learning how your idiot perceives him- or herself in the context of his or her personal realities. Luckily, this book is written by a recovering idiot who is okay with who he is. Before we're finished, you'll be well versed in idiot-speak.

A dog who thinks he's a cat will ultimately be harder to deal with than a dog that's okay with what he is. Hampered by lack of a common language with animals, we might never get the chance to fully explore the question. Yet, in many ways, you face a parallel dilemma with your significant idiot.

Gender-ism and Animal-ism

Men and women have been compared to dogs and cats since ancient Egypt—probably before. Dogs, as I interpret the species, are more or less tuned out of the big picture and find great delight in small pleasures. I envy dogs. Similarly, the essential characteristic of clueless creatures, great and small, is a limited to nonexistent awareness of how their words and actions affect others. Most dogs, despite certain idio-t-syncratic behaviors are, for the most part, harmless, friendly, well intentioned, and even sentimental.

They are, nonetheless, essentially clueless when it comes to social graces. Their marvelous sensibilities in other areas, such as detecting illness and danger long before medical science or your own radar picks up a blip, are especially endearing.

The worst thing you can do to other humans is misdiagnose cluelessness and use idiot intervention techniques on non-idiots. Treating people with certain other personality disorders, such as narcissism, as idiots could cause more trouble than you care to deal with. There is always hope that an innocuously clueless idiot might someday, somehow catch a clue. My fellow recovering idiots and I are living proof of that.

Speaking of misdiagnosis, cats are shrewd, strategic, calculating, and callous big-picture thinkers who are completely committed to the satisfaction of self. Truthfully, so are dogs; only on a smaller scale and strictly in the moment. Dogs also think happiness comes from pleasing the dog owner, a twisted perspective by which they abdicate an immense amount of power that no self-respecting cat would ever part with. Cats understand power and know how to use it. Any recovering idiot worth his or her battle scars knows loud purring from a cat rubbing against him or her is a siren's song of exploitation and manipulation. Never let it be said of a cat, "But, she loves me."

That's one of the reasons people say that dogs have masters and cats have servants. If people aren't the cats' servants, why do they clean cats' toilets? People expect their children to be operating independently in that arena by the time they're 3 years old. To those who think dogs are as intelligent and shrewd as cats, why are cats allowed to relieve themselves in the house while the dog has to go out in the rain and snow?

I know a fellow and his wife who have a cat and a dog, and they play the appropriate (servant/master) role for each animal. In the marriage, the husband doesn't even try to pull the lord and master routine, bless his heart. As a result, both husband and wife are quite content. A man trying to play lord and master of a happy home is as laughable as a dog trying to play lord and master to a cat living under the same roof.

Keys to living with an idiot

⇨ **Ask the animal question.** What animal does your significant idiot remind you of, and would you have one for a pet? Doing a stream of conscious exercise and naming the first critter that comes to mind when thinking of your spouse, significant other, siblings, children, parents, in-laws, friends, bosses, or coworkers will tell you at least three things. First, is this other person likeable in his or her present state? Second, is it truly his or her behavior over time or your accumulated bias that led you to choose his or her alter animal? Third, which of you is higher on the food chain, you or the idiot? The animal you associate with other people says as much about you as it does about them.

⇨ **Ask a denial-piercing question.** If living with an idiot is problematic, is the behavior that annoys you the exception or the rule? That is a denial-piercing question. Think before answering. Admitting that the idiot annoys you most of the time can make you wonder how and why you got involved to begin with. If you hate alligators and other belly-crawling reptiles, and yet that's how you categorize your significant idiot, why are you with that person? Are you looking for a pair of alligator boots? Could that person really be a fuzzy bunny and you merely need to clean your glasses? Probably not.

⇨ **Qualify your information.** My criteria for seeking feedback and guidance in most things is twofold: (1) Has my mentor/counselor experienced similar circumstances? (2) Has my mentor/counselor grown as a person because of it? If the answer to number one is yes and number two is no, you might find yourself just swapping miseries. Yes to both questions means you can trust the information you're getting—and it probably won't come in the form of advice. It will be shared experiences. How are you perceiving the significant idiot in your life? How are you perceiving yourself? Mentors and counselors, caring friends, fellow group members, or anyone without a dog in your fight can lend objectivity in a safe environment. Who to trust is ultimately a personal issue. However, getting outside feedback about what you're going through can be the difference between change for the better or same old, same old.

Rescuing, Reality Check, Recovery

The Student Becomes the Teacher

I hope you didn't think I would let Shirley languish in the bottom of the quicksand pit. I live for heroic moments. I tied a rope to a tree, the other end to my waist, dove in the quicksand, and fished around until I found her. She wrapped her arm around my neck, and I pulled us to safety moments before she strangled me.

"What took you so long?" she gasps as we sprawl on the ground, covered with quicksand.

"That's it?" I ask in amazement. "No 'Thank you for jumping in and rescuing me'?"

"Is that why you did it?" she asks right back. "To get an attaboy?"

She had me there. I've been a rescuer for so long, I've stopped asking *why*. "You might be right," I sigh half-heartedly.

"Well," she continues. "It's a good thing you did it or I'd be dead. So, thank you."

That seemed appropriate under the circumstances, regardless of my intentions.

"You're welcome."

This happens to me quite a bit. Not the quicksand, but being corrected and/or enlightened by the person I think I'm helping. No matter how often wisdom more profound than my own comes when I least expect it, from people I least expect it from, I'm still amazed how arrogant I can be as to think I'm the only one who can be a conduit for enlightenment. I work with people all the time who are bound up in issues the likes of which Houdini couldn't escape from, and, in the middle of their turmoil, those I'm helping end up teaching me something about myself. We should welcome good ideas wherever we encounter them. And we should embrace the truth, whoever speaks it.

Denial Cinema:
Turning Snapshots Into Epic Motion Pictures

Outside the field of psychological research, ordinary people, such as you and me, don't seem to conduct many longitudinal studies on relationships. That doesn't stop people from constantly trying to fix or tinker with them. People often seem to have short memories, even though they know at some level that behavior over time is the best indicator of an individual's true motivations and predictor of future behavior. I often encounter people who act surprised, hurt, or angry that a friend, sibling, spouse, parent, child, coworker, or boss behaved in a certain way.

My first question is, "When has this person acted any other way?"

Nine times out of 10 I'm told, "Well, never, I guess." Or, "There was that time in 1989...."

I don't even need to know the offending party. It's that predictable. Memory loss is not the problem here. We all have ways that we *want* our friends, siblings, spouses, parents, children, coworkers, or bosses to behave. When they behave in a manner contrary to our desires, we act surprised and wave it off. We call it the exception, not the rule, when in fact it's quite the opposite.

It's much easier to spot when you're not the person engaged in the denial. When I encounter someone acting in their usual fashion, and a friend of theirs, spouse, boss, or whomever says, "Gee, (s)he's never acted like that before," I cast my eyes skyward in a prayer for the one in denial and sigh to comfort myself. Even as I witness such denial taking place, I know I'm just as likely to commit the same act when I least expect it and my denial will be as transparent to others as theirs is to me.

When others act in a way that pleases us, even if they only demonstrate pleasing behavior 10 percent of the time (if that much), we tend to say, "That's the (fill in the blank with spouse, significant other, sibling, child, parent, in-law, friend, or coworker) I know and love."

This tendency to make your wants the rule and disappointments the exception just seems to come naturally; even if the good or acceptable behavior only takes place once in a blue moon. Those dealing with a difficult person might capture moments when he or she is behaving nicely (perhaps when sleeping), snap a mental picture of the tranquility, and create a continuous loop for themselves. That way they can watch the continuous loop and pretend they're in a perfect relationship. It's a neat trick if they could pull it off. Eventually, though, the film wears through and snaps.

The View From the I-zone

If you can accept that a snapshot is just a snapshot, you're on your way to recovery. Although an idiot is just an idiot, they do have good moments. To make more of the good moments you have with your significant idiot, consider what recovery looks like for him or her. Just as Shirley taught me a thing or two when I least expected it, you can learn from the significant idiot in your life.

Those of us who proudly call ourselves Recovering Idiots began our recovery journey by accepting how cluelessness makes our lives unmanageable. We'll never achieve perfection, but faithful adherence to the process will make us easier to tolerate as we work day by day to get a clue and exit the idiot zone. That's good news for those who are desperately seeking a happier and more fulfilling way to live with us. They don't want to arbitrarily dismiss us, but there's only so much a person can take.

There are many groups for treating codependent thinking disorders like the one I struggle with, such as Adult Children of Alcoholics, Al-Anon, and Co-Dependents Anonymous among them. (See *www.stanice.com/links.html* for a list of about 100.) Some claim that self-destructive behaviors—extreme and excessive exercise, eating, not eating, spending money, shoplifting, sex, gambling, working, not working, and abuse of alcohol and other substances people sniff, snort, shoot, or smoke to self-medicate—are merely symptoms. To be successful, recovery programs must ultimately deal with the poor judgment that leads to these behaviors.

"-Isms"

You've no doubt noticed by now that there are many "-isms" in recovery lexicon. Although we at Idiots Exposed have learned to value actions more than words, it helps to have the vocabulary to discuss the skills and behaviors we know we must employ once we stop talking about them. All recovering people make up new "-isms" when the mood strikes. When I add the suffix "-ism" to the end of a word, it feels like I'm exposing a little secret and dragging it out of the dark recesses of my psyche into the light of day. There I can tackle it.

Think-ism

I agree that success over time probably depends on reframing the corrupted cognition that has ceased to function properly. Zig Ziglar calls it "stinkin' thinkin'." But, as every recovering relationship junkie has heard a thousand times, you can't think your way into right behavior. Right behavior begets right thinking. If thinking could cause miracles to happen, I would have won the lottery, been elected president, married Markie Post, and cured cancer before I was 35.

To recovering idiots like me who once believed we could outsmart our more sinister angels, this is a bitter pill to swallow. It's difficult to accept that the same intellectual capacity we thought could lift us above problems less enlightened people struggle with would sabotage our own happiness and ability to relate to others. At IE, we come to accept that we've out-thunk ourselves, outsmarted ourselves, and our intellectual tonic is more deadly than the disease. The Thursday night regulars say, "Our best thinking got us here."

Just Do It-ism

> "Let one therefore keep the mind pure,
> for what a man thinks, that he becomes."
>
> —The Upanishads

> "We are what we repeatedly do.
> Excellence, then, is not an act, but a habit."
>
> —Aristotle

Which is it, then? Thinking or doing? Thanks to authors such as H. Jackson Brown (*Life's Little Instruction Book* series), Robert Fulghum (*All I Really Need to Know I Learned in Kindergarten*), holy scripture, and a legion of self-help authors, the principles of successful living and right thinking are well documented and easily accessible. Your undoing is in the doing, or, more appropriately, in the *not* doing. The life-changing potential I've discovered in 12-step programs is vested in developing and *using* new skill sets.

We all know the uplifting thoughts that reflect fuller, happier lives. Heck, we've memorized most of them. We read them in daily devotionals and on calendars. We crochet them into throw pillows. But any 12-step regular will say that without doing the next right thing, then the next, and the next, one little glimmer of self-doubt can immobilize you or, worse yet, send you spiraling back into your dark and comfortable caves of self-destructive, but all-too-familiar thinking.

Contrast the words of James the apostle with the Nike slogan. James wrote that faith without works is meaningless. Nike exhorts "Just do it." Both are correct in their own way. James's comment contains the belief that action, while important, should still be informed by values, context, and overriding principles.

The advertising copywriter who came up with Nike's slogan subscribes to the Lao-tse notion ("A journey of a thousand miles...") that we can't get anywhere until we've started. That's cool, too. However, the Nike slogan leaves the door open for misuse. For many, action is first and foremost to relieve impatience. How many times have you said, "I'm bored, let's do something"? Doing anything just to be doing something is folly for children, risky business for adults, and ultimately unfulfilling.

Bottom line: Thinking alone won't change anything, and doing is best when thought out ahead of time. Still, there are some things that all the thinking and doing in the world won't change, such as someone else's attitudes and behaviors—pray for acceptance. For the things you *can* influence and change—pray for courage. In those situations, you have an obligation to yourself to invest in making things better.

The futility of attempting to control with thinking is illustrated in the Zen proverb "If we understand, things are just as they are; if we don't understand, things are just as they are." Of course, we could be equally Zen-like if we said, "If we believe O.J. is innocent of Ron and Nicole's murder, the killer is still on the street. If we believe O.J. murdered Ron and Nicole, the killer is still on the street." Either way, certain things will just be what they are, and certain people are just going to be who they are.

In stark contrast to navel gazing, consciously choosing right behaviors through optimal thinking gives wings to your best intentions. In the end, actions, not words, express your most honest intentions. We all have a belief system guiding our actions, whether we're aware of what it is or not. I created a synthetic reality that spiraled into itself for many years before it reached critical mass. And I've never experienced a more hollow feeling than accepting at long last that my best intentions produced the worst possible outcome.

With the help of my Higher Power, I've moved beyond being an average, garden-variety idiot to being an idiot willing to do the work. No longer will I be a mere weed in the garden of life, I'll be the gardener. To be specific, I'll tend *my* garden. The work, of course, is faithfully following the principles of the program I've chosen and applying the steps to all of my affairs.

That's my approach. Yours might be different. As the saying goes, "Take what you want and leave the rest." Not everyone needs to be so formalized. You can choose a program that's right for you, subscribe to a guiding philosophy, and then avail yourself of the best wisdom attainable, use your best judgment, pray hard to the God of your understanding, and then start focusing on the next right thing.

Walking Toward the Light-ism

If your significant idiot has never parked his or her butt in a metal folding chair in the Methodist church basement, there is no doubt a legion of "-isms" infesting his or her daily grind like cockroaches. One thing to be said in favor of cockroaches: they at least have the decency to stay out of sight during the daytime. Rarely do they show their ugly selves in the light, preferring to do their dastardly dirty work under the cover of darkness.

I once worked in a warehouse, and on the night shift, the lights were turned off in the break room where the communal refrigerator was located. Cockroaches were drawn to this breeding ground of countless molds, fungi, and toxic bacterial composites to forage for food. But when the lights were turned on, they scattered, running back under base molding, into cupboards, between floorboards, under the refrigerator, anywhere away from the light. Yuk.

One caveat about the cockroach metaphor: some personal demons are tougher characters than cowardly cockroaches. As a neophyte in recovery, I thought that getting my stuff out on the table and into the light of day was going to have the instant, effortless, and universal effect of switching on the light above the warehouse refrigerator. When I started sharing my character defects in group—that is, shining the light on them—my "cockroaches" didn't all scatter.

Sure, most of them did. But some of my cockroaches and I go way back. The older ones bear a stark resemblance to Tony Soprano and his goons. Instead of scattering, they stood there defiantly with their arms folded as if to say, "You want a piece of us? You're not getting rid of us that easily." Indeed, ruminating on the problem won't replace it with anything better, which brings me back to the "do it-ism."

That's a major difference and distinction between therapy and recovery. In therapy, people tend to take a flashlight and crawl into the dark caves of their psyches to peek at the bizarre and often frightening "-isms" that lurk there. In recovery, people drag their "-isms" into the light for everyone in their *fellowship of equals* to see. In most cases, they aren't nearly as frightening in the light as they were in the dark. Taking positive steps to get what's inside outside is the primary agenda of group work. It's almost always helpful. I've never known the recovery process to harm someone or exacerbate bad behavior. Some people claim it has saved their lives, marriages, families. To each his or her own.

Fake ID-ism

One of my character defects that didn't run away in the light of day was a false self-image. If I multiply myself by the number of relationships I tried to base on a false identity, the result is consistently zero. Know anyone like that? If you're struggling to maintain a kind thought toward the significant idiot in your life, you might consider that he or she could be something or someone other than what you originally thought. Are *you* something or someone quite different than what you originally presented to the idiot? Did you present yourself as smaller than you really are, or larger, in order to *fit* into the relationship you wanted so badly? Is it all of the above? Reality abuse messes things up every time. Trying to manufacture reality invariably leads us down that road paved with good intentions, and we all know where *that* road leads.

When we try to invent our own reality, we risk being found out for the frauds we really are. We also risk being diagnosed as psychotic and committed to Bellevue. Yet, the deception might not be intentional. I really thought I was supposed to be an alpha male. Even after reading *Why Men Are the Way They Are* (Berkley Publishing Group, 1990) by Warren Farrell, I *still* thought I was supposed to be an alpha male. Even after Warren and I became friends, I still thought I was supposed to be an alpha male.

In the end, to have an honest relationship, I had to accept that I'm not the classic, dominant lord-and-master type alpha male I was socialized to be. Now, I feel much freer just being me; hopefully kinder, more patient, caring, and tolerant than when I believed I was the smartest person in the world. I'm not claiming to be anywhere near perfection. Never will be. Being perfect is more pressure than I care to deal with, thank you.

Impulse-ism

A good friend of mine in IE constantly reminds me that happy and fulfilling relationships require new skills and habits, more new skills and habits, and even more new skills and habits. It never ends. Recovery is a life sentence to feeling better. (Otherwise, life can be a terminal illness.) I'm not allowed to say, "I tried doing the next right thing a time or two, it didn't work, so I decided to fall back into impulse-ism." Deciding, re-deciding, and deciding all over again tomorrow to place thoughtful action ahead of acting on impulse is fundamental to successful relationships.

"But, Dr. John," Shirley interrupts. "Isn't impulsive action, action all the same? If we're not supposed to over-think, isn't impulse a good thing?"

"Ah-h-h-h," I sigh with the confident coolness of a Zen master. "Taking thoughtful action requires a certain amount of subtle finesse." That, and a lot of practice. It's my Goldilocks Theory. Under-thinking can lead to remorse, regret, and/or resentment. Flying off half-cocked is never a sane or systematic approach to positive behavior. Over-thinking can lead to immobilization, inertia, and/or insomnia. The optimal scenario is just enough thought to reason out the best and most appropriate action in any given situation. Optimal or judicious thinking, as Goldilocks would say, is applying the amount of thought that's "just right."

To paraphrase Dwight Eisenhower, truly important things are seldom urgent and urgent things are seldom truly important. Eisenhower saw no value in living crisis to crisis. There are times you feel you must do *something*, such as deciding how you're going to live with your significant idiot without harming the idiot or yourself. In these moments you need to follow a process that flows out of an ongoing program of self-awareness, enlightened thinking, and changed behavior. When you feel an irresistible impulse to do *something*, it's important to focus on doing the *right* thing. The old saying is still true: even when there never seems to be enough time to do it right the first time, there always seems to be time to do it over again.

Keys to living with an idiot

⇨ **Seek reality.** Seek reality as it is, not how you imagine it to be, how you want it to be, or how some misinformed parent, friend, or romance novel *said* it should be. Triangulate your information. Run a reality check with someone who thinks like you think. Run another reality check by asking for feedback from someone who doesn't think like you at all, but who has no reason to be misleading. Finally, ask the idiot. Have a conversation. You can take whatever the significant idiot in your life tells you—in context *and* considering the source. Somewhere in the middle of that triangle you will find reliable information. You need reliable information to keep it real.

⇨ **Accept yourself.** Accepting yourself as you are doesn't mean you shouldn't invest in your own personal growth and development. Accepting *who* you are is the starting place. People who feel deep sadness can't merely snap their fingers and become happy. Even if you're only temporarily in a sad place, an instant remedy is not feasible. Repositioning yourself vis-à-vis the real world is the best option for experiencing greater happiness, but only if your perception of the real world is accurate. If you're going to learn how to live with an idiot or live well in spite of the significant idiot in your life, you must start from where you are.

⇨ **Act.** Don't just stand there, *do* something. Are you willing to do the things you're impatient for your idiot to do in order to enhance the relationship? Or will you sit back, wait, and complain? What will happen if you stand at the edge of the healing waters beside your significant idiot, waiting for him or her to go in first? Archeologists in the next century will find two skeletons at the edge of the healing pool. You have the option to do what you want your idiot to do. Show the way. Be the big person. If the idiot doesn't respond, you're in training for a happier life regardless. Taking initiative is the fastest way to free yourself of the constraints and limitations of idiot-ism.

Big Decisions, Little Brains

> "It is the chiefest* point of happiness that a man
> is willing to be what he is."
>
> —Desiderius Erasmus
> (*Yes, he really said "chiefest.")

Millions of people before me have asked, "Why am I attracted to the type of people that pour gasoline on the flames of my personal torment?" To my knowledge, nobody's offered a truly comprehensive answer. A partial answer covers how we're drawn to certain character flaws like moths to flames, saying we're most comfortable in familiar waters, even if they're stormy and dangerous. The part I feel remains unanswered has to do with attraction. I can understand on an intellectual and emotional level the appeal of familiarity. But just because I know what it's like to have poison ivy doesn't mean I'm going out looking for it.

The intangible element of attraction has much to do with fulfillment. All of the influences in our lives, especially those formulated in early childhood, create a paint-by-numbers portrait of who we think we're supposed to be based on external expectations of who we *should* be. Then we proceed to paint.

Some people resemble a page in a coloring book more than a paint-by-numbers set. With a coloring book, the image is there, defined by simple lines. In a paint-by-numbers set, the colors are already chosen. In a coloring book, the choice of colors is left up to you, which explains why I've never worn the correct shirt with the correct tie in my life.

For some unknown reason, we're expected to file a flight plan for our life long before we're old enough to have a pilot's license. By the time we *are* old enough to have a pilot's license, we've stopped asking, "Why am I flying in this direction when my destination is over there?" We just keep flapping our wings.

The things you really want and need to be fulfilled in relationships and life in general are often left off the map or painted the wrong color. The only way to find them is to accidentally stumble across them. And even if you do, you'll probably say, "Funny, this place isn't on the map. I might as well keep going." You fly away from the very thing or the kind of person who is best suited to your long-term happiness.

If my flight instruments were that miscalibrated on the macho alpha male thing, how far off course have I drifted in other matters? Another frightening yet fascinating aspect of personal growth: Once you begin to realize how much you don't know (and never knew, but thought you did), you realize that everything not grounded in solid faith and trust is shifting sand.

To reconcile the incongruity between what I thought I was supposed to want, and what was truly best for me, I created a grand scheme consistent with the way I interpreted life. How in blazes am I supposed to create a grand scheme for life when I don't have the patience to order a car with the upholstery I want? I just settle for what's on the lot, sign away the next five years of income, and drive away, anxious to begin my buyer's remorse.

If I waited for what I wanted, otherwise known as delayed gratification, I might actually experience gratification instead of buyer's remorse. But because I can't wait, buyer's remorse, otherwise known as
common sense, advises me to cancel the order, purchase something I
can afford, and save a year's worth of income in interest alone.

To a lifelong controlling dependent such as myself, a grand scheme
means a *way to control life*. What's the use of being a control freak if
I don't roll up my sleeves and start controlling? Of course I can't
really control anything, so I engage in some serious imagination-ism
and, voilá, a new reality is born. As I mentioned before, the flight
plan I filed for my life was for an alpha male. That's like filing a
flight plan for a Boeing 747 and showing up in a hang glider. No
matter how many times you hear it, the truth hurts, especially when
it collides with false reality.

The words of an old-timer at my first Idiots Exposed meeting still
ring in my ears, "The one thing all of my failed relationships had in
common was me." Romantic, marital, professional, social, I was there
to see every one of them end. Not that every one has ended. I'm not
that bad for heaven's sake. But in those that did end, I played a part.
The old-timer's comment was a hammer and I was the nail. Despite
my headache, I was intrigued by the revelation. Now, simply knowing
the truth has set me free from a lot of playacting that gets me nowhere. I'm free to be myself.

Keys to living with an idiot

⇨ **Be proactive, not reactive.** Keeping your impulses in check
   starts by accepting reality. Are you acting or *reacting* to the
   idio-t-syncracies of the significant idiot in your life? If you're
   reacting, do you react to completely predictable behavior
   with judicious thinking? Are you ready to invest that much
   scrutiny to determine how idiotic those idio-t-syncracies really are? More importantly, is your relationship worth enough
   to anticipate and stay ahead of your friend, sibling, spouse,
   parent, child, coworker, or boss? If you believe you're dealing with an idiot, wouldn't it feel a little silly to be caught off
   guard?

⇨ **Be authentic.** Are you willing to be who you really are? Are
   you willing to let your significant idiot be what he or she

really is? Will you come off your position far enough to find common ground and possibly some resonance with your significant idiot? You should not ask your idiot to do anything until you're willing to be completely honest about your relationship, your role in it, your expectations, and your limitations. And then it's still up to your significant idiot to decide if he or she will join you in refurbishing the relationship.

⇨ **Find your strength in who you are.** You are never more powerful than when you're operating from your essential nature. You shouldn't put much stock in attitudes and behaviors other than your own. In your strength, which comes from who you are, you can be tolerant and patient with those who operate from a different place than you do. Your greatest strength might be expressed in stillness. If you decide to leave or abandon the relationship, will you depart in strength or in weakness? Will you blame the idiot or confess that there might have been some "stinkin' thinkin'" going on.

Meet the Inner Idiot

Once I realized there *was* a clueless me inside the clueless me, I was at last poised to calmly accept and even forgive cluelessness in others. If there is any hope for living a happier, more fulfilling life with your significant idiot, it must start with *empathy*. You must exercise that withered, atrophied, 98-pound weakling empathic muscle. Pump it up until it looks like the Governator of California. The stronger you become, the more of the real you there will be for others to connect with and bond to.

Your promise of a happier more fulfilling life rests not in changing the significant idiot in your life, but in idiot-proofing your chicken-soup-soaked soul. This can be accomplished by empathically walking the proverbial mile in his or her moccasins, finding where your experiences overlap, and building on the commonality.

Chapter Summary

An early and essential step to living successfully with the idiot both outside of you and the idiot inside of you is accepting who you are in the real world. You must also accept who others are. These assessments are best made through thoughtful reflection on real behavior over time; not excuses or rationalizations for behavior. The more you can ground yourself in reality, the better your footing will be when the storm strikes. The storm I'm talking about is resistance to change. Anything that will make what you have today better tomorrow is change.

You can make transitions easier by making note of your "-isms." It's your thinking that needs to be realigned. As your thoughts become better grounded in reality, conscious and deliberate behavior must follow. You have the opportunity to reinvent the environments you share with the significant idiot in your life. But it will take consistent application of new skills and habits to get that done. It's up to you to take charge of those things you can change. Let the rest go. If you don't step up, the idiots will be in charge—with your permission.

To-do list:

☑ Ask the animal question.

☑ Ask a denial-piercing question.

☑ Qualify your information.

☑ Seek reality.

☑ Accept yourself.

☑ Act.

☑ Be proactive, not reactive.

☑ Be authentic.

☑ Find your strength in who you are.

Chapter 3

Not All Idiots
Are Created Equal

IF NOT EVERY IDIOT IS A spouse, friend, family member, in-law, co-worker, counter clerk, or employer, and not every spouse, friend, family member, in-law, coworker, counter clerk, or employer is an idiot, who are these people and why do they drive you bonkers so much of the time? I've designated the following six categories to simplify idiot-ology and provide a practical way to get your arms around the issue of living with idiots. They were not-so-scientifically selected on the basis of personal and professional experience dealing with them, and being one or more of them at any given point in my life.

Gonzo Typology

I learned the term "gonzo" when it was used by one of my literary inspirations, Hunter S. Thompson, to describe a style of sports journalism in which he simply wrote notes in a spiral notebook about what was happening at an event, the way he experienced it, in real time, and then he turned in the notebook afterward without editing. I've adopted and adapted the term because gonzo anything is more fun than the way we're "supposed" to do things. Stylistically, gonzo typology is more consistent with a book called *How to Live with an Idiot* than, say, the *Diagnostic and Statistical Manual of Mental Disorders, fourth edition* from the American Psychiatric Association.

Life Fountains and Black Holes

I've reduced the human race to two broad categories. Machiavelli had his *lions* and *foxes*. Carl Jung had his *perceivers* and *judgers*, *introverts* and *extroverts,* and so on. Harville Hendrix has *isolators* and *fusers* at the extremes of his continuum. I have *life fountains* and *black holes.* It's a more poetic way of saying *givers* and *takers,* those who make deposits into life's bank account, and those who make withdrawals.

We are all variations on the Life Fountain vs. Black Hole theme. Virtually every one of us possesses and demonstrates characteristics of both. One of the principles of Idiots Exposed is that we're all doing the best we can with what we have to work with. We're all children of our Higher Power. Judge not, lest we get gonged.

Like most things in the natural universe, there are healthy and not-so-healthy aspects to both Life Fountains and Black Holes. Givers can give for unhealthy reasons and Takers are capable, under the right circumstances, of receiving instead of taking. There's a big difference between graciously receiving and taking.

Overall, there are those who seem to be instruments of dispensing all that's good in the universe while others suck it up like enormous cosmic vacuum cleaners. Although my name *is* Hoover, I'm not in the vacuum category. I belong to the not-so-rare splinter strain of the species that you will momentarily come to know as a Category II Giver.

Humans are complex creatures who often appear to one another as clueless when their true natures are simply masked by our complexity. Then again, sometimes we're just clueless. Sometimes a cigar is just a cigar, right Sigmund?

Life Fountain Subtypes

Category I Givers

Life Fountains are Givers, although their motivations can vary. Category I Givers generally consider themselves unworthy and undeserving of the good things in life. That's their motivation for giving the shirts off their backs. They don't necessarily feel anyone needs their shirts more than they do, they simply believe they deserve them less than anyone else. I'm not saying Category I Givers are spineless, but they are technically invertebrates. Let's call them *amoebas*. Somewhere along the line, their sense of self-worth was permanently deleted from their operating system.

Category I Givers see life as a ladder and themselves at the bottom. Amoebas consider everyone else above them. You could say they have low self-esteem, but that would be an understatement. The meek receptionist at the public access television station in Al Franken's hilarious movie *Stuart Saves His Family* (1995) is the poster child for the Category I Giver amoeba.

Category I amoebas give to assure their positions remain subordinate to everyone else. The privilege of being less than zero is all the reward they seek for their giving. This type will buy every magazine subscription and set of encyclopedias door-to-door salespeople have to offer. Category I amoebas are catnip for telemarketers. When a telephone solicitor calls during dinner, the Category I Giver says, "I'm sorry I was eating when you called." At least Category I Givers don't expect anything in return from the Takers on the Black Hole side of the equation. Amoebas can pretty much operate independently and, I assume, be relatively happy.

In the spirit of open and honest disclosure, I have amoeba moments. In radio and television interviews I've done about *How to Work for an Idiot*, when the interviewer says, "I'm afraid we're about out of time," without thinking I say, "I'm sorry." What's that about? Is it because I appreciate the interview so much, I'm having such a good time, and/or enjoying the exposure for the book to the degree I feel a need to apologize? I'm getting something nice, so the amoeba in me responds as if I don't deserve it—as if those few moments of heaven were but a fool's paradise.

I have enough Category I Giver amoeba in me to buy tickets to the police and firefighters' charity concerts every year. Even the ones sold by boiler room telethieves who give 10 to 15 cents on the dollar (if that much) to the charity they purport to represent. Since I've been in recovery, I've taken to saying, "I'll send my $40 directly to the benevolent association, what's the address?" Call terminated.

Category II Givers

Rather than refer to people who consistently demonstrate enlightened self-interest in personal relationships, I've identified the most appropriate furry mammal to serve as a surrogate in this category. The beaver is a tireless worker. Industrious and dedicated, this eager

animal will flatten forests and alter the course of rivers to create a safe, secure, and isolated lodge for the spouse and the little beavs. The beaver is the poster child for how I interpret many of author Melody Beattie's codependent characterizations, capable of enormous effort to create a dam, a pond, a home—literally and figuratively—a place for the beaver *not* to be alone.

Codependent beavers (co-beavers) are capable of giving everything they have to others for the unexpressed (and slightly devious) purpose of receiving some love energy and appreciation in return. Oops. The approach doesn't work; unless the other party is also a Giver. In that case, he or she will give the co-beaver love and appreciation without the co-beaver's having to kill him- or herself to earn it. The mere fact that co-beavers constantly complain about how unappreciated they are should be proof enough that love can't be earned. Trust, yes. Love, no.

Those who consider themselves *recovering* co-beavers are shocked and horrified to discover their motives are not pure. What should be and what *is* are two different things. For the most part, people give to get. Gifts are often but bait in the snare.

Category II co-beavers attempt to capture and control others so they won't be alone. Through that curious and mystical combination of nature and nurture, most of them believe they're not worthy of being loved and they're not interesting enough to hang around with unless they compensate with their strategic giving and nurturing.

Not all beavers are codependent. The *bucolic* beaver is a laid-back, easygoing sort that works hard, provides for his or her dependents, and doesn't need or expect much in return except what a significant other is willing and able to give. The ambitious *achiever* beaver works hard at achieving aggressive and lofty goals, yet is still a well-balanced beaver in terms of what he or she is willing to give and accept in return. For the most part, bucolic and achiever beavers have healthy boundaries. They know what they are about and keep their attitudes positive and in perspective.

Category II co-beavers can act like imposters in beaver pelts. Unlike their more authentic and genuine furry friends, the bucolic and achiever beavers, the co-beaver's neediness can be camouflaged by nurturing and caregiving. They can actually fool significant idiots in their lives some of the time. The Category II co-beaver's highest aspiration is to fool all the idiots all the time. They try to make a compelling case by claiming that people need them, when in fact it is they who are scared to death of being abandoned and left alone. So they'll do anything and everything to keep others around.

The co-beaver will cook meals, wash and iron clothes, clean the house, vacuum dog hair off the sofa, and pay the bills. (Just please, please don't leave the lodge. But if you must leave the lodge, please stay in the pond.) Category I Giver amoebas will do all of these things and then go away on their own figuring they're not worthy of anyone's company to begin with. Category II co-beavers fell trees, build dams, and construct lodges to make themselves worthy of hanging around. I guess you could say they're one step ahead of the amoeba.

The attraction of Givers to Takers is most apparent on the level at which completely unworthy people (the amoeba's self-image) and only slightly more worthy Category II Giver co-beavers need someone willing to receive what they give in order to fulfill their destiny. The co-beaver's motives can be hidden so well that even the beaver has forgotten what they are. But they're there. Co-beavers would never invest so much effort for no reason.

Want a plot twist more bizarre than the concept of giving in order to receive? After giving till their fingers are raw and their bank accounts are drained, co-beavers can wind up resenting the very people they waited on hand and foot and spent all their money on. More specifically, Category II Giver co-beavers run the risk of resenting the difference between the level at which they give and the level at which Takers give back, which is like night and day. Bucolic and achiever beavers, with more realistic expectations of themselves and others, are less likely to build up resentment.

If co-beavers are lucky enough to have paired up with bucolic or achiever beavers, they will weather the co-beavers' nutty behavior pretty well. Bucolic or achiever beavers might even find the co-beaver's frenetic shenanigans amusing and endearing. If co-beavers are really lucky and inherit emotionally healthy in-laws, friends, coworkers, and bosses, their resentment factor will be greatly reduced. But co-beavers are famous for attempting ill-advised cross-species relationships or relationships with equally codependent beavers, neither of which turn out well as a rule.

It's hard work gnawing down trees with your two front teeth, dragging the logs to the stream, and slapping mud between them with your tail all day. Once the co-beavers realize the real reason they're doing all that, they tend to place both hands on their scalps and yank as hard as possible. How idiotic can they be, especially if they're trying to hang on to a Taker from the Black Hole family? Takers are not going to give anything back unless it suits them. They're *Takers*. Co-beavers working themselves to death so Takers have a nice situation to come home to and all they can do is yawn and ask, "When do we eat?"

This is idiotic. Co-beavers might as well come right out and say (but of course, they will *never* actually say) the deal is this: I promise to gnaw through tree trunks, flood streams, and build lodges for you, and you promise not to leave or send me away. They don't say these things out loud or even consciously acknowledge them because to do so would make them sound pathetic. So, why is it that when they give and the Takers don't leave, they become resentful? The Takers are still around, holding up their end of the unspoken bargain. What's the problem?

Why are co-beavers so utterly irrational in this regard? Simple. Their unworthiness sandwich is only a few slices of bologna thicker than the totally pitiful Category I Giver amoeba's mustard sandwich. Yet, it's the only way they know how to hook and imprison those whose validation they think they need like all living things need water and oxygen. Or so they think until they get into recovery. Recovery, like Idiots Exposed, is learning better ways of thinking.

The Santa Claus syndrome: Servant or sucker?

Many Takers who fall in the Black Hole category don't believe Givers are for real. As willing as they are to take all that others are willing to give, Takers nonetheless consider pure giving from the heart to be a figment of childish imagination. They figure anybody who acts like a servant must really be a sucker. They suspect the only possible motivation for the giving is to get something in return, which about sums it up for Category II Giver co-beavers. Not only are Takers notoriously ungrateful, they are absolutely right on the money about the co-beaver's motives.

Category II Givers are a splendid and sorry bunch, all at once. While many beavers live well-balanced lives of giving and receiving, co-beavers are definitely giving with strings attached. Check that, *ropes* attached. They have expectations. Their expectations are their best-kept secret, not grounded in reality, actual experience, or statistical probabilities, but they're expectations just the same. When their expectations are not met, they become resentful.

Part of the misguided thinking common to Category II co-beavers, and the reason many are in recovery, is the expectation that their fantasies will somehow become real. One fantasy is that someone who is programmed to take will do so only if they have something of equal value to exchange. Of course, it is all contingent on Takers going through radical transformations that defy reason and logic. Hang around recovery meetings long enough and you'll hear someone say, "Expectations are just resentments waiting to happen." Amen.

Category III Givers

There is a Santa Claus, although Takers will never fully believe it. There are healthy and mature servants; those who give because it's the right thing to do. They don't give to please or to receive anything in return. They are just doing the next right thing by extending love into the universe. Category III Givers are better grounded  than Category I or II Givers, which gives them a good foundation from which to enrich other people's lives.

Someone suggested I associate the dolphin with the altruistic Category III Giver. (Despite appearances to the contrary, I'm not trying to write *Son of Animal Farm* here.) The dolphin gives us the impression that genuine regard and oneness with the universe is a conscious dolphin choice over aggression and antisocial behavior. Perhaps. Perhaps not.

To me, altruism, or giving with no expectation of return, is among the highest levels of human actualization. Humans have the transcendent ability to reflect on situations and consciously put others first when they so choose. I keep the Category III Giver in human form because to reach Category III on the Life Fountain side of the proposition requires the highest exercise of free will. As much as I love Flipper's perpetual smile and clicking, I don't think he has free will.

Category III Givers are generative in the sense that psychology luminary Erik Erikson meant the term to be used. Generativity, it is said, refers to the extension of love into the future. That suggests a person has evolved beyond him- or herself to the point that he or she can look outward and give to others in a meaningful and selfless manner. It also requires solid footing and a well-balanced self-image because the giving is going outward with no expectations. The hope (not expectation) is that someone will benefit, if not today, in the future.

To me, the ability to genuinely act in an unselfish, altruistic manner and extend love into the future implies a real relationship with a Higher Power. After all, belief in a future requires faith. We don't know what's out there, but I believe what is true today will still be true then, whenever then is. The Higher Power that truly orders the universe will be as omnipotent in the future as now and in the past. Ergo, the love we extend is a good investment. If I didn't believe there is a future and a Higher Power sovereign over my life, I might live totally for the moment and torch everything I don't use myself.

Being brutally honest about my own intentions, I usually venture into Class III Giver territory only when I feel my Higher Power looking over my shoulder. Wrong motivation, I know. There's nothing wrong with trying to please or merely demonstrate obedience to the God of my understanding with good behavior, but trying to perform a little sleight of hand and fool an omniscient being just makes me look silly—even when everybody to the right and left of me thinks I'm generous and caring.

My personal goal is to graduate from a disingenuous, if not well-intentioned, Category II Giver co-beaver to a genuine altruistic Category III Giver. While I'm at it, I'll be satisfied to lose those pitiful Category I Giver amoeba habits, too. I succeed in short spurts, which I plan to extend as my new skills and habits become stronger.

I'm also learning that some self-absorbed Takers will take from generative Category III Givers all day, calling them suckers. But a genuinely accommodating Category III Giver altruist won't subject him- or herself to that type of insatiable scenario for long because there is no ultimate good in it. Just because generative, or selfless and altruistic, people act unselfishly doesn't mean they're stupid. Quite the opposite, a Category III Giver altruist is anchored in reality and has expectations more grounded in reality than Category I and II Givers combined.

Life Fountain Summary

The Life Fountain subcategories are pretty straightforward:

⇨ **Category I Giver amoebas:** Very nice folks, but spineless for the most part, and afraid of their own shadows, as well as everyone else's. Have Girl Scout cookies to sell? Go to their house. Need someone to watch your pet and water your plants while you're out of town for a month? They'll do it even if you're a perfect stranger. Ambitious amoebas can generate great amounts of income. But they need accountants and lawyers to keep them from giving it all away.

⇨ **Category II Giver beavers:** Industrious, hard-working furry critters. Bucolic and ambitious achiever varieties are well-balanced beavers. Co-beavers keep busy giving, giving, and giving some more; attaching strings and expectations to everything. Their worst nightmare is to build the dam, flood the stream, and have nobody to share the lodge with. Resentment builds and compounds until the sound of a flat tail smacking the water can be heard for miles around. Promise to love a co-beaver and he or she will follow you anywhere, and carry your luggage.

⇨ **Category III Giver altruists:** Give the human race most of the good name it has. They think outside of themselves and seek the best solution for all concerned. They're genuinely caring and compassionate and don't let shame and selfishness bind them up. Altruists are ultimately accommodating and the rest of us can feel guilty by comparison, but that's our problem, isn't it? They follow the 12-step recovery rule, putting on their own oxygen masks first before helping those around them.

Keys to living with an idiot

⇨ **Act as if you're worthy until you start to believe it.** If you can't convince yourself you truly are worthy, learn to act like it. In the case of the amoeba, he or she needs to avoid becoming an inverse idiot. There's giving and there's being a damn fool about it. Acting worthy is difficult for amoebas, but if they imitate their favorite television or movie star, they'll make a marked improvement right off the bat. Amoebas can pretend as if they expect as much from others as they give. Category I Giver amoebas needn't worry about becoming selfish. It's not in them.

⇨ **Monitor motives.** Why do only co-beavers run and hide at that suggestion? Category II codependent Givers must fight an uphill battle against the denial and rationalization they've practiced since they were little beavers. If outcomes are not what they want or expect, their motives are probably as much to blame as the ingratitude of their Taker targets. It won't hurt those who are co-beavers to pay attention to how the bucolic and achiever beavers handle themselves. They aren't afraid of their motives and don't mind talking about them with anyone.

⇨ **Give selflessly.** Give with no expectation of recognition or return on investment. You can help out a stranger who needs it and keep your identity secret. You can mail an anonymous donation to the home of someone you know can really use the help and never reveal where it came from. Think these things are hard? Try putting a large amount of cash in the offering plate at church so there's no tax deduction. If doing these things makes you feel good, you're a Category III Giver. If they are routine and there is no sense of proportion involved, you're probably a Category I Giver. If selfless actions make you sweat, you're probably in the co-beaver region of the Category II Giver.

Black Hole Subtypes

Category I Takers

Also known as garden slugs, couch potatoes, or breathing sofa cushions, these nearly lifeless creatures have earned a bad reputation among partners who want even a minimal amount of excitement in their relationships. Just as the distraction of television in the 1950s seemed to invite inactivity in men and women, young and old, the advent of the home computer and lax enforcement of physical education in schools has increased the size of this passive population.

In days of old, women began reclining on sofas and eating chocolate only after they were married. The same was largely true for men. They usually didn't become permanently embedded in La-Z-Boy recliners with beer cans in their hands until after the first child was born. Today, everything is changed. Children are watching MTV from their cribs, not taking their first steps until they're 4 years old, and only then to make a run to the refrigerator.

When I was a kid, I couldn't wait to get out and play. For children nowadays, being sent outside to play, away from the television, DVD player, computer, and Nintendo, seems like punishment. Accordingly, there is now more body fat and less muscle per pound of adolescent than ever before in the history of the human race. The garden slug is rapidly becoming mainstream.

The Category I Taker garden slug, as a Black Hole category, refers more broadly to people who barely contribute, if they contribute at all, yet expect to enjoy the fruits of everyone else's labor. Ain't that just like a 14-year-old? (Some 14-year-old's anyway.) Garden slugs will contribute if compelled to do so, but their efforts are predictably accompanied by groaning, much whining, and will be left half-completed (with the slug nowhere in sight) when you go back to check. The noise from the whining can be so annoying that parents, spouses, and others eventually stop asking and the garden slugs become part of the upholstery.

Personality-wise, Category I Taker garden slugs are the "B" side of Category I Givers. They can even make happy couples, if you can call them happy. The Category I amoeba is the alpha and the Category I garden slug is the omega. They fit together like concave and convex, hand and glove, Democrats and tax increases, Republicans and golf. Tab A into Slot B. Nature's most perfect opposites. The garden slug could care less why the amoeba serves hand and foot. The slugs' motto: "Just keep it coming," or, as they say in the South, "Bring it on."

Category II Takers

The classic dichotomy of large income vs. quality time with family and friends defines Category II Takers, otherwise known as jaguars. Author Warren Farrell (*Why Men Are the Way They Are*) claims that

working long and hard to provide for the family is a form of nurturing. He further contends it is most often a form of male nurturing, which has drawn criticism from some females who think a male jaguar should be able to generate lots of money *and* be home every evening at 5:30 to play with the kids and help them with their homework.

Perhaps this is possible, perhaps it is not. Either way, it rarely happens. There is a business and political food chain in Western Civilization on which more aggressive animals tend to eat less aggressive animals. Statistically, driven people who earn the big promotions and even bigger bucks usually work long hours and weekends. Time with the family suffers. Paradoxically, they often find time to play golf. Work hard, play hard.

How can financial providers of epic proportions be Takers? Jaguars drain equity from the relationships they're involved in, unless it's with a mistress or lover, in which case there is no equity, just a lease with an option to purchase. Even though they bring home big bucks, they are Takers in that their hard-driven work practices and alpha-cat-lifestyles are not family-inclusive. Nevertheless, jaguars, when they show up, expect the family to be home, intact, and happy. When spouses and children express feelings of neglect from the absentee spouse or parent, the jaguar points out how nicely the family lives and how expensive such a lifestyle is, thereby justifying his or her scarcity around the homestead.

Marriage made in a place that starts with "H"

Category II Taker jaguars often pair up with Category II co-beavers in one of those cross-species affairs, and they take all the beaver is willing to give under the pretense that turnaround is fair play for the lifestyle the jaguar provides. This is a matter of negotiation between partners and has to be considered on a case-by-case basis. The jaguar and the beaver actually might not be half bad for each other, providing the jaguar has a romantic streak wider than a Sharpie.

Children have a bad habit of expecting consistent nurturing from both parents. Where a jaguar and a busy co-beaver are involved, children come to realize that's too much to ask. But some sort of balanced effort would be nice. In the jaguar/beaver coalition, or lack thereof, one parent is essentially absent from the home, while the other is left gnawing, damming, and building. All things being equal, kids sometimes wish their jaguar dads would take a day off now and then to spend with them, and they wish their mother beavers would learn to play golf. If the dad is a co-beaver and mom is the jaguar, the kids just stop inviting their friends over.

Many female beavers married to male jaguars live lonely lives in gilded ponds only to wake up one day and realize they married their fathers. Their entire marriages are spent trying to acquire the love and warm fuzzies they never got from Dad. Of course, they get no warm fuzzies from their jaguar for the same reasons they got no warm fuzzies from their fathers. There's no money in warm fuzzies. Can you find the clueless creature in this picture?

These wives are usually eager to please if not altogether beaver-like, and they keep beaver therapists in business. Trying to earn Daddy's love never quite worked out, so they marry someone very similar in temperament and keep trying. God bless their never-say-die attitudes. Category II Taker jaguars and Category II Giver co-beavers can both work themselves into early graves, but they do so for entirely different reasons. All too often, the co-beaver is hell-bent on closing the gap between self and significant other while the jaguar is just as hell-bent to put work between self and intimacy. The chase is on. Beavers seldom run down jaguars.

Category III Takers

You can be in a room for three hours before you realize there's a garden slug in there with you. When a whirling vortex enters a room, everybody stops what they're doing and looks. No matter what room they enter, or what activity is taking place, people can't *not* notice a whirling vortex. This person lit him- or herself on fire somewhere in early puberty and is still burning. Gaping spectators apparently have never seen 5 to 6 feet of burning nitrogen before. Once they catch a glimpse of a whirling vortex, it's difficult for them to look away.

A whirling vortex is a walking, talking firestorm. The intense heat from a firestorm creates an artificial tornado that sucks oxygen from the atmosphere into the vortex to feed the flames. Anyone who has spent much time in the presence of a whirling vortex knows what it's like to have the oxygen sucked out of his or her lungs.

Whirling vortexes are high entertainment for ladies and gentlemen, boys and girls of all ages. Even animals can't help but to stop and stare. Fish in aquariums press their noses to the glass, dogs freeze in mid-scratch, and cats stop grooming themselves. People are simultaneously fascinated and appalled by whirling vortexes. Hollywood networks and studios pay millions for television and film rights to their outrageous behavior.

Those with no lives of their own are helplessly drawn to these incredible creatures who gobble up life around them. Category I Giver amoebas try to service whirling vortexes in their invertebrate way. But, like moths to a flame, are burned to a crisp. Whirling vortexes, with their voracious appetites for one-way love and sex, are answers to a co-beaver's prayers. Or so many co-beavers think.

"At last," muses the co-beaver, "here is someone who can't possibly gnaw down his or her own trees, drag them to the stream, and build a dam, pond, or lodge. Now my life will have meaning. The whirling vortex, although not a beaver, will nevertheless need me." A co-beaver's radar sweep for emotionally unavailable partners can spot a whirling vortex three states away. The co-beaver's fur prickles, stands on end, and the beaver's big, flat tail slaps the surface of the pond in sheer delight. The clinical diagnosis for this is: beaver-in-love.

Everything a Category II Giver beaver can build, a whirling vortex can instantly consume in his or her perpetual conflagration. The whirling vortex's insatiability is job security for the co-beaver, as the furry creature rebuilds everything the whirling vortex burns down, blows away, or floods out. Until the human torch suddenly goes out, leaving a singed widow.

It's hard to say no to a whirling vortex. That only makes him or her burn hotter and suffocate more people as precious oxygen is sucked from innocent lungs. It's best not to go near them to begin with. But try keeping the moth from the flame; you can't fight instinct.

Drama queens, kings, princes, princesses, and princes/princesses in training are subtle variations of the whirling vortex phenomenon. But these lesser vortexes are like dust devils compared to Hurricane Charley. Sometimes a Category II Giver co-beaver can whip him- or herself into such a frenzy of giving and demanding appreciation that she or he appears to be a whirling vortex. A trained clinical eye can instantly diagnose them as only a minor atmospheric disturbance. Sometimes a jaguar can get to chasing his or her tail so fast that he or she appears to also be a vortex. But co-beavers and jaguars will eventually slow down enough to be seen for what they are. A true vortex continues to whirl almost indefinitely.

You don't meet whirling vortex Category III Takers, you encounter them. And talk about taking. It's take, take, take until the Giver has nothing more to give. The Giver suddenly finds him- or herself alone. Imagine what it's like standing in the path of destruction immediately following a killer tornado with clothes hanging off your weary bones in tattered rags. That's what life can be like for survivors of a whirling vortex.

As a clinician, I've dealt with vortex survivors and it's not a pretty sight. As a recovering Category II Giver co-beaver, I've survived relationships with whirling vortexes, coming out of the experience 2 inches shorter than I started, bankrupt, and with a distinct limp. As long as I stay faithful to the principles of my Idiots Exposed recovery, I will either be able to present myself at some point in the future as a mature partner for a whirling vortex, able to establish and maintain healthy boundaries, or be smart enough to run in the other direction as fast as possible.

When I ask many Category III Taker survivors if they would do it again, there's no hesitation. They say, "Are you out of your mind? I'll never go through that again." Liar, liar, pants on fire. Of course they do. I have yet to meet a tried and true co-beaver Category II Giver who recognizes the error in his or her ways on the first, second, or third try.

Sure, it was the most frightening and ultimately painful experience of the survivors' lives, but they can't stay away. Parents, mothers in particular, try to urge their children, especially adolescent girls, to steer clear of whirling vortexes at school. Of course their children ignore them and continually come home in tears, wearing only tattered rags. Black Holes and Life Fountains both start showing telltale characteristics early in life.

Black Hole Summary

The Black Hole subcategories are pretty straightforward:

⇨ **Category I Taker garden slugs:** Inanimate objects for the most part. Breathing sofa cushions have developed the impression somewhere along the line that to be loved means to let someone else sustain one's life. This can happen to children of amoebas. On the other hand, this learned helplessness can also be an act of repressed anger; a passive-aggressive way to get even with a dominant, wing-clipping mother and emotionally absent father, or vice versa. If an idiot has barely moved in months, some will embark on a seek-and-destroy mission into the idiot's secret agenda. Others will just vacuum around them, dust them off occasionally, and go on with their lives.

⇨ **Category II Taker jaguars:** Driven to succeed. These highly productive creatures can be walking, talking dichotomies. They provide a good lifestyle, but spend little time with the family enjoying it. They can expose subdominant Taker characteristics in a Category II Giver co-beaver. Someone who thinks true love is gifts and/or being well-provided for by the Category II Taker jaguar can stay in denial a long time before suspecting there's something rotten in the state of Denmark. The jaguar is a master of mixed signals, which can fool anybody at any given time. Co-beavers in denial, or who are too busy gnawing down trees to notice, are especially susceptible.

⇨ **Category III Taker whirling vortexes:** Receive the highest Nielsen ratings. They get everyone's attention, at least initially. Amoebas will lay offerings at their feet and go away quietly. Altruists will smile at the temporary distraction and move on to calmer waters. Category II Giver co-beavers have been known to handcuff themselves to the whirling vortex's ankle. Whirling vortexes are every bit as needy as co-beavers and don't even pretend there is a fair economy of exchange. Category III Taker whirling vortexes feel they deserve anything that comes into their sight just because it comes into their sight. They are the eternal victims of some injustice. Anything or anyone that would deny them anything they desire is seen as unjust or persecution.

Keys to living with an idiot

⇨ **Be the windshield, not the bug.** Be the gardener who evicts the slug. If you feel your destiny is fulfilled by waiting hand and foot on a breathing sofa cushion, your self-esteem could be at the bottom of the well. Catholics have a concept called penance, but even a Franciscan wouldn't expect you to spend your entire adult life tending to a garden slug. If you contemplate the ideal life and your role in it, does the picture include a couch potato?

⇨ **Seek balance.** If you're the jaguar, you probably feel you're in perfect balance. Life in the fast lane, occasionally pulling over for some quick warm fuzzies from the fam, and it's back to the races. If you're the jaguar's significant other, you couldn't be more out of balance. Few will be reading this book if they aren't teetering or at least listing this way or that. Over time, the trade-off you've created between lavishness and love begins to sag in the middle like a cheap mattress and it threatens to give way. If you're a garden slug's partner, the trade-off is constant companionship (if you can call it that) to avoid being completely alone. With a whirling vortex the trade-off is an adrenaline rush to escape a boring existence.

⇨ **Get off the tracks.** If you don't want to be struck by a speeding locomotive, don't stand in the only place a locomotive will strike you. If you don't want to be swept up in a whirling vortex, go down into the storm cellar when the tornado sirens blare. You saw what happened to Dorothy when she ignored the warnings and set out to find Toto. Sometimes, a whirling vortex is so magnificent to behold that you can become immobilized and frozen in your tracks. You know exactly what's about to happen, but can't move. How often must you almost be sucked in by the force of the speeding locomotive before you learn not to play near the railroad tracks? Don't hang with dangerous people in dangerous places. If you need a thrill that badly, consider skydiving.

Chapter Summary

People are made up of some combination of these six categories (amoeba, co-beaver, altruist, garden slug, jaguar, and whirling vortex). Each person has dominant characteristics embellished by subdominant themes. People are animals trying to become human, children trying to grow up. The good news is that people are doing the best they can with the information in their personal databases. Hurtful and/or self-destructive behavior is an indication that they need more and better data. Or, perhaps, they might just need to trust it more.

Unfortunately, working with corrupted files might have become so familiar that people don't know any other way. It doesn't occur to them to search the Web and download fresh information. That's where they can become effective change agents—at the point of learning more about who they are, more about why their significant idiots are the way they are, and how to best respond. The more you learn, the more you realize you don't know.

I believe amoebas, beavers, altruists, garden slugs, jaguars, and whirling vortexes do the best they can with what they have. In relationships, you are part of what the other party has to work with. Living with your significant idiot and/or your inner idiot in happier and more fulfilling ways requires following the advice of Teddy Roosevelt: "Start where you are, use what you have, and do the best you can." Reading this book might not be the beginning of the journey. It's probably not the end. Hopefully, it's a fun and informative place to visit along the way.

To-do list:

- ☑ Act as if you're worthy until you start to believe it.
- ☑ Monitor motives.
- ☑ Give selflessly.
- ☑ Be the windshield, not the bug.
- ☑ Seek balance.
- ☑ Get off the tracks.

Chapter 4

Composite Idiots

IF YOU'RE HAVING TROUBLE PICKING out the significant idiot in your life from among the six descriptive categories, it's probably because few people are purely one thing. People are all composites of multiple influences. A pinch of this, a dash of that, a shovelful of other stuff. Even spineless-yet-lovable Category I Giver amoebas have moments of fearless fortitude. Solar eclipses happen more often and, even then, these moments are mostly limited to daydreams. Yet, amoebas at least *think* about acting courageously. In the end, gonzo typology holds that people are predominantly one thing with diminished dominance in other things mucking up the mix or, more positively spun, creating the unique personality DNA that makes each person special. Whichever category traits ring truest will require most of your attention.

If you think in terms of multiple intelligence or perhaps spiritual gifts, each person is a slightly different concoction. Some males have stronger female energies than other males and some females have more male energy than other females. Some females have more male energy than males, and vice versa. We're all uniquely situated somewhere on a variety of continuums: passive vs. aggressive, quiet vs. outspoken, shy vs. bold, neurotic vs. psychotic, and so on.

Idiots in the Eye of the Beholder

Carry this thought to its logical conclusion and nobody is a complete idiot. Everyone has a clue about something, at some moment in time. Remember the autistic character played by Dustin Hoffman in the film *Rain Man*? He wouldn't have much luck as a customer service representative at Wal-Mart or selling insurance. But as a card counter in Las Vegas, a conjurer of rocket fuel algorithms, or a predictor of statistical risk-management probabilities, he's light-years ahead of me.

Flip that thought over like a pancake and realize that people all have their idio-t-syncratic moments. They all have an inner idiot to deal with. There are certain subjects and certain times when they're all essentially clueless. You could take the whole notion of multiple intelligence and claim, using similar logic, that each person has multiple blind spots. Each person has a blind spot selected from a range of multiple blind spots available to them. It seems as if most people can be idiots some of the time, some can be idiots most of the time, but none are really, truly, absolutely, positively idiots *all of the time.*

What are we then? It could be that we're lesser idiots pointing accusing fingers at greater idiots and/or greater idiots wondering why lesser idiots are so upset with us. Even though I am considered by many to be a competent communicator, I'm still caught flat-footed in situations where only a modicum of attentiveness would have kept me out of harm's way. Other people who don't demonstrate appreciable communication skills have no trouble being heard and understood. Perhaps it's the naiveté or transparency of their message. Perhaps it's the naiveté or transparency of the messenger. There is much more to communication than meets the eye.

Complementary vs. Symmetrical Relationships

Who are we dealing with in our lives and why? I mentioned the term *economy of exchange* in Chapter 3 in reference to how beavers and whirling vortexes are never quite able to reconcile their balance sheets—not that it matters a hoot to the vortex. By economy of exchange, however, I'm referring to more than the sum total of Giver deposits vs. the sum total of Taker withdrawals. I'm referring to the fact that relationships, especially the dysfunctional ones, are mostly complementary.

A complementary relationship is one in which one person's weakness is counterbalanced by another's strength, and vice versa. If both parties contribute equally in terms of what the other wants and needs, the relationship can work. But if, for example, I'm addicted to a substance or self-damaging behavior and you're addicted to me, the result might be disastrous as we both try to overdose on our substance of choice. I had a clinical supervisor in California who used to say we're all addicted to something or someone. "It's just a matter of what's in our jug," she said. If I'm a substance abuser, you can chase me down my spiral, but you'll always be at least one step behind.

A person with an addicted personality has a tough decision between what to give up first, the addiction or the enabler—the substance itself or the person who helps you continue the addiction. Obviously, most of us would recommend giving up the substance, but that would still leave one active addict. If all that's left for the recovering addict is the daunting prospect of facing a flaming Category II co-beaver while sober, let's hope it's not too far from the wagon to the ground.

A complementary relationship means you'll spend precious little time (or little of *your* precious time) in the same place. When you're up, the other person will be down, and when the other person is down, you'll be up. The only time the two of you will meet is passing through the middle, and there'll be scarcely enough time to wave. That's a tough way to live with someone you care about. It must be true that opposites attract, but they seldom bind.

In the symmetrical relationship, both persons' strengths might combine to build a business and/or political dynasty, such as Bill and Hillary Clinton. A symmetrical relationship can also mean that both people's weaknesses might combine to make one huge weakness a la *Days of Wine and Roses* (1962), a movie wherein two alcoholics drink themselves into abject poverty hand in hand. In a symmetrical relationship, both persons' strengths might also try to occupy the same space in the universe and knock each other off the tightrope.

Generally speaking, clinicians recommend symmetrical values in relationships. Democrats should socialize with, befriend, marry, and give birth to little Democrats. Christians should mate with Christians for the greatest chance of emotional closeness and support. In other words, why invite conflict? There is enough friction to go around as it is.

Symmetrical relationships are only dangerous in extreme behavior. If you can live within a reasonable envelope, your similar temperaments, interests, and beliefs will encourage you to spend more time in the same place and space. Spelunking with a partner who shares your love for deep, dark caverns will go a lot farther than hooking up with someone who is claustrophobic to spend an afternoon underground watching you having fun (assuming he or she can see in the dark). Skydiving with someone who is afraid of flying will dampen your enjoyment if you're the least bit sensitive to your friend or partner's feelings. The reluctant sky diver won't enjoy watching you have fun (assuming he or she has his or her eyes open) if she or he has to make the leap with you.

Positive and Negative Economies of Exchange

Because people have a tendency to waffle a bit between their primary and secondary Giver or Taker categories, as will anyone with whom you are involved, the greatest chance for happy and fulfilling relationships will occur when the things you are most willing and anxious to give strengthens the bond between you and your partner. The things the other person is most willing and able to give will do the same. That's a positive economy of exchange, and it's symmetrical in nature.

A negative economy of exchange is the opposite. What you are most anxious to give invites the other person to move further off center and deeper into nonproductive and even destructive behavior, or at least makes it easier for him or her to go there. Note that you can't cause another adult to make poor decisions, but you can pave his or her road to hell with your best intentions. If your best intentions are really a covert plan to capture and hold the unsuspecting person within your nurturing web, how can you be critical of the type of person you've chosen to ensnare?

A futile dance of denial and destruction occurs when others demand to be given that which drives them further into negative and destructive behavior. Although fully aware of the potential consequences, people give them what they ask for anyway. It goes without saying, as one person spirals toward self-destruction, he or she is not providing love and nurturing to his or her significant idiot, which in the case of the Category II Giver co-beaver, fuels the chase down the spiral in hopes of catching up and getting some attention.

Shirley Fires Back

"You can't blame me for my husband's, parents', adult child's, or friend's bad decisions," Shirley fires off as if she were never submerged in quicksand at all.

"Certainly not," I agree. "Or the *good* decisions."

"Don't agree just to placate me."

"I'd never do that, Shirley," I assure her. Perhaps there might be times when placating her would be the lesser of available evils. But on this point I really *do* agree with her. "I don't think anyone should feel guilty, especially for things they don't have the power to do in the first place."

"Once they're no longer children, dependant on me to make decisions for them," she goes on, "their decisions are their own."

"Right."

"If they choose to think, say, or do destructive things, they're going to do them with or without me."

"Absolutely."

"So, what does it hurt if I make life a little easier for all of us?"

"You're a sneaky beaver," I say with a smile, peeking at her between my thumb and index finger, which I'm holding about an inch apart. "You had me this close to buying in until you got to the part about *what's the harm?*"

"You can't have it both ways, John," she says confidently. "You said so yourself."

"True, I said that. But the troubling issue for me is not having it both ways, but having it one way and making it *appear* as if it's another way. That's not honest."

"Now you've lost me," Shirley says. "I'm not sure what you're saying, but I'm pretty sure I don't like it."

"I'll tell you up front that this is a difficult pill to swallow, no matter how much I sugar-coat it. I know because I'm still trying to force it down my own throat."

"Can you bottom-line it for me," Shirley suggests, sounding more like my editor all the time.

"We don't cause and can't cure or control good or bad decisions made by other adults," I say.

"Right," Shirley agrees.

"People will think, say, and do what they will—with or without our assistance."

"I seem to recall saying the same thing moments ago," she points out with a hint of pending victory in her voice.

"Correct," I say.

"Thank you."

"The crafty part of distancing ourselves from decisions made by others is the smug place it allows us to occupy."

"Careful, John," Shirley warns.

"Referring only to my own experience now," I assure her. "I once enabled with the best of them, telling myself the other person was going to do whatever the other person wanted to do, with or without me. I went ahead and enabled in part to prove the other person's behavior didn't affect me. That was a lie on my part to begin with. But the bigger lie—one I didn't consciously realize I was telling myself and everyone else through my behavior—was that my enabling wasn't hurting anyone."

"I thought we just agreed we can't cause, cure, or control...."

"That's right," I continue. "But my plea of innocence was a smoke screen. The harmful effect of my enabling was mostly on me, not the other person. I wasn't being honest enough to admit that the eager and busy beaver the other person saw was furiously trying to build a lodge and surrounding pond that were inescapable. The other person believed, for a while anyway, that I was gnawing through tree trunks, building a dam, a lodge, and a pond for our mutual benefit."

"Weren't you?" Shirley asks, suddenly concerned.

"To the extent that it would make things comfortable for the two of us, it was a good thing. But," I sigh, "I wasn't honest about my true intentions, even with myself, and that's never a good thing."

"You lied?"

"Not exactly," I say evenly. "I didn't know I had ulterior motives until my ulterior motives finally caused the relationship to crash and burn. But, hey, enough about me...."

"Not so fast kemo sabe," she says, holding her hand up like a traffic cop.

"Doesn't that mean 'trusted scout'?" I ask.

"Don't try and change the subject."

"Sorry. This medicine isn't tasting very good. The more I try to explain my co-beaver behavior, the more I realize how destructive it was."

"If I'm hearing you right," Shirley interprets, "you're saying that enabling a garden slug, jaguar, or whirling vortex is not hurting them *directly* because they will do what they will do no matter what?"

"Something like that."

"So we're both saying the same thing?"

"If it stopped there, I wouldn't be gagging on this pill," I say. "Enabling the other person didn't help them any, and it *definitely* hurt me. By denying or ignoring my self-serving motives in the relationship, I set myself up for failure, and caused us both pain."

"What if you were just doing the best you could with the knowledge you had?" she added, giving us both a softer place to fall.

"You're right, Shirley," I answer, accepting her offer. "But sooner or later, after a string of failed relationships..."

"...or giving up on a long-term relationship and just going through the motions..." she inserts.

"...I owe it to myself to reflect on what I'm doing and why. Even more so, I owe it to my partner, parent, child, coworker, in-law, friend, or complete stranger to be as honest and authentic as I can be. I can't be honest if I don't look inside regularly and ask the hard questions."

Shirley looked at me for a long moment. "The bottom of the quicksand pit wasn't all that bad now that I think of it."

"Oh, come on, Shirley."

"You're saying that a healthy relationship depends on me doing all the heavy lifting."

"I'm saying that a healthy relationship begins with doing my *own* heavy lifting. The other person's heavy lifting is up to them."

"What if the other person won't do theirs?"

I gave her a knowing glance, complete with raised eyebrows. We didn't say any more to each other. But I knew that she, like me, had to face the frightening-yet-liberating prospect of abandoning old habits in favor of new ways of living with the idiots in our lives. I just hoped it wasn't frightening enough to send her racing for the quicksand. For me, I was starting to get a clearer picture of how Givers and Takers manage to get so tangled up.

Keys to living with an idiot

⇨ **Observe category behavior over time.** The idiots in your life are composites of different categories, as all people are. If you take a snapshot at any moment in time and assume that's the primary category this person operates from, you might get lucky. You might not. Don't leave it to chance. Being observant over time is the best way to tell for sure which primary category you're dealing with. Keep a journal; it is pattern-revealing. That knowledge will be the foundation as you try to find more meaningful ways to live with your idiot. Too often, people commit to relationships based on a snapshot of a moment in time. The law of averages catches up, as it always does, usually long after the proposition of ending the relationship has become sticky and painful.

⇨ **Do a symmetry check.** Have you stopped to consider if the relationship between you and the other person in question is complementary or symmetrical in nature? Has your personal equity in the relationship risen or fallen over time? How about the other idiot? Are you rising or falling together, or are you headed in opposite directions? When you have cause for celebration, is it muted by the depression the other person is feeling? Or do the two of you laugh together and cry together easily?

⇨ **Ask the right questions.** Only honest questions get honest answers. If someone asked you right now what the motives are behind your behavior, could you name them with a reasonable amount of certainty? If what you do doesn't make much sense on the surface, you need to ask why you're doing it. If what you're doing is a direct violation of what you say you believe in, you *really* need to determine why you're doing it. Exploring your inner agendas and accepting what you find there sets you up to be more honest and authentic with others. Honesty and authenticity are critical to a fulfilling relationship of any kind, especially for the long haul.

The Cross-Category Myth

There is a reason God didn't instill a desire in the lower forms to breed across species. But they, like humans, can and do interbreed within the species. An industrious Category II Giver beaver can lapse into Category I Giver amoeba spinelessness under pressure or into Category III Giver altruism in shining moments of inspiration, depending on the circumstances. Although Category I Giver amoebas might have rare moments of altruistic Category III Giver fantasy, genuinely altruistic Category III Givers virtually never relapse because there is strength and wisdom in having seen the view from the mountaintop. Category I Giver amoebas cast their gaze submissively downward as a rule. Altruistic Category III Givers cast their eyes outward and up, and thus see the big picture. Category II Giver co-beavers never take their eyes off their significant others, not wanting to miss that possible instant of affectionate recognition.

What if many categories are involved? What if it's raining and the sun is still shining? Will they get soaked and sunburned all at once? I doubt it, but, more importantly, I don't care. If you're digging that deep, you're probably well beyond pay dirt. If you are convinced your idiot is the cause of all your problems, but you are the cure for his or her unhappiness, you're swimming in the Niagara River, above the falls, dangerously near the edge.

Bad news for mistresses of the world: some jaguar Category II Takers extract emotional equity from their families while pouring out adoration on an extracurricular lover. Nevertheless, the Taker is still a Taker, and the moment the lover caves to the pressure, he or she will recognize the jaguar is taking from him or her, too. Sometimes a busy-but-abandoned co-beaver laps up adoration from an adoring admirer only to have the admirer rip off a mask revealing the Taker underneath. Another beaver is fooled again. That can mean either the end of the beaver's emotional vacation or a challenge to take his or her game to the next level and marry the fraud in hope of changing the person.

Multiplicity

When all is said and done, each person is *primarily* a Taker or a Giver. Although at some level we engage in both behaviors. To possess equal proportions of both would call for a true multiple personality in which complete dimensions of the psyche are split off from one another. Takers can move up and down the scale from garden slug, to jaguar, to whirling vortex, but they will virtually never be true Givers. Even so, people don't spend much time in categories other than their own.

As Shirley and I discussed, people sometimes operate in their primary category and *call* it something else. This can be a devious misrepresentation, or an outright act of denial. Some mother-in-laws present themselves as altruistic Category III Givers in order to stay connected and in control of their children's lives. Some mother-in-laws really *are* altruistic Category III Givers. Some are co-beavers with loaded checkbooks.

Some Takers give very public philanthropic gifts to create the illusion of being altruistic and receive the adoration and praise that comes with being the big benefactor. Altruistic Category III Givers don't expect praise and adoration for their giving and often play it down to the point of giving anonymously. I knew a man, now deceased, who gave millions to colleges, hospitals, and museums. His name never went up on a building until he married a Taker. Then *their* name was suddenly everywhere.

Category Identification

Masking

Although Takers are Takers and Givers are Givers almost without exception, it's often difficult to recognize which is which. First is the issue of masking. Eager co-beaver Category II Givers disguise their true intentions and behaviors so as to control outcomes. Masked motives, they reason, don't frighten away unsuspecting targets.

Altruistic Category III Givers purposely don't call attention to their selfless behavior and, as a result, receive less recognition than they deserve. They're okay with that. Category I Giver amoebas tend to be so invisible to the general public that they don't cast a shadow on a sunny day, much less need a mask.

Category II Taker jaguars often mask their taking as providing. Stormy Category III Takers can turn on the tears and become convincing helpless victims on cue. No one would believe they could suck oxygen out of lungs. Category I Taker garden slugs won't exert the energy to find where they left their masks, much less put them on. Garden slugs, bless their hearts, are refreshingly shameless about their laziness.

Denial

Denial is the second reason identification of Givers and Takers is difficult. People see in others what they want to see and frequently refuse to see what's really there, especially if it's inconsistent with their fantasy. If it doesn't fit your script to be associated with a garden slug, then you pretend he or she is simply resting up to conquer the world—tomorrow. Garden slugs, as I just pointed out, don't need no stinking masks. Masks require more effort than slugs care to exert. Whatever they decide to do, if anything, they'll be well rested for it.

My script as a co-beaver has traditionally cast me in the role of small "s" savior and has called for an injured, tortured soul in distress for me to rescue. Sometimes I had to use a little imagination to come up with an injured, tortured soul that fit my requirements. It was, therefore, incumbent upon me (while continuing my worst practices) to take what was perhaps a mildly injured ego and turn it into a catastrophe. If

I ever became involved with a true catastrophe, my actual powerlessness to change anything would be exposed for the myth it is. In the bad old days before Idiots Exposed, I felt it was safer for me to pretend. Sing along:

> Oh, denial will usually fail you,
> 'cause the truth can always nail you.
> Accept what you already know,
> Let it go, let it go, let it go.

Balance

A third reason none of the six broad types I've described might be popping out is because you have a reasonably balanced significant idiot. You may be reasonably balanced yourself. You might have a person who gives *and* is willing to receive in a healthy way. Notice I didn't say *take,* I said *receive.* Receiving is a gracious act of accepting what is offered. Taking is dining and dashing, grabbing and going, or snatching and running. A reasonable balance between giving and receiving can set the stage for a copacetic relationship between Category I amoebas and Category II beavers, or Category II beavers and altruistic Category III Givers.

On rare occasions, things might work out between Category I amoebas and altruistic Category III Givers, providing the spineless amoeba can force him- or herself to graciously receive some measure of affection and nurturing from the altruist. Conversely, an altruistic Category III Giver won't be comfortable with only receiving. "Please, please," begs the altruist, "let me give you *something.*" The altruist/ garden slug combo is rare, although they seem potentially compatible. Despite first impressions about opposites attracting, the ultimate Giver won't bond with the ultimate sponge. Oil and water there.

Cohabitating Category I Taker garden slugs are rare. It can happen, but that leaves no one to do the shopping and laundry. Two Category II Taker jaguars can look beautiful to the outside world. But if they're to last for long, they need to be on their game or have low emotional needs. Two Category III Taker whirling vortexes? That's what proverbial "Hollywood" marriages are made of. Great ratings, but quickly canceled. The Chicago Cubs will sooner win the Super Bowl than a pair of whirling vortexes stay married 18 months. A pair of Category I Giver amoebas can become a bootlicking team I suppose, but I hope they'll keep that to themselves.

The most successful relationships, in my estimation, are between altruistic Category III Givers who understand and appreciate the value of being a gracious receiver in addition to being a selfless giver. The conspicuous absence of false expectations leads directly to an absence of resentment. Even a pair of Category II Giver co-beavers can make a decent go of it if they can keep their control issues in check.

Idiots: Now You See Them; Now You Don't

With cluelessness as the dominant defining characteristic of an idiot, those most likely to qualify are Category I and II Giver amoebas and co-beavers. They simply refuse to recognize or acknowledge their own lopsided behavior and how it affects themselves and others. Category III Givers are probably out as idiots, although anyone can be clueless every now and then. Being a genuine, generative, altruistic creature requires an acute awareness of the world around them and the universe at large.

Category I Taker gardens slugs as idiots? I haven't known many intelligent garden slugs. But they could be a lot more aware of the game they're playing than you realize, which would tend to disqualify them as genuine idiots. They always seem to hook up with some visible means of support. Is that luck or cunning? I personally suspect that breathing sofa cushions are not all that lucky.

Are Category II Takers idiots? Jaguars are rarely as clueless as they claim to be when pleading innocence. Working multiple relationships requires cognitive complexity (mighty fast thinking and talking). Jaguars are strategic and calculating. Definitely not *complete* idiots. Potentially cruel and selfish, yes. Clueless, no.

Category III Taker whirling vortexes can be clueless, and indeed many of them are. Whether that's by choice or convenience, it doesn't matter. They attract hearts to them like metal shavings to a magnet. As Stephen Sondheim wrote in one of his zillion or so insightful lyrics, "Who needs Albert Schweitzer when the lights are low?" Whirling vortexes are fine with leaving the clues for others to find.

Idiot Meets Idiot

With luck, your nice and normal partner, parent, sibling, friend, child, or coworker is most likely a *cuddly* version of one or more of these broad types, even if she or he is, by definition, an idiot. The question is not "Is my partner an idiot?" A more helpful question is "When, how, and under what circumstances does my partner, parent, sibling, friend, child, or coworker and I become co-idiots?" As a recovering idiot, I can testify that it's easier to spot cluelessness in others than it is to take ownership of my own. To say there is no cluelessness in me means there is no truth in me either.

Usually, where there is idiocy, there is more than one contributor. There is nothing more potentially devastating or possibly hilarious than two inner idiots just below their hosts' conscious recognition. Inner idiots don't cease to exist just because your radar fails to pick them up. Inner idiots are masters at evading detection.

Remember, individuals have a dominant Giver or Taker type, mixed with a pinch of higher- and/or lower-level categories. If someone had but one personality component and you had the same one, it could be multiplied by itself and there would still be but one to deal with. But relationships are not only difficult, they're mathematically impractical. If each person had two components, and they were multiplied, they become four; three for each would be nine; and so forth. Two people can quickly become a complex couple who need a calculator to get to the end of the day.

Keys to living with an idiot

⇨ **Be flexible.** Practice staying loose. Determining which category your significant idiot's in doesn't mean your thinking should become fixed and rigid. Living in the midst of a dynamic and volatile world as we do is like standing with our ankle caught in a wolf trap in a hailstorm. People can and will switch and swap behaviors without consulting you first. Don't try to prepare for every possibility. Instead, you can set your mind to accept the outcomes of others' behavior, as well as their true motivations, whatever they might be. Heck, you don't even know what kind of mood *you're* going to wake up in tomorrow.

⇨ **Be aware.** Replace denial with awareness to complement your acceptance. Just because you're learning to be more accepting of variable outcomes that might not be to your liking doesn't mean you should wear a blindfold. By stripping away the fog of denial, real behaviors of real people will become less surprising and therefore less disruptive to your equilibrium. You'll miss your magical thinking now and then, but once aware, you won't want to go back into the fog.

⇨ **Do the math.** Being flexible and aware positions you to make informed and intelligent decisions instead of defensive ones. If wholesale changes are called for, you can base your new choices on characteristics that add up in your favor. Two plus two only equals seven to someone in extreme denial or to a colossal idiot. Knowing and accepting how people are likely to behave, based on adding up your own experiences, gives you an enormous advantage in deciding the most appropriate physical and emotional closeness or distance to serve your long-term emotional health. If you're up to your eyeballs in idiots, you must decide if you can expect anything better without making sweeping changes in how you choose friends, pick partners, or spend time with family. All the effort you put into a relationship, if multiplied by zero from the other party, usually produces zero relationship.

Chapter Summary

People are complex composites. (There are three types of beavers alone.) Despite the fact that each of us is predominantly characterized as a Life Fountain (Giver) or Black Hole (Taker), people can spend time appearing to be in various subcategories. The best way to know who you are and who others are is to observe over time. That way you can more reliably diagnose your dominant type and category.

Observation, awareness, and flexibility are among the keys to dealing with annoying behaviors that block your sense of fulfillment. By acting smarter and thinking more clearly, you can get a handle on the complexity of cross-category relationships and position yourself to be happier with the hand you've been dealt. By making these things habits, even recovering idiots such as myself begin to look less idiot-like.

To-do list:

- ☑ Observe category behavior over time.
- ☑ Do a symmetry check.
- ☑ Ask the right questions.
- ☑ Be flexible.
- ☑ Be aware.
- ☑ Do the math.

PART II

THE SEVEN RELATIONAL SINS AND SOLUTIONS

Chapter 5

The First Relational Sin and Solution: Anger vs. Anticipating

The Seven Relational Sins and Solutions

"Bless me, (insert the name of your Higher Power here), for I have sinned." By relational sins, I'm talking about thoughts, words, and actions that diminish rather than enhance a relationship. I leave the moral issues to you and your Higher Power. Most people agree adultery, as in sexual intimacy with someone other than your designated spouse, is a moral sin as well as a drag on the relationship. However, my list of relational sins (listed in alphabetical order, not order of importance) focuses on underlying character issues that can set off a chain reaction of undesirable behaviors.

Cluelessness often equals oblivion. Is acting like an idiot, without technically *knowing* it's misguided behavior, a sin as I've just defined it? To strict legalists, ignorance of the law is no excuse. In the case of your significant idiot, there might be a whole lot of misguided behavior going on beyond the idiot's awareness.

I believe sin is intentional. It happens when we know what's right and intentionally do otherwise. That's when we put our own will in front of You-Know-Whose. A young child doing something out of pure ignorance triggers a different emotional response in me than a child doing something with premeditated malice or forethought that she or he knows to be wrong. This begs the question, "Does your idiot know better?"

Clueless idiots usually aren't aware of the consequences of their actions, so they can misbehave boldly with no knowledge of why others are getting so upset with them. As a recovering idiot, I can say from experience that we, like puppies, sometimes need to have our noses rubbed in it a few times before we get it. With our noses full of it, we graduate from cluelessness to potential sinners. That's why you, not the significant idiots in your life, are reading this book. It's a kinder, gentler way of gaining insight and learning to deal with us. We all need forgiveness now and then. Raging idiots also need remedial training.

There are many things all people know better than to do, but they do them anyway. Telling little white lies when they think it will diffuse or avoid an ugly situation, exceeding the speed limit when we think the traffic will bear it, and eating a piece of cheesecake when on a diet are a few innocently innocuous examples. As the stakes go up, people might be tempted to sin more boldly. Cheating on income taxes, fudging on a job application—just imagine the possibilities.

Putting Away the Hammer

Taking care of yourself is a constant theme in recovery, not just idiot-ism. I keep reminding myself of that as I explore things people do wrong in relationships, because I don't want to begin hammering anybody over the head, especially myself. It goes without saying that the significant idiot in your life might sin abundantly, but that's not something you can control. I've chosen to focus on your own behavior and how you respond to the behavior of others because that's where you *do* have some control. I know how tempting it is to hammer on the poor, defenseless idiots in your life. I've been hammered on plenty, and often for good reason. But fair is fair. If you don't like hammer marks on your head, you need to find a more effective way to deal with your significant idiot as well.

Just because the heaviest load for improving relationships tends to wind up on the shoulders of the person who cares most passionately about the quality of the relationship doesn't mean you shouldn't be aware of what each person is adding to the mix. Each person must make decisions based on the best information available. Knowledge of your own contributions, positive or otherwise, as well as the contributions of others, helps everyone make the most informed and mature decisions. It also makes you less likely to wield a hammer.

Jumping up and down and pointing an accusing finger at whomever is aggravating you at any given moment or over a lifetime might seem like fun, burn calories, and relieve a lot of pent-up tension and anxiety, but it's not going to produce a happy and contented relational environment. Besides, why are you so agitated anyway? The level of hostility you feel at any moment toward a spouse, significant other, sibling, child, parent, in-law, friend, or coworker is probably a direct reflection on how poorly you've dealt with them as much as it reflects the gravity of their misbehavior. In other words, there's a whole lot of sinning going on. Let's be slow to point fingers and fast to seek solutions.

Anger

Anger is a natural emotion. It's natural to feel angry when things don't turn out as planned or people don't behave as you'd like them to. The emotion is a good indicator that you are frustrated, disappointed, insulted, and/or hurt. Dealing with anger through humor, perspective, and other diffusing techniques I touch on in this book will provide options in dealing with people whose words and actions trigger angry responses.

Anger becomes a problem when it becomes your choice. Choosing to let the anger speak for itself limits or eliminates positive options. I've spent a great deal of my life choosing anger, feeling self-righteous and justified the whole time. But no matter how justified I felt in any given situation, I can't recall a single instance when my anger made me feel better in the long run. Neither did it get me what I wanted any more reliably than being reasonable.

Like anyone else, I became angry when I felt cheated, betrayed, unfairly attacked, and/or lost something I wanted. Even when I was *truly* cheated, betrayed, and/or unfairly attacked, anger didn't restore what I felt I had lost. I've lost precious personal and lucrative professional relationships by choosing anger. I speak from much personal experience and loss when I start my list of relational sins with choosing anger.

Anger affects Life Fountains and Black Holes differently, just as Life Fountains and Black Holes express anger in different ways. The paint-by-numbers images of amoebas, co-beavers, altruists, garden slugs, jaguars, and whirling vortexes will continue to fill in as the relational sins are listed relative to each Giver and Taker category. Knowing how others experience and practice each relational sin will not only help determine how you can best live with these people, you can also more clearly see yourself in the picture.

Life Fountains

Anger and Amoebas

When lowly Category I Givers encounter anger, they close their eyes and cover their heads. These are not people who harbor any pretense that they can withstand a massive assault, nor mount one. Speaking for myself, the more fiercely I am attacked, the more I tend to assume an amoeba-like posture. Generally speaking, when they encounter threats less than or equal to their power to resist them, the fight response becomes an option. When the threat is too overwhelming, flight is the best option.

Category I amoebas aren't up to much of any challenge, hence the old duck-and-cover routine. Fortunately, amoebas don't do much of anything to attract an attack. It's hard enough to tell when they're around. Amoebas can get caught in the wrong place at the wrong time, which has produced some of the funniest comedy routines in the history of television, motion pictures, and vaudeville.

When a Category I Giver amoeba expresses anger, the scene can be comedic. How frightening can a single-cell creature be? One of my most amoeba-like experiences occurred when I was working as a substitute teacher in a kindergarten class. There was no quieting those kids. I tried entertaining them with reading, singing, arts and crafts, and children's videos. Each diversion lasted 10 minutes at most before they started climbing into closets, rifling through the teacher's desk, or punching each other.

My kindergarten substitute teaching career ended in a deplorable scene with the matronly elementary school principal chewing out the entire class for making enough noise to be heard across campus. We stood, heads bowed, as she ripped into us. I think she was most disappointed with me. At least I took the brunt of the scolding. But I couldn't seem to do or say anything, even at the top of my lungs, to make a dent in the kids' frenetic behavior. That's amoeba-like powerlessness.

Amoebas might not express anger as a rule because they know how silly it looks on them; like me when I tried to herd kindergarteners. The amoeba might also be a relatively serene being who doesn't experience a great deal of incoming or outgoing anger. If amoebas pair up with abusive partners or go to work for bullying bosses, there could be a lot of ducking and covering. Having few expectations, by nature, amoebas tend to experience less frustration and fewer disappointments than the rest of us. Without fuel for anger, amoebas don't have much use for agitation. We'll know a furious amoeba is about to attack when we hear the words, "Uh, excuse me...."

Angry Beavers

We've all met them. If you're like me, you've been one. What usually makes co-beavers angry is not receiving the recognition and appreciation they feel they've earned with all their tree felling, damn damming, pond filling, and lodge building. If they go to all that trouble *and* make dinner, the least their idiot can do is show up. They keep a firm grip on one end of the rope they attach to everything they do. When they yank hard, they expect something to come flying their way. When it doesn't, they're tempted (sometimes beyond their ability to resist) to wrap the rope around their significant idiot's throat.

Just because Category II Giver beavers choose anger doesn't mean they'll be obvious about it. Co-beavers are known for their passive-aggressiveness. After the co-beaver has dropped enough not-so-subtle hints where everyone is sure to stumble over them, their partners, children, friends, in-laws, coworkers, or pizza delivery person will invariably ask, "What's wrong?"

"Nothing," says the beaver, clicking his or her tongue against those massive incisors and tapping out a busy tempo with his or her flat tail.

"Oh, come on," the idiot pries. "Something's wrong, I can tell."

So it goes.

The most disarming move the alleged offending party can make with a passive-aggressive co-beaver is to say, "Okay. If you say nothing's wrong, that's good enough for me." And walk away. The co-beaver will chase down his or her partner, child, friend, in-law, coworker, or pizza delivery person, saying, "Since *you* brought it up, I'll tell you what's wrong."

Some wily veteran co-beavers can hold a grudge for years, keeping careful score of every debt that's not acknowledged or paid back. Often, the benefactor doesn't realize she or he owes for the service.

Sarcasm is a favorite weapon of the passive-aggressive Category II co-beaver. Sarcasm is spineless anger. It's dishonest and doesn't contribute to a solution. Theoretically, nobody is supposed to notice a sarcastic remark, but the beaver is disappointed if no one does. If someone mentions the sarcasm, it's vehemently denied. Yet, how are words capable of tearing flesh not supposed to be noticed?

Using sarcasm is like jumping up and down behind the person we're upset with and making faces and rude gestures, until that person turns around. Then we stand still and smile sweetly. Sarcastic remarks are more of an indictment against the sarcastic person's character than punishment for the alleged offender. If I did all the jail time I deserve for being a sarcastic co-beaver, I'd never see the light of day again.

My problem is that I *feel*—if I openly share my anger and frustrations—people will dismiss them. Worse yet, they could point out it was probably my own unreasonable expectations that brought them on anyway; in which case, they would be right. I hate it when that happens. But it's hard to part with thinking and responses as old and familiar as favorite slippers.

Beavers can blow up, but it requires a lot of pent up pressure. As Category II Givers, co-beavers don't feel worthy of love and attention just because God made us. So, they work hard and sacrifice to compensate. That same mentality doesn't allow for permission to be angry or to express themselves. That's why they resort to sarcasm and other indirect ways to express dissatisfaction.

None of this stops us from building up steam fueled by disappointments and dissatisfaction. Like amoebas, beavers who feel no permission to discuss their frustrations or anger don't feel permitted to explode over it. When a beaver finally explodes, there are pieces of pelt everywhere. Better to find a healthier way to express anger.

Co-beavers can be the nail instead of the hammer. This is because their smothering nurturing irritates the heck out of their nurturees until *ka-bloom*, the person or persons they have been serving hand and foot explode at them. This takes co-beavers by surprise because they can't understand how anyone can be upset with their endless kindness and caring.

If the kindness and caring comes from a place of genuine concern, and not from a need to be loved, people don't tend to react that way. Wounded co-beavers need to realize that their intentions become transparent when they are too insistent and persistent that others accept what they're giving. It's not their fault others choose anger.

But they can't deny their role in creating discomfort and aggravation that leads toward that choice.

In some cases, beavers become scapegoats. Anger that has nothing to do with them comes their way regardless. If the co-beaver has established a track record of irritating the other party or parties with excessive nurturing, any little thing the beaver does could be named as the reason for the displaced anger. The angry person loses the chance to deal with whatever it is that's really causing the anger, and the co-beaver suffers unnecessarily. In the end, beavers, like the bucolic and the achiever, that draw and maintain healthier boundaries around their own behavior become less susceptible to the anger of others.

Altruistic Anger

Connecting these two words is almost oxymoronical. "Kind words turn away anger," says the Good Book. Regardless of what Higher Power you subscribe to or even if you subscribe to a Higher Power at all, it's common sense. People often get frustrated and angry when they feel ignored. The emotional maturity that led to an altruistic Category III Giver attaining his or her prestigious Life Fountain category includes the value of listening.

Listening to a person who doesn't ordinarily feel listened to, and speaking soft encouraging words won't generate anger. Genuine listening and sensitive comments will often de-escalate an angry person. What the truly altruistic Category III Giver *won't* do is patronize or talk down to an angry person (or anyone, for that matter) because that involves judging. An emotionally mature person does not judge.

When anger is directed their way, true altruists bear it graciously. It's no fun for anyone to experience anger, incoming or outgoing. But understanding they are probably not the real cause or target of someone's anger is also part of the wisdom that accompanies emotional maturity. For the one withholding kindness, an act of kindness by someone else can result in feelings of guilt. If and when altruists do something likely to elicit an angry response from others, they probably anticipate the possible response. The altruists do it regardless because their action serves an overall purpose worth the bump in the road.

Because altruistic Category III Givers base their decisions on good judgment, regrets are few. Mistakes happen, though. I never called them saints. Yet, awareness keeps Category III Givers from making bungling a habit. Just as classic idiots lack awareness of how their words and actions affect others, altruists have enhanced awareness. If what they do is likely to ruffle feathers, they will be prepared to handle the flapping. The Category III Giver altruist is also mature enough to understand that doing the next right thing can give others an excuse to push back, even when the pushing has nothing to do with the altruist's actions.

In extreme cases of injustice, the altruist might embark on a campaign of righteous anger to get some changes made. If Carrie Nation's "hachetation" thrashing of saloons in Topeka, Kansas, in 1901 wasn't righteous rage, I don't know what is. I lift a glass of chardonnay to her memory now and then. Angry behavior, even based in righteousness, is still tricky business.

Black Holes

Anger and the Garden Slug

Category I Taker garden slugs don't have much use for anger; it takes too much energy. You might get a rise out of them if you block the television set or are late delivering their dinner. Generally speaking, though, they are pretty laid back. If they do get frustrated with you for not feeding or caring for them properly, they are most likely to express it in a sarcastic remark or whining. Like amoebas, slugs are invertebrates, albeit on a much larger scale. Also like amoebas, slugs can change their contours constantly to meet the contours of whatever recliner they're occupying.

If there is any alpha-male energy in garden slugs, they might bellow when they want a cold beer. But excessive complaining and moaning coming from the upholstery probably means a Category II jaguar has a hangover, is in a funk, or a Category III vortex, temporarily spun out of the whirl cycle, is imitating a garden slug. In either case, Category II and III Black Hole Taker types are more suited to expressing anger than garden slugs.

Garden slugs are the recipients of anger from frustrated partners, parents, in-laws, employers, and anyone else expecting some type of interaction. Anger directed at garden slugs won't have much effect. They're used to it. If they gave a hoot how people feel about them, they'd already be doing something useful.

The best way to get a garden slug's attention is to stop waiting on him or her hand and foot. About the time the slug starts using body fat to stay alive, he or she will start moving. Setting and enforcing boundaries with a breathing sofa cushion will require growth and development on the part of the person who has, to that point, lived only to serve—strings or no strings. A humorous (or perhaps pathetic) scenario is a Category I or II Giver amoeba or co-beaver who hollers perpetually at a garden slug, knowing full well the slug won't be affected, yet continues hollering as he or she carries the pizza to the coffee table.

Anger and the Jaguar

Cats have tempers. Category II Taker jaguars are fully capable of expressing their dissatisfaction when things don't go their way. Jaguars can use their superior strength, speed, and agility to outmaneuver their prey and slice them to bits. Slicing to bits is extreme and unusual behavior for jaguars. A sharp scratch or two will get the point across without permanently disfiguring or disabling the partner, parent, child, coworker, employee, friend, or whomever.

Jaguars are so skilled and proficient at getting what they want professionally that they expect the same results from their social relationships. If the jaguar is the primary provider for a family, the big cat feels entirely justified in exerting whatever strength, speed, and predatory skill is necessary to keep his or her dependents in line. If only that effort took into consideration input from the other parent, or trusted adviser, that would be a cat of a different color.

Nobody is going to call a partner who values input and equal participation from the other partner an idiot. Accusations of "idiot," or worse, start flying when listening stops, thoughts and feelings are not considered, and jaguars start overpowering others. That's the risk we take with jaguars. The same sleek, sexy, muscular frame, incredible speed, and predatory confidence that attracted us to begin with can instantly be used against us in a fit of rage.

Although jaguars are at the top of their food chain, amoebas and beavers from the Life Fountain Giver family still often think they have a score to settle with the big cats. Jaguars don't even acknowledge a raging amoeba, except perchance for a good laugh. Beavers pose no appreciable threat to jaguars either. They can aggravate jaguars, which never turns out well for the beaver. Beaver vs. jaguar, jaguar vs. beaver, you do the math.

Anger and the Whirling Vortex

Believe it or not, whirling vortexes are so inherently insecure that getting angry at them only increases the fury of the storm as they try to calm their own nerves and deal with the emotional static. Nine times out of 10, a whirling vortex isn't going to notice an amoeba is even present, much less respond to an amoeba's anger. Vortexes and slugs have no use for one another and seldom occupy the same address. Altruistic Category III Givers are intelligent and mature enough to steer clear of whirling vortexes. They're content to let them whirl on their own. Incidents where vortexes are angry with altruists for not giving them what they want in a moment of desire are rare, although they do occur.

Vortexes and jaguars rarely serve each other's needs and therefore aren't often seen together, except when a beautiful vortex is a trophy for the jaguar. But a beautiful whirling vortex requires such high maintenance, and jaguars are so narcissistic, that such a pairing is usually short-lived. Whirling vortex vs. jaguar battles are something to behold, though. A lot of shrieking wind and snarling cat, with the cat slinking away afterwards looking as if it were drenched with styling gel and blown dry with the jet blast from a Boeing 747.

Jaguars are much more likely to pair up with a beautiful young trophy beaver and co-beavers are just as likely to yearn after a whirling vortex. That means co-beavers spend a lot of time aggravated that the whirling vortex, a Category III Taker, is not responding to whatever the co-beaver is giving. The co-beaver erupts and the vortex is set off in response. If the vortex doesn't simply blow into the next town to find some more appreciative company, he or she might fight back.

Saying no to a whirling vortex is unacceptable, plain and simple. Vortexes don't understand the word no. It does not compute and only makes them mad. Whirling vortexes explode into anger at the mere mention of the word. The storm of anger a whirling vortex is capable of emitting is so terrifying, co-beavers learn to stuff their anger and wish garden-variety idiots could be as fascinating as whirling vortexes. But alas, they are not.

The storm of anger a whirling vortex exudes can appear to be a chaotic collision of righteous indignation, accusations of mostly imagined transgressions, pure unadulterated rage, shaming, and self-pity. It's not a pretty sight. But whirling vortexes feel they have been violated, even if the beaver or whomever they're involved with has given up everything.

Somehow, when a whirling vortex crunches the numbers, the beaver, altruist, amoeba, or jaguar owes him or her.

After a blowout with a whirling vortex, it's not unusual to find a ragged, penniless co-beaver with snatches of fur missing. At that same moment, the whirling vortex is crying his or her eyes out in front of a new admirer, gaining lots of sympathy as the vortex tearfully recounts how he or she was victimized by the beaver. To anyone except another whirling vortex, it is difficult to get your mind around how a vortex comes to such conclusions. An exception is new admirers who choose to believe the whirling vortex is a normal (although incredibly attractive) human being.

Keys to living with an idiot

⇨ **Admit anger.** Because anger is a natural emotion, there is no shame in admitting you experience it. The sin occurs when you consciously choose anger over healthier alternatives. Adjusting attitudes and expectations can avoid future anger. The really big sin occurs when you choose anger and *deny* you've chosen to use it. When you are disenfranchised or otherwise powerless, anger can make you feel momentarily empowered and vital. Sooner or later, natural results prove otherwise. You'll just end up getting madder.

⇨ **Accept that others get angry.** If there is anything people fear more than their own anger, it's anger in others. Amoebas, who constantly change shape anyway, change into wallpaper or window blinds when there is anger around. Co-beavers gnaw, dam, and build faster to try and make the anger go away. Altruistic Category III Givers take a deep breath and accept that some anger is inevitable. They then do what they reasonably can to improve the situation and beyond that, leave well enough alone. Couch potatoes might raise their eyebrows, but generally tune out anger in others. Jaguars snarl and arch their backs, and whirling vortexes increase their wind speed. All would do better to let other people have their feelings without reacting.

⇨ **Make a different choice.** When tempted to give in to anger and be swept down that momentarily gratifying spiral, you can aspire to be an altruistic Category III Giver and put the anger in perspective. You know anger is an available choice. But so is removing yourself from the situation long enough to consider which of your expectations were not met and what basis you had to make such expectations in the first place. Consider what Jesus would do. What would Gandhi do? Abraham Lincoln? Helen Keller? Ronald Regan? Bill Clinton? David Letterman? Martha Stewart? You don't have to get very far outside of yourself to realize that there are other people who might respond very differently to a similar situation. So can you.

Anticipating

Anticipation is an antidote to anger. As a solution, anticipation displaces the sin of anger by occupying the same space and time. But don't confuse anticipating with assuming. Assuming can be dangerous because it involves prejudging and invites false expectations. If your attitudes, responses, and remarks are based on presuppositions, they might (and probably will) reflect and perpetuate prejudices and biases you don't want. Even though people naturally became cynical over time when they think and act in certain ways, their cynicism is based on expectations as much as it is on their actual behavior. Sure, they might still act like lemonheads, but anticipation will position you to make lemonade.

When you assume that someone is going to make you angry, you've already gone there. More accurately, you have chosen anger before the other person does anything. Anticipation means emotionally preparing yourself to stay loose and be prepared for a variety of scenarios. You can't reasonably expect others to change what they say and do. By anticipating, however, you can remain flexible about your role in the situation. Because anticipation covers a wider variety of possible outcomes than the one you're customarily resigned to, you remain open to subtle positives in what your significant idiots might say and do.

There is a sales technique called *cooling the mark*, which involves pushing a potential customer's thinking slightly outside his or her box. The salesperson doesn't push so hard or suggest new ideas so radical that the customer bolts and runs. But with numerous nudges, customer objections begin to diminish as customers open up to ideas they would have ordinarily pushed back. Clinicians call the process systematic desensitization. I call it adjusting the boundary.

Children are masters at this technique. "Mom, do you remember how much you wanted me to learn to ride a bike?" the kid starts out. "There's a really great bike down at Wal-Mart that you ought to see." Wives and husbands use variations of this technique on each other, as do children in the playground. "Honey, do you remember that power drill you said we couldn't afford unless it was on sale?" Each one is cooling the mark. Ethically, I'm okay with persuasion as long as it stops short of manipulation. Cooling the mark can be used for anger control. "Mom, you know how the pastor said we should be slow to anger?" the little boy asks. "You know the big picture window in the Wilson's house next door...?"

Even after the value of anticipation is well established, when sufficiently riled, it's hard not to jump straight to anger. Anticipation can reduce the destructive force of anger by cooling your own marks. Anger is an after-the-fact response when your expectations are not met, unless your accumulated cynicism has brought you to the point of pre-anger. Either way, if your expectations are continuously not met, you might eventually remain in a state of perpetual anger; in which case, you need to reexamine the way you form your expectations. Some people hitch their emotions to a fantasy that, to more reasonable people, appears to have little or no chance of coming to pass.

Without arbitrarily throwing a wet blanket over healthy ambitions, it can serve you well to reign in your wilder expectations—especially those that depend almost exclusively on someone else conforming to behavior on your terms. Placing your happiness in the hands of others is a risky proposition, especially if the people to whom you hand over your happiness are, well, idiots. More bluntly, if you allow others you consider less emotionally and/or intellectually equipped than you to control the outcomes of your best-laid plans, will the real idiot please stand up?

If you anticipate, you won't be taken by surprise. Instead of becoming angry, you give yourself the option to say, "I was aware this might happen. It's not the end of the world." Or, "I knew this was a possibility. On to Plan B." By anticipating, you rehearse what might happen, if only to have alternative scenarios filed away in the corners of your mind.

If things don't turn out the way you want and you blow up anyway, saying, "I *knew* this wasn't going to work. I *knew* my (fill in the blank) wasn't going to do what I wanted him (or her) to do," you really didn't anticipate. Instead, you wagered all your hopes on the performance of others and prayed for a miracle, which is very different from anticipating the range of outcomes that might occur.

Shirley's Suggestion

"My daughter-in-law is dead-set on ignoring me," Shirley complains.

"I'm curious why you feel offended when she makes up her own mind."

"It's not like I'm asking her to reverse the flow of the Mississippi River," Shirley justifies. "I walked into their house last week and asked why she hadn't moved the plant in her kitchen closer to the window as we had agreed."

"Did she really say, 'Yes, Shirley, I agree the plant will be better next to the window'?"

"I think she said something more like, 'Fine, whatever.'"

"Has she ever snapped to and followed every suggestion you had for her?"

"When she and my son were first married, she listened quite well," Shirley recollects fondly. "But even then I suspected that she was simply trying to placate me."

"Since then?" I ask.

"Like pulling teeth."

"Do you think your son and daughter-in-law are happy to see you come for a visit?"

"No."

"Why not?"

"My son has accused me of trying to run their lives."

"Would you like them to eagerly anticipate your arrival?" I ask.

"That will be the day," she says sarcastically. "But those are my grandchildren."

"Would you like them to invite you more often?" I continue undaunted.

"That would be wonderful."

"Would you like to leave with a smile on your face and their faces, too?"

"I'd love to go there just once without my visit ending in a fight," she says hopefully.

"Could you prepare a speech before you visit next time?"

"What kind of speech?"

"Plan ahead of time to compliment your daughter-in-law on how nice her house looks. No matter how terrible you think it looks."

"That would be a lie," Shirley snorts with righteous indignation.

"That would be a kindness," I assure her. "Sometimes discretion is the better part of honesty."

"If I compliment her when I go in the house," Shirley contemplates, "she'll be more receptive to my suggestions? Is that what you think?"

"Almost," I say. "Anticipate what she would most like to hear you say. Praise her home when you arrive. Do you anticipate she'd like that?"

Shirley sighs and nods her head. "Oh, yes."

"Anticipating how she might interpret your suggestions," I go on, "you might hold off until she asks for your advice."

"What if she never asks?" Shirley shrieks.

"Silence is golden."

Shirley terminated the conversation at that point. I hadn't sufficiently cooled my mark. I pushed her outside of her box too far and too fast. But I'm confident she'll be back. The seeds I planted will take root if Shirley really wants to have a happier and more fulfilling relationship with her son and his wife.

I wanted to pick up the phone and call her daughter-in-law because she could have put anticipation to good use. Without even meeting these people, I was willing to bet dollars to doughnuts the daughter-in-law probably dreaded her mother-in-law's visits. But did she anticipate them? The difference can be profound.

If the daughter-in-law does her best to suck it up and hopes for the best every time the mother-in-law announces a visit, she probably also prays, through some miraculous Divine intervention, Shirley will be a new person when she arrives; not critical, judgmental, or full of advice. There's nothing wrong with praying, mind you—as long as you pray for the right things. If you pray for the serenity to accept the things you cannot change, like some mother-in-laws, you will position yourself emotionally to anticipate outcomes other than the ones you want, and be more willing to accept whatever comes your way.

The beauty in this is that your happiness suffers less damage. You can live a calmer, more serene life. Upon Shirley's first piece of advice, the daughter-in-law probably pulls her husband aside in the laundry room and snarls through clenched teeth, "Your mother *always* does this. If she gives me any more advice, I'll scream." How much nicer it would be for them to anticipate Shirley's behavior (based on a lifetime of experience). The daughter-in-law and her husband can then look at each other and sigh when Shirley launches into a litany of suggestions.

Instead of stuffing anger, forcing smiles, and placating Shirley's suggestions, they can say, "It's great to have you here, Mom. Let us tell you what we have planned for the day." What they're *not* saying is, "Mom, we knew you would come in here and try to control everything in our lives. That's how you are. That's how you've always been. We love you, but we're not going to relinquish control of our lives just so you can have a life." That's the conversation Shirley's son and his wife might want to have in private as an act of anticipation. Based on the same years of experience, Shirley's son and his wife can stay one step ahead and plan activities they know Shirley and her husband will enjoy.

Life Fountains

Anticipate Like an Amoeba

Anticipation appears to come naturally to amoebas. Despite being single-cell creatures, they tend to be intelligent and reflective. However, their expectations are about as low as their self-esteem, which indicates they are not making use of anticipation as much as they're setting their sights so low that any outcome is acceptable.

In that regard, I guess they're being realistic, which is a good thing. But I'd rather base my anticipation on a realistic-yet-wider range of possible outcomes. We do have some influence on how and when things take place. That's why Reinhold Niebuhr's Serenity Prayer includes the part about the "...courage to change the things I can." Although amoebas aren't exactly using anticipation to its full extent, anger is not a characteristic commonly associated with amoebas.

Beaver Anticipation

Left to their natural inclinations, Category II Giver co-beavers can conjure the most unrealistic expectations at the expense of healthy anticipation. Their sense that superior tree felling, dam and lodge building, and pond filling skills will cause others, jaguars and whirling vortexes in particular, to fall in love with them never holds up in practice, but they keep trying just the same. They wind up angry every time.

A healthy dose of anticipation can eliminate most of that. Of course, the co-beaver would have to admit his or her ulterior motives and accept outcomes less than the fantasy endings filling his or her imagination. Co-beavers are most in need of anticipation, but the least likely to employ it. This is yet another example of how they paint themselves into corners and then get upset because they can't get out.

Anticipatory Altruists

These ultra-mature Category III Givers have no trouble understanding or using anticipation as a hedge against disappointment and frustration. Whereas amoebas appear naturally inclined toward anticipation, altruistic Givers really do scan the range of options available to them before they act, and they carefully consider the equally wide range of possible outcomes. Unlike any other type of Life Fountain, altruists will do something, even if they anticipate a difficult outcome. They weigh decisions based on best outcome. If they feel it's the best thing to do for the most people concerned, they step out boldly and pay whatever price is necessary.

Black Holes

Anticipation and the Garden Slug

Anticipate what? A television service disruption in the area? Garden slugs don't expect much of anyone except perhaps the servers of their immediate needs. Anyone predisposed to waiting on a couch potato hand and foot is unlikely to rebel and give the slug anything to complain about.

Garden slugs might anticipate over a long period of time—years, to be exact—the possibility of exhausting their amoebas or beavers. But such a conflict would be so long in coming that the garden slug could hardly be expected to stay focused that long. If the garden slug's partner, parents, in-laws, children, or friends anticipate anything other than an imitation of an inanimate object, they haven't been very observant.

Anticipation and the Jaguar

Anticipation takes on a lesser role in the life of jaguars because their solution to disappointments is to crash through whatever the problem is with more power and volume. Jaguars are self-propelled for the most part and do for themselves rather than wait for others to do for them. This is a primary reason they tend to be the movers and shakers on this planet. They don't like to wait on anyone or anything. If they don't like something, they change it. If they don't like someone, they change people or sideline the one who has outlived usefulness and add a new model.

Jaguars are capable of using anticipation in a healthy way, but have little need to. Those who want to learn a better way to live with jaguars need to anticipate a jaguar's probable reaction to a variety of situations if the coexistence is to be peaceful. Jaguars won't respond as much as they'll react. But they'll react in predictable ways. If their significant others care enough to study them over time, anticipating their behavior won't be difficult and there will be few surprises. To amoebas and beavers in particular, that means reducing or removing unreasonable expectations in favor of anticipation. When anticipating a jaguar's next move, ask, "What would a pure predator do?"

Anticipation and the Whirling Vortex

Whirling vortexes can be as heedless toward anticipation as they are toward anything else. They often expect the best from everyone around them and anticipate the worst. Because they can transform themselves into victims in front of your very eyes, vortexes probably won't admit to anticipating something even if they do. More often than not, anticipation won't serve a worthwhile purpose for the whirling vortex any more than it does for a jaguar. If something makes whirling vortexes angry or disappoints them, they don't stew on it; they huff and puff and blow the problem away, along with anyone in their path.

Anticipation is a more valuable tool for those who stand to get hurt in the hurricane-force winds and gnashing teeth of angry vortexes, jaguars, and beavers. Yes, beavers. Perhaps even more deadly than an angry whirling vortex or an angry jaguar is a more intensely hyper-codependent beaver who has been scorned or ignored once too often. The more over the top a co-beaver is, the more predictable the behavior.

If we have a raging co-beaver on our hands, we know why. He or she just wants to be acknowledged and appreciated for the enormous sacrifice he or she has made without anyone requesting said sacrifice. The jaguar is nearly as predictable. But a whirling vortex can come at you from any direction, at any time. Even the vortex might not know what's going on emotionally, except that she or he is upset, and that's enough. Anticipation, as it applies to a whirling vortex, needs to be generalized to cover unclassified and unanticipatable blowups. When the whirling vortex goes off, don't act surprised or panic. Take a deep breath, sigh, and think, "Here we go again. This too will pass." Then head for the storm cellar.

Keys to living with an idiot

⇨ **Nip anger before it nips you.** Once you let anger dictate your behavior, it's too late to "unring" the bell. If anger is truly based on your expectations not being met, it's pretty obvious that anger can be reduced by adjusting expectations. Easy to say. But people often feel as if they have no choice but to be angry. Then behavior follows that you're not proud of or, worse, further damages relationships. If you want to live with an idiot in a happier and more fulfilling way, you need to go about the business of finding alternatives to anger. This doesn't mean denying anger as a natural emotion, but instead taking charge over the things you have the ability to change.

⇨ **Stop assuming.** The idiots in your life might give you ample reasons to assume they'll disappoint you. But that still doesn't relieve you of your role in the debacle. Learning from past experience what might happen in any given situation is smart. But bringing your own bias and prejudice to the party doesn't help. If you base expectations on false assumptions, the outcomes will be predictably disappointing. It can be as simple as *garbage in, garbage out.* When you base expectations for the behavior of others on assumptions, it's almost like daring the idiots to disappoint you.

⇨ **Anticipate.** This is a much better habit than assuming. When you anticipate, you take away the idiots' power to disappoint you. You also remove much of your basis for anger. The range of possible outcomes you anticipate might include some assumptions, but there will be much more on the menu. Anticipating is based on experience, which you can recall yourself, or learn from others who know someone you're dealing with. (Of course, hearsay always brings up the consider-the-source issue.) Anticipating is taking effective control of our attitudes before the attitudes of others can set our emotional agenda.

Chapter Summary

Anger vs. anticipation. Anger usually means you were caught unprepared, or didn't bother to think ahead. Part of preparation is setting reasonable and realistic expectations. Anticipation plays a large role in avoiding the reactive knee-jerk type of anger. Anger can only be productive when it is recognized as an indication of how you are tuned in to the world around you at any given time. Choosing anger as a response is never productive except in the most extreme situations when righteous indignation is the only way to go. But I can't think of when that would have ever served me best.

Anger and anticipation play different roles in the case of the Life Fountain family vs. the Black Hole family. More innocuous personalities such as amoebas, bucolic beavers, and altruists from the Giver camp and garden slugs from the Taker camp are not big anger choosers. For more dramatic characters such as jaguars and whirling vortexes, anger is usually part and parcel of their private and public personas. Co-beavers can spend a lot of time being hurt and angry, but they tend to play it out in more subtle ways.

Choosing anger indicates that preferable options have not been considered; at least not *thoughtfully* considered. If one or more of the parties in a relationship chooses anger, meaningful communication is doomed for the duration of the anger. When trying to live a happier and meaningful existence with the significant idiots in your life, anger will always be a setback. Anticipation is a first step toward lasting improvement.

You can give yourself a way out, and avoid arbitrarily anticipating the worst. You can remain flexible enough to be pleasantly surprised if your spouse, significant other, sibling, child, parent, in-law, friend, coworker, or boss shows signs of improvement.

To-do list:

- ☑ Admit anger.
- ☑ Accept that others get angry.
- ☑ Make a different choice.
- ☑ Nip anger before it nips you.
- ☑ Stop assuming.
- ☑ Anticipate.

Chapter 6

The Second Relational Sin and Solution: Blaming vs. Re-framing

FOR DECADES, MENTAL HEALTH and personal growth counselors have advocated replacing "You" statements with "I" statements. There are exceptions. If the "You" is followed by a compliment such as, "...are so beautiful," great. If the "You" is followed by an instruction such as, "...need to take a left, cross the bridge, the shop is on the corner," no problem. If the "You" is followed by a new car as in, "Congratulations, you are the ninth caller," terrific. But a "You" followed by an accusation is blaming.

Statements beginning with "I" imply acceptance of responsibility. Some crafty critters try to sneak around the "I" statement with, "I feel bad when you act *like a big, fat jerk.*" Or, "I don't know what to do when you *act like an absolute moron.*" "I" statements are reserved for accepting personal responsibility for our feelings, our thoughts, and our actions. If a cheap shot hitches a ride on a statement of ownership for our feelings, all bets are off. We might as well have started with the word "You...."

All of us want to be heard. When an accusing statement starts with "You," the accused won't hear any of the words that follow. The accused tunes out the accuser in self-defense. If the accused does take it in, the accusing "You" statement will probably be followed by an equally accusing "I" statement such as, "*I* have a problem controlling *my* anger? Excuse *me*...?"

Blaming

We've all played the blame game. It would be nice if it were only a game. To many, it's a hobby. To others, it's a serious avocation. To yet others, blaming is a way of life. To those who feel the need to be perfect, blaming can be a survival skill. If the only shot I have at being loved and accepted is to be perfect, I must not be at fault for anything. Just being *suspected* of wrongdoing or imperfection is unacceptable. Accepting responsibility for anything negative will leave a blemish on my "perfect" record.

A person might or might not be guilty as charged for doing something negligent, knuckleheaded, or hurtful. Facts could prove or disprove the accusation if the blamers and blamees don't get caught up in a storm of denial, counterdenial, attack, counterattack, and counter-counterattack. Despite being slightly less abrasive than criticism, blaming is still a losing game. Anticipating future behavior based on historic behavior helps avoid situations that wind up in blame.

Idiots from every category, even recovering idiots such as myself, tend to play the blame game when they're insecure. An interesting side note: For an essentially clueless idiot to actually feel insecure is a hopeful sign. Being insecure implies idiots have some conscious or unconscious awareness that they are out of their element, and functioning beyond their capabilities. Having the feeling at all is, in itself, a clue. At least they're feeling something, which offers faint hope they will *get it* someday.

Idiots blame others for their acts of incompetence and/or insensitivity to avoid responsibility for correcting the problem. Idiots don't feel competent to correct problems, so they figure it makes no sense to acknowledge any part in them. This might be good thinking if idiots weren't so clumsy as to leave fingerprints on stupid mistakes. All recovering idiots have perfected the innocent expression and signature response, "What?"

Nice Try

I've mixed colors in the washing machine often enough to prove this concept. When my significant other holds up formerly white articles of clothing, now pink, green, or blue, I can see the blame in her eyes. I flash a too-defiant-to-be-completely-innocent expression, blink my eyes twice, and say, "What?" Lamely questioning, "What?" never gets me off the hook, but in that moment I feel connected to the worldwide family of idiots.

Those of us who attend Idiots Exposed meetings feel we have more pressing demands on our time than to separate whites and colors in the laundry. What those important things are I can never remember because the unpleasant aftermath of dyeing whites the color of my new sweatshirt is so memorable. The parable of the laundry illustrates how futile it is to duck blame because, when the whites become pink, pistachio, or chartreuse, there is no one *else* to blame. The dog didn't put the sweatshirt in there. I don't have children. Recovering idiots are our own adult supervision. How frightening is that?

A skilled blamer would instinctively put it back on the other party saying, "If you would do the laundry, this wouldn't happen." When an idiot is caught red-handed, it's over. I don't know how many times, dating back to college, a roommate has said, "You owe me a new set of towels." That comment, although a "You" statement, assigns responsibility where it belongs in a matter-of-fact way. I suppose he could have said, "I'll expect a new set of towels tomorrow." Same point, no "You" statement.

Holding someone accountable, as my roommates did, is different from blaming. To say, "We need to do something about this problem," is different than saying, "You idiot." Holding people accountable, if it's within your power of persuasion or negotiation to do so, is something you can do to take care of yourself. Accepting responsibility for things you do is equally important.

If there was someone to blame for the new colors in the laundry, idiots like me could keep goofing up with impunity. Fortunately, with nowhere to run and hide, clueless idiots are faced with the choice of exerting the infinitesimal amount of effort required to separate clothes or keep getting hammered. It takes quite a bit of hammering and pink underwear before those clueless creatures come around. If blaming is replaced with holding them accountable, say, in their wallets, they'll come around faster.

What happens when an idiot is blamed for something that's not his or her fault? That could mean that blaming is being used to transfer responsibility from where it belongs to an unsuspecting and innocent person. The idiot's fault or not, if blaming is perceived as an act of aggression, the facts of the matter get lost in the blamee's struggle to shed blame or discredit the blamer.

Extremism—Positive *and* Negative

As much as I'd like to see all blaming come to an end, pretending that nothing ever goes wrong and therefore no one bears responsibility, much less blame, is a dangerous road to travel. The perpetually positive (see no evil) thinkers ("Things just happen, nobody's to blame") can fall into this crowd. Only circumstances can be responsible. Those who *want* to gossip and blame are always irritated when a perpetually positive thinker says, "Well, she has been under a lot of pressure lately," or, "His father was an alcoholic," or, "(Fill in the blank) is in the White House." Nothing is ever anybody's fault.

Perpetually positive Pollyanna thinkers feel holding people responsible for bad choices is cruel and unusual punishment. This is a feel-good philosophy intended to make perpetually positive thinkers feel good. It doesn't do anything to promote the growth and development of people who are captive to their own thinking and judgment disorders. The metal folding chairs in the basement of the Methodist church on Thursday nights are full of IE people trying to accept responsibility for their thinking and judgment disorders in order to make better choices in the future. They don't want anyone making excuses for them.

At the opposite end of the continuum from the perpetually positive thinkers are the perpetually negative thinkers. Habitual blamers fall into this population. Everything is somebody else's fault. It's hard to say which extreme is worse—perpetually positive or perpetually negative. Suffice to say, avoiding either one is a good idea.

If you're a blamer, as I was for much of my life, your default settings automatically send you into a blaming mode when you are uncomfortable with something or someone. When it's too uncomfortable to accept that you're contributing to your own discomfort, the spiral will continue—like a dog chasing its own tail. Around and around and around we go. Like the perpetually positive thinker, this mind-set doesn't promote growth and development of the individual. Worse yet, it doesn't make the blamer feel better. The blamer claims it does, but then why is he or she always so angry and/or depressed?

Life Fountains

Blaming Amoebas

Amoebas make terrific scapegoats. Most Category I Giver amoebas wouldn't think of blaming others for things they do. Amoebas are more likely to accept responsibility and take the blame for things others do. Amoebas don't take on the sins of others out of the goodness of their hearts. They do it primarily to avoid conflict.

I recently experienced one of those you-don't-realize-you've-slipped-into-amoebaland-until-it's-too-late moments. I was walking out of a store at the same moment another person rushed in. If I hadn't been paying attention and taken evasive action, there would have been a collision. The other person was moving fast and caught me by surprise. Unsure what amount of potential hostility I was facing in that nanosecond, my instinctive amoeba response was summed up in the two words I spoke: "I'm sorry." People don't even need to ask amoebas to absorb blame. It just happens.

Blaming sessions can become spirited and potentially hostile. Amoebas will do anything they can to keep the volume down. If that includes taking the blame for things other people do, amoebas will. The catch-22 occurs when the amoeba takes the blame someone else is eager to shed, and the amoeba winds up catching *more* grief than he or she originally would have if the amoeba had pushed the blame back across the table at the truly guilty party.

A classic plot for sitcoms is the hapless amoeba absorbing blame to keep things copacetic only to find out that his or her troubles are just beginning. The more the amoeba tries to keep things peaceful, the more he or she complicates and aggravates the situation. The more things go wrong, the more blaming there is to do. The more blaming there is to do, the more there is for the amoeba to absorb. Being single-cell creatures, constantly changing shape, amoebas can swell up with blame until they finally explode, becoming confetti.

Blaming Beavers

Being primarily a member of the Category II Giver beaver family, my amoeba-like behaviors are diminishing with time, especially as I make progress toward more altruistic pursuits. The subheading "Blaming Beavers" is an intentional double entendre. Beavers can be the scapegoats in relationships. In other words, they can be *blamees*. Of all the beaver varieties, the co-beaver is most likely to be tagged with blame for the actions of others. They can also be fierce blamers.

Bucolic beavers aren't very quick to do anything hasty, which includes accepting blame for something that's not their fault. They're too laid-back and easygoing to get caught up in someone else's urgency. Ambitious achiever beavers make better choices as a rule, despite the intensity with which they pursue success. Unlike bucolic beavers, achiever beavers will consider certain situations urgent and time sensitive. But they will be judicious about what they consider urgent. This, in part, is what helps them become successful.

Achiever beavers have been heard to utter the popular comeback: "Lack of planning on your part does not constitute an emergency on my part." Spending precious time and energy deciding who should be blamed for something is not an efficient or ultimately profitable use of time or energy. If the blaming is trite and inconsequential, bucolic and achiever beavers might shoulder responsibility just to keep the ball rolling rather than get bogged down in minutia. Neither do these two reasonable beaver types try to push responsibility for their own actions onto others. As a result, bucolic and achiever beavers are pretty easy to get along with.

If anyone tends to give beavers a bad name, it's the co-beaver. In this case, the bad name is associated with the blame game. Many co-beavers engage in a vicious cycle of accepting blame for the actions of others, principally jaguars and whirling vortexes. The co-beaver's reasoning and motivations are simple: "Take their burdens on my shoulders and they'll appreciate me more."

Not. Jaguars and whirling vortexes are never going to fully appreciate sacrifices made by the long-suffering co-beaver. Over time, the co-beaver is going to lose patience with the jaguar and/or whirling vortex and start resenting them. What began as voluntarily taking on blame that didn't belong to the co-beaver degenerates into the Category II co-beaver blaming the jaguar or whirling vortex for his or her unhappiness.

With the co-beaver blaming his or her significant idiot for the burden of blame the significant idiot never asked the co-beaver to assume in the first place, the unfortunate cycle of blame closes around the co-beaver's head. The co-beaver blaming the jaguar or whirling vortex for something they aren't really guilty of is like piling up more wrongs to make a "right." If the co-beaver had maintained a healthy boundary, taken responsibility for his or her own transgressions and no others, the cruel ordeal could have been avoided. It's a good thing beavers can operate in mud, because co-beavers have a habit of stepping in it.

More than any other Life Fountain Giver or Black Hole Taker life-form, the co-beaver is most often locked in pursuit of perfection. While pursuing perfection, they will probably be overtaken by frustration. To keep that perfection scorecard unblemished, perfectionists try to avoid anything that might open the door for blame. In extreme cases, co-beavers will blame others when things go wrong as a result of co-beaver behavior. Perfection is preserved; for the moment, anyway.

Better to be a bucolic or achiever beaver. I imagine it would have been more peaceful to be a full-time amoeba. Being a co-beaver, up to my incisors in the blame game, led me to take on enormous and unnecessary emotional burdens. Getting out of the blame business lightened my load enormously.

Altruistic Blaming

Thanks to the lofty, big-picture thinking altruistic Category III Givers are famous for, they never waste time or energy on anything as non-productive and potentially destructive as pointing fingers. It takes maturity and wisdom to gain enough emotional altitude to see that blaming serves no good purpose. I've found that the altruists in my life are great role models and advisers, often seeing things in ways I would never have thought of. The more contact I have with them and the more I learn from them, the more I become like them.

Like Goldilocks's porridge, thinking can be too positive or too negative. The altruistic Category III Giver is the best example of thinking that's "just right." Perpetually positive thinking, to the point of blocking reality, is dangerous. Perpetually negative thinking is equally dangerous when it hides anything positive in the real world from view. The co-beaver who has slipped into perpetual negativity can find happiness only in the fantasy world he or she imagines will come to pass when everyone thinks and behaves as the co-beaver thinks they should.

An altruistic Category III Giver doesn't fall into this trap. By keeping a healthy perspective, the altruist finds an optimal balance by considering things in context. That places the altruist's thinking in the middle of the positive to negative continuum with the ability to flex. Blaming or refusing to accept responsibility are both deep ruts in the road of life. An altruist appreciates why co-beavers might become excessively negative or naively positive, but won't fall into or get stuck in either of those ruts.

Being aware that ruts exist is the best way to avoid falling into them. Altruists, who can see self-destructive behavior for what it is, don't dismiss responsibility the way perpetually positive thinkers do to avoid enforcing consequences or a possible self-indictment. Altruists do not engage in blaming either. Being aware of who is responsible for something doesn't necessarily mean lowering the boom on them. If the altruist is responsible for something, negative or positive, he or she will accept blame, or praise. The point is to remain flexible, and learn from mistakes, the things that cause pain, ways that don't work, as well as things that bring joy and peace.

Choosing to remove blame as a weapon from our personal arsenal is a step toward greater maturity and patience for the idiots in your life. Responsibility must stay in its appropriate place, but blaming can go away and stay away. Holding others accountable without judging them is an emotionally mature thing to do. Holding myself accountable without judging is equally mature. This is the benchmark altruistic Category III Givers set for the rest of us.

Black Holes

Blaming and the Garden Slug

Category I Taker garden slugs will blame anyone for anything that annoys them if they feel it's worth investing the energy, which they rarely do. What appears to be a live-and-let-live attitude on the part of the slug is really just a capitulation for lack of energy. If pressed hard, a sluggish Category I Taker will attribute his or her actions (or lack thereof) to a backache, toothache, hangnail, exhaustion syndrome, or (fill in the blank) being in the White House. These are the most lame forms of blaming imaginable. Even the slug doesn't expect anyone to take him or her seriously. But who cares? The slug is not going anywhere anyway.

A co-beaver who ends up with a slug spouse or slug child can (and probably will) blame the slug for all kinds of things. The slug, however, has a retort for everything. If the co-beaver says, "You're the reason nothing gets done around here." The slug will say, "If you want (fill in the blank) done, do it yourself."

This is actually sound advice if you can forget for a moment who it came from. As soon as you start expecting others to do things and become annoyed when your expectations are not met, you have crossed into the blame zone. Anticipating what a garden slug is likely to do and likely not to do is a good hedge against disappointment and emotional turmoil. I go back to my stock question, "When have you ever known this person to act any differently?"

Try to out-blame a slug and the slug will out-excuse you every time. If you sarcastically ask, "Have you forgotten how to take a shower?" the slug will say, "The commercials aren't long enough." Some annoyed spouses have even said things such as, "If I had known how exciting you were, I'd never have married you." Uh-huh. How about the killer line for sluggish kids, "If I had known you would turn out like this, I'd have sent you back." Too late. For the 30-year-old still living at home, "We didn't spend our entire retirement fund paying your college tuition for 10 years so you can tie up our television playing video games." Some slug-wranglers get lucky and their breathing sofa cushions venture out and become productive citizens. For the rest, better get a second job, folks. Nobody's getting any younger.

Blaming isn't going to propel a Category I Taker garden slug into action. You might as well decorate around him or her. Maybe even build a small addition off the back of the house; park him in there with a TV, sofa, and remote; and connect the addition with a hidden door so company will never know the slug is still around.

If a person works two jobs to make ends meet and comes home to collapse on the sofa, that's not a garden slug. It's more likely an exhausted amoeba, or bucolic or achiever beaver. Sometimes a Category II Giver co-beaver will work him- or herself to the point of exhaustion, collapse on the sofa, and then start blaming him- or herself for being lazy. Don't confuse the symptoms. A Category I Taker garden slug is lazy and makes no apologies for it. Changing expectations will achieve better results than playing the blame game.

Blaming and the Jaguar

Jaguars are fast and sleek. They will turn any blame you send their way against you. If you plan to lay blame on a jaguar, expect to have it thrown back in your face with a comeback such as, "What are you talking about?" This classic jaguar question is not denial. It's a spacer. While you are busy explaining what you're talking about (the jaguar already knows more of what you're talking about than you do), the jaguar is inverting everything you say to place the blame squarely back on your shoulders. Many jaguars are so convincing that you come away from the confrontation shaking your head, wondering what just happened, and when (exactly) you went insane.

The jaguar's guilt is never really in question. But it's still your fault. It matters little whether a beaver, amoeba, altruist, or garden slug has a legitimate beef with a jaguar, they're all going to be out-maneuvered. Altruistic Category III Givers won't often be found in compromised or diminished positions vis-à-vis jaguars because they're usually smart enough to avoid such snares. But on that rare occasion when an altruist is standing eyeball to eyeball with a defensive jaguar, count on the altruist to be wise enough to walk away and pursue the matter with a higher authority or chalk it up to experience.

A garden slug in a similar situation will walk away because walking takes less energy than fighting or petitioning a higher authority to hear the grievance. An amoeba will slink away not feeling worthy of the battle. The only character who poses an appreciable threat to the jaguar in the blame game is the whirling vortex. More on that in a moment.

Only beavers seem to be willing to take on an opponent they have no hope of defeating. In this case, the jaguar. Bucolic beavers, true to their descriptive name, understand what a waste of time blaming is. Ambitious achiever beavers don't want to waste time or energy on something that doesn't promote success and well-being. Only the self-righteous and long-suffering co-beaver is left to take on the jaguar, this time trying to blame the big cat for something the feline did, but won't own up to.

Jaguars always have arsenals of blaming accusations at their dis-posal. In the event they are blamed for anything, they are prepared to turn the tables quickly and decisively. Jaguars rarely need to take the offensive with blaming. Co-beavers get their tails twisted frequently enough to throw blame a jaguar's way, but the jaguar just extends a paw and swats it back at them.

If co-beavers, in relationships with jaguars, ever stop blaming for whatever reason, the jaguars might pick up the load. Jaguars have been known to take out their frustrations on their families, even when they're frustrated about how things are going at work, how they played golf that afternoon, or because things are turning dicey with the mistress.

For the co-beaver, blaming is supposed to affix responsibility on the shoulders of the one responsible for something. For Category II Taker jaguars, blaming is a powerful tool for shifting responsibility to someone else, regardless of how much or how little they deserve it. I can't say it serves no purpose for anyone. Even though jaguars are proficient at transferring blame, it doesn't ultimately help them become happier jaguars, which supports my earlier contention that blaming doesn't do anyone any real good. There are no winners in the blame game.

Blaming and the Whirling Vortex

Blaming backfires when used against a jaguar. Try to lay blame on a whirling vortex and it's literally blown back in your face. Despite their incredible energy and high volume, whirling vortexes are insecure at their cores. At some level they are fully aware of how guilty they are for various crimes and misdemeanors. Blaming them for the things for which they are truly guilty will turn a minor squall into a full-fledged hurricane.

If blaming serves any good purpose, it could be as a lie detector for whirling vortexes. If you accuse whirling vortexes of something they didn't do, they barely notice. There is no inner conviction eating away at them. Accusing a whirling vortex of something for which he or she bears no responsibility will barely rate a strong gust of wind in defense.

Accuse whirling vortexes of things for which they are responsible, and you'll get blown into the next county. Whirling vortexes don't claim to be perfect. When they go into their poor, poor, pitiful me routines, they confess to all manners of grievous infractions, if it gets them something. But for some odd reason, when they get caught with their hand in the cookie jar, so to speak, and it's not their chosen time in the confessional, don't be the one to point it out.

When they're in their pitiful mode, whirling vortexes can look and act a lot like garden slugs in the way they shift responsibility away from themselves. They believe they are ultimately forgivable, which is a good Judeo-Christian principle. However, the forgiveness they expect is not based on grace, but on the outrageousness of their excuses.

Consider the testimony of a whirling parolee: "If my momma had let me eat candy as a child, I wouldn't have gorged myself on it as a teenager away from her watchful eyes. Then I wouldn't have had a toothache that night, and gone looking for some Anbesol in the drugstore pharmacy after they had closed. Being so dark in there, I accidentally snatched up all their narcotic pain medications and sold 'em behind the bowling alley." How can we not forgive such a victim of cruel and unusual circumstances?

Keys to living with an idiot

⇨ **Don't point.** Remember the old saying that an accusing finger pointed at someone else leaves three more accusing fingers pointing back at you. As soon as you feel compelled to point at someone else, you need to wag that finger back and forth in front of your nose as if to say "ah, ah, ah," move on to Plan B (B as in "better" idea). Pointing is an impulse for many people. If you continue to practice the habit, you're not facing stiff enough competition. After a lifetime of pointing my index finger at amoebas and weaker beavers, I stuck it in the face of a whirling vortex and nearly had it torn off. It was a painful, but good lesson. Of all the bad things we can do with our fingers, pointing the fickle finger of blame is one of the worst.

⇨ **Avoid the blame game.** Many people who feel maligned, used, or abused think their revenge is in blaming others. Depending on the parties you are blaming, you can get away with this behavior all, some, or none of the time. In any case, blamers never endear themselves to blamees. Blaming a 98-pound amoeba who can't fight back resolves nothing. Blaming a 298-pound garden slug who just rolls over and goes back to sleep resolves nothing. Blaming an altruistic Category III Giver just makes you look foolish. Blaming a jaguar will lead to you being led away in a straightjacket. Begin blaming a whirling vortex and your body might never be found. Blaming yourself just makes you unhappy.

⇨ **Seek solutions.** It's a much healthier way to expend time, energy, and resources than blaming. If you truly want to live a happier and more fulfilling existence with the significant idiot in your life, blaming won't get it done. In fact, it will only make things worse. Next time you're tempted to lay a heap of blame on some dodo, you need to think of words you can speak and actions you can undertake that will produce a solution. Blaming is the cheap, easy, and useless way out because it never leads you out. If you stop abdicating so much of your responsibility to others with poor track records, you won't end up with a heap of blame to distribute. You can do things yourself or find someone more reliable. If you stop accepting responsibility that doesn't belong to you, you'll have less reason to blame yourself.

Re-framing

You can come to understand your life in a new way by putting the picture you have of your life in a new frame. The frame around your life portrait can also be called your worldview. The current frame you have is made of your existing beliefs, biases, prejudices, and paradigms. When is the last time you re-framed? Never? Perhaps you've tried unsuccessfully to change reality within your old frame. I did. As your life portrait changes, is your frame changing with it?

If the realities of life beyond my control are not going to change, what hope is there I can feel any better about myself and my relationships with others? Why not just accept how I feel, find something or somebody to blame, and at least get my frustrations off my chest? You can feel differently about the realities of life, that's why. It's not easy. It takes patience, persistence, perseverance, and a new picture frame, but it can be done.

In the previous chapter I spoke of choosing an alternative to anger rather than trying to just push it aside, bury it, or deny it exists. Ridding yourself of blame is another choice you can make. When you evict something from its traditional place in your life, a vacuum is created. Things can seem hunky-dory for about 24 hours, and then you hear it. That loud sucking sound is all kinds of mischief being sucked in to fill the vacuum—thoughts and behaviors potentially more damaging than the stuff you just cleaned out.

Your mantra needs to be: *Clean Out and Fill Up.* Cleaning out alone won't work because of the vacuum/sucking thing. Trying to cram mature thinking and behaviors into a space already overflowing with misguided thinking and behaviors is not, well, mature. You need to get rid of the old to make room for the new. It doesn't happen all at once. It's sort of a one-to-one exchange.

You can think of your reservoir of stinkin' thoughts as Ping-Pong balls filling a dry swimming pool. Taking an old one out and replacing it with a new one, one at a time, is going to take a while, hence the persistence and perseverance. Without the support of a recovery program, support group, or trusted adviser of some kind to provide encouragement, most people will barely get started before they throw up their hands and say, "This is stupid."

Another way of looking at this process is taking life, with all its realities, out of your old picture frame and putting it in a new one. You can think of your life portrait as unfinished because your life is unfinished. The portrait, as it has been up to this point in your life, is what it is. Re-framing can give it new meaning. With new meaning, you can add to the portrait in ways you wouldn't have thought of before. Left in its old frame, you wouldn't have seen the potential and new possibilities in the new portrait.

Re-framing is sometimes all that stands between blaming and seeking solutions. Re-framing could also be thought of as rethinking. You could say that your early childhood developmental issues gave you a particular way of making sense out of the world around you—an eyeglasses prescription of sorts. Instead of going back for regular exams to see if the prescription was still helping you to see things clearly, you left it the same intensity while your vision changed, until everything became distorted.

Just wiping off the lenses once in a while helps. But for some reason, people don't try to see more clearly until the pain of distorted vision becomes too great to bear. Some people never clear up their vision and die miserable. It's happened in my family, and I'm happy to say it's a family tradition our current generation is breaking.

That's one reason why I joined Idiots Exposed. All of my best-laid plans and grand schemes got me nowhere in relationships. I slipped further down my co-beaver spiral until I admitted I was truly powerless. It would take intentional, deliberate behavior, guided by an intelligence greater than my own, to climb back out. A noble undertaking, considering how many Ping-Pong balls were in my swimming pool.

Re-framing how I view the world and my role in it has changed everything for me. Finally accepting the futility and destructive nature of blaming has released me from that prison cell where I made wrong decision after wrong decision. Although I won't say I've exactly left the institution, I've replaced a slew of old Ping-Pong balls with new ones.

Shirley's Suggestion

"I don't need to re-frame anything," Shirley assures me. "The idiots in my life need the new picture frame. Not me."

"That's a variation on the theme," I chuckle.

"Don't mock me."

"Sorry."

"I'm serious."

"But are you happy?"

"Not yet."

"Wait a minute," I say. "I remember now. You'll be happy as soon as the idiots in your life think, say, and do what you tell them to think, say, and do."

"...tell them to think, say, and do," Shirley says in unison with me.

"I thought you were going a different direction with that."

"I was," Shirley says. "But nothing changed."

"What did you expect to change?"

"I expected them to start thinking, saying, and doing what I wanted without me telling them."

"Surely, you jest."

"Not funny, John."

"It sounds as if you're still blaming others for your unhappiness."

"Why shouldn't I? It's their fault."

"If you could command them to do one thing and one thing only, Shirley, what would it be?"

"To be happy."

"If they would just be happy, you would then be happy?"

"That's all I've ever asked of them really."

"Until they're happy, you can't be happy?"

"How can I be?"

"Why don't you decide to be happy first and show them how?"

"That's not how it works, Doc."

I could see it wasn't working for her. In Shirley's old picture frame, she can only conceive of being happy if those around her are happy first. She doesn't see the need for a new picture frame, yet. It is as if Shirley cautiously, almost reluctantly, lifts one old Ping-Pong ball out of the swimming pool and kicks a bucket full of others she has removed back in. To her credit, just picking one up now and then puts Shirley on a faster track.

Life Fountains

Re-framing Like an Amoeba

Amoebas are reluctant to re-frame their thinking because they have become so familiar with their subordinate roles. I won't go so far as to say they're comfortable, but they've reached equilibrium where things make sense. For an amoeba to re-frame his or her portrait would take an enormous motivation, such as a religious conversion, long-term psychotherapy, or a tax incentive.

Having said that, an amoeba's new frame, should he or she ever acquire one, will hopefully bring out the positive contribution amoebas make in their own lives and the lives of others. With the enhanced positives should come enhanced relationships as the amoeba's self-equity increases. A new and better frame will make any life portrait look better; even an amoeba's.

Beaver Re-framing

Shirley is a Giver with an aversion to receiving, despite her penchant for demanding. She is such a Category II Giver co-beaver that the other beavers tease her about her buckteeth. I understand her because I'm only a few Thursday night meetings ahead of her. Although there are many bucolic beavers near and familiar to her, it still doesn't seem to matter how undemanding she could be and still be a beaver. Neither does her exposure to ambitious achiever beavers seem to interest her in re-framing her blaming in more productive and positive ways.

All of the activities co-beavers engage in are designed to frame a sense of truth and reality based on what co-beavers believe they are missing in their lives. That's why they work so industriously at constructing a new reality. Imagine for a moment a busy and insufferably eager co-beaver suddenly gets a glimpse at life as it could be: boundaries in place and respected, decisions made in the best interest of everyone involved and accepted, permission for all creatures to be as they are, and permission to not associate with those whose behaviors are upsetting.

Of all the characters in this drama, one would think a beaver could gnaw down a tree and construct that new picture frame lickety-split. The problem with co-beavers is they don't work on their own frames. As Shirley points out, they feel it's their job to re-frame *everybody else's* thinking. They try to squeeze everybody's portraits into their old frame. With that, they cross the line and their best-laid plans and grand schemes fall victim to failed ambition. You can re-frame your own portrait of truth and reality—no one else's.

Re-framing Altruists

Although altruistic Category III Givers view life through a realistic frame to begin with, they appreciate the need to continuously reinvent the frame to make sure they don't get locked into stilted thinking. It's not that altruists do everything right, but they are the quickest of all the Life Fountain or Black Hole types to learn and apply new knowledge. More than being quick learners, altruists are curious.

A curious learner will reexamine the way she or he looks at the world on a regular basis. Developing a more curious picture frame for his or her still unfinished life portrait makes it more interesting and, ultimately, more functional.

Black Holes

Re-framing Garden Slugs

Garden slugs won't be looking for a new frame through which to view life, but they may, perhaps, look for a bigger television screen. Something has to motivate these people. The biggest re-framing issue *you* face is finding fresh new ways to look at your slug. Everybody has something that energizes them. In the case of a breathing sofa cushion, you might need to get a completely new optician's prescription to find it. If you want to invest that much energy in a garden slug, that is.

Chances are he or she has long ago given up on his or her favorite avocations and resigned him- or herself to a passive lifestyle. There's no sense in caring more for their happiness than they do.

On a positive note, sluggish Category I Takers make it easier to see how re-framing the way you view and respond to others is the polar opposite of blaming. Blaming a passive garden slug for all sorts of ills and aggravations in life is as easy as falling off a log. Like many easy roads to travel, blaming the slug, or anyone else for that matter, doesn't lead anywhere useful or productive. Not only is it easy to see the slug is not responsible for anything worth blaming, it's equally easy to see how much we are *not* to blame for their condition. I'm never surprised to hear that someone has re-framed his or her life portrait and a garden slug was somehow left out of the new frame.

Re-framing Jaguars

The jaguar's keen ability to make others feel guilty for their own transgressions is a sinister form of de-framing. De-framing is a form of undoing. Guilty parties often defend themselves by blaming their accusers of wrongdoing. When clear water will reveal corruption, the corrupt muddy it. Jaguars are good at de-framing whatever we try to re-frame. This is not a good talent in the hands of a Category II Taker. Most people involved with jaguars (especially co-beavers) go through endless blaming and forgiving cycles before they finally decide "enough is enough," and resolve to change something in their approach. Jaguars are clever manipulators; expert in the use of smoke and mirrors. They alter the context of a situation, real or imagined, to make themselves appear blameless.

The co-beaver's desire to get along with everyone and stay attached plays into the jaguar's ability to de-frame on demand. Jaguars can be charming manipulators in how they go about it. This leaves the difficult job of truly re-framing the relationship to the co-beaver. What else is new? Anticipating the possibility a jaguar might attempt to de-frame a situation is a first step to building a bigger and more realistic frame around the jaguar's temporary and opportunistic frame.

The most difficult aspect of re-framing a portrait including a jaguar is abandoning the long-cherished hope and dream the jaguar will keep his or her promises. Some promises might be kept, especially the financial ones. Yet, keeping your old frame in place is to bet the farm on the jaguar keeping *emotional* promises. You've invested much, consciously or unconsciously, in your old frames.

Re-framing Whirling Vortexes

It's difficult to keep a Category III Taker whirling vortex in any kind of frame. The vortex moves too fast. The micro approach to keeping perspective on a whirling vortex is to use a moving frame. But that isn't the kind of perspective that will lead to better decisions and responses over the long term. It will just keep you chasing a vortex that has much more wind power than you do.

To avoid keeping yourself in a constant state of reacting and playing catch-up to a rapidly moving atmospheric disturbance, you need to stand back and adopt a broader perspective. In the same way building a frame large enough to contain the jaguar's infinitely adaptable and flexible de-framing is challenging, constructing a frame large and comprehensive enough to wrap context around a whirling vortex is not a job for the weak spirited.

Even if whirling vortexes want to build a contextual frame around their life, which they almost never do, they won't have time for framing in the conventional sense of the word. He or she views life more as a series of snapshots; used for a moment and then tossed aside. Vortexes are not big-picture thinkers. Instead of stepping back and considering the wide shot, they remain forever on a tight close-up of themselves.

If you're dealing with a whirling vortex, you need to become a competent re-framer as quickly as possible. Because blaming will only make the vortex whirl faster, your only hope for peace and serenity resides in your ability to construct a context within which your guiding principles of patience, tolerance, respect for self, and respect for others can survive and thrive.

Keys to living with an idiot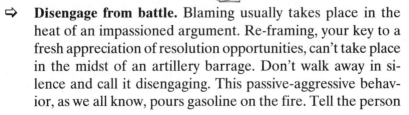

⇨ **Disengage from battle.** Blaming usually takes place in the heat of an impassioned argument. Re-framing, your key to a fresh appreciation of resolution opportunities, can't take place in the midst of an artillery barrage. Don't walk away in silence and call it disengaging. This passive-aggressive behavior, as we all know, pours gasoline on the fire. Tell the person you're angry with that you are taking a time-out because the conversation is not working for you. Tell him or her you're not giving up on finding a resolution and you'll be back after you've had a chance to sort out your thoughts. The other party will no doubt think you're going away to reload your canons. But you know better. You need to check your frame and, if you've slipped back into your old frame, you'll re-frame as necessary.

⇨ **Re-frame the game.** Blaming only reinforces the bias and prejudice within your old frames. When you surrender to the impulse to blame, you abandon any hope of improving the situation. Blaming always elicits a negative and defensive response. Blaming is an unpleasant experience, although in different ways, for both the blamer and the blamee. By rein-vesting energy from blaming into re-framing, you open up the possibility of a more copacetic relationship with idiots near and far. By re-framing the game, you establish new rules of engagement that, in turn, can produce new results.

⇨ **Return with a solution.** When you have a chance to think rationally, think not of revenge and winning. Think instead of creating a context in which both parties can be happy. If you have been conditioned to fight pitched battles, your mind immediately goes to counterstrike strategies. Switch gears. Coming up with a few well-thought-out solutions will take some effort. Writing down what you want before reentering the conversation helps keep what's being said clear and less volatile. Complete capitulation is not an acceptable solution. If you anticipate, you won't be caught off guard by the way the idiot responds to your conciliatory offers. Stick with it. Your significant idiot might not agree immediately to your proposed solutions. Once they're out there, you might need to disengage again and give the solutions time to incubate. Time can heal many things if you give healing enough time.

Chapter Summary

Accusations don't win friends or influence people. If the accusation is false or off target, the response might be anything from mild to hostile. If the accusation is accurate, it could mean war. The most ferocious counterattacks are usually in response to being caught saying or doing something the perpetrator knows to be wrong. If it's war you want, just blame someone for something about which he or she already feels self-convicted.

Re-framing the context in which you interpret hostility or neglect on the part of idiots in your life can open opportunities for solutions you can't think of while operating within your old frame. The essence of the term "idiot" is automatically attached to accusations and blame. Re-framing issues and situations provides a chance to see the other person as something other than an idiot, which is a foundation for a better relationship. A word to the wise: re-framing means giving up a lot of uncomfortable-but-familiar stuff to gain mysterious-but-promising new stuff. Anticipate new stuff to feel weird. Weird can be good if you stick with new and improved behaviors long enough for them to take root.

To-do list:

- ☑ Don't point.
- ☑ Avoid the blame game.
- ☑ Seek solutions.
- ☑ Disengage from battle.
- ☑ Re-frame the game.
- ☑ Return with a solution.

Chapter 7

The Third Relational
Sin and Solution:
Criticizing vs. Complimenting

DOGS POOP ON RUGS. It's a natural thing. Preventable, hopefully, but natural nonetheless. How that gets drawn into the middle of our human squabbles is unnatural. "If you had walked the dog like I asked you to, he wouldn't have pooped on the rug." Blaming. "I should have known there would be poop on the rug if I left the dog alone with *you.*" Criticizing. Criticizing and blaming are two different things, although they can overlap. We tend to blame ourselves and others for creating or exacerbating bad situations.

Blaming attacks actions or behaviors. Criticizing, as I'm using the term, attacks a person's character. Some argue that criticizing is positive, necessary, and appropriate—calling it constructive. I often ask people to critique my work in an effort to remain objective. Critiquing, by prior arrangement, *is* a helpful exercise. But unsolicited "critiques" are not helpful if they're character attacks in disguise.

I say, if *criticism* is positive, necessary, and appropriate, it's probably *solicited feedback.* Unsolicited criticism can be damaging, unless the recipient has the emotional maturity to consider the source and circumstances of the criticism, and keep it in perspective. Armed with this shield of emotional maturity, the recipient is likely to learn as much about the critic's worldview as anything useful from the criticism.

Shirley Weighs In

"I don't criticize," Shirley insists. "I advise."

"That's good to know," I affirm.

"I wish you'd explain that to my daughter-in-law."

"Let me guess," I begin. "Your daughter-in-law misinterprets your advice as criticizing?"

"Yes. And I don't know where she gets such an idea."

I furrow my brow and look at Shirley inquisitively. That's all it takes.

"I'm serious, John. I give her advice, but I don't criticize her."

"Ah."

"There is a difference," she insists.

"How does advice differ from criticizing, exactly?" I ask.

"I'm trying to help."

"But she still hears your advice as criticizing?"

"Yes," Shirley says. "Criticizing doesn't help. Even I know that."

"Why do you think criticizing is *not* helpful?"

"Because people don't ask to be criticized," she scoffs.

"Does your daughter-in-law ask for your advice?"

"No."

"I'll bet she doesn't find your advice helpful, either."

"How did you know?"

"Lucky guess."

"Now I suppose you're going to tell me I can't give *advice*?"

"We're part of a fellowship of equals, Shirley. I can't tell you to do or not do anything."

"I know," she says. "But the meeting's over. I'm curious to know what you really think."

"I think that if your daughter-in-law, son, sibling, friend, spouse, or anyone else close to you treats your advice like criticism, they are feeling criticized."

"That's impossible."

"It's more than possible, Shirley. That's what's happening."

"This isn't fair," she snorts. "If I can't give advice, how am I supposed to help?"

"By asking."

"Asking what?"

"How can I help?"

"If I ask how I can help," she protests, "it will leave it up to them to tell me."

"Indeed it will."

"And what if they say they don't need any help?"

"Guess you get a vacation," I say.

Shirley folds her arms, slumps back in her chair, and announces, "That's just unacceptable."

Advice and Criticizing: Peas in a Pod

I know where Shirley's coming from. It's far too easy to criticize and call it advice. It's all too frequent for well-intentioned advice to be interpreted as criticizing by the receiver. By the time I say, "I didn't mean it like that. *You* took it the wrong way," it's too late. It would have been better if I had anticipated how inflammatory my words might be and *pre*-adjusted my comments. Blaming the receiver for taking the message the wrong way or misinterpreting my intentions is a tacit admission that I need to become a better communicator.

Shirley is right about different intentions between advice and criticizing. Advice is either well intentioned; meant to help; or, in its sinister state, an attempt to control others. Even well-intentioned advice can be received as veiled criticism. Advice is a slippery slope. The person who feels compelled to give advice might be following an unconscious agenda to make themselves feel better by putting someone else down.

Sitting in metal folding chairs in the Methodist church basement on Thursday nights, we often share with one another how easy it is to backslide into advice-giving, and, in doing so, criticizing. That's how Shirley and I got on the topic. Regular IE folks know how toxic criticizing can be. Criticizing sends a clear and unmistakable message that something is wrong with the other person's character. Maybe there is. Maybe there isn't. But it's our Higher Power's job to make that call. It's our call to decide how we're going to respond to his or her behavior.

Hidden Message?

When offered unsolicited advice, you can sense the real message is that something's wrong with what you're doing and/or how you're doing it. If it's something innocuous and obvious, you probably won't let it bother you. You might appreciate it. You might even say, "Thanks."

I'm old enough to predate automatic shut-off valves on gas pumps. I've stood daydreaming next to a gas pump more than once until someone suggested, "You might want to shut that off." Gas overflowing from the tank onto my shoes grabbed my attention and I didn't take offense at the advice. I was more worried about open flames.

Unsolicited advice still runs the danger of offending the advisee. I appreciate, and frequently solicit, advice from trusted advisers. Yet, when someone gives me *unsolicited* advice, right or wrong, my first instinct is to push back. I fear they're trying to control me. People hear and act on positive messages. People instinctively resist being controlled or told to change. The implication, "You're doing it wrong," carries the additional weight of negativity. Words such as "no," "don't," "stop," "never," "should," and "shouldn't," especially when part of unsolicited advice, elicit negative responses no matter what behavior they're associated with.

No matter how helpful the advice is, my knee-jerk response is: "What's wrong with the way *I'm* doing it?" Even if there is a better way to do something, it seldom feels good when someone else points it out. As I've become more comfortable and confident with my problem-solving and decision-making skills, the less advice and criticism trouble me.

You aren't responsible for everyone's default settings. Some people get their backs up at nearly everything said in their presence. Some people will let the most vitriolic slings and arrows bounce off their armor like water off a beaver's pelt. There is a wide continuum of sensitivity in between. Open wounds notwithstanding, unless people thoughtfully consider the words they use, their messages are not going to be received the way they are intended. If people spew out words without thinking, chances are slim the receiver will *get it* the way they want their message to be *got*. The receiver might just shrug off the source.

There are still moments when advice and criticism amplify my own insecurities. Whenever unsolicited advice or criticism is given, unspoken, unanticipated, and powerful messages come through to the receiver along a continuum of sensitivity. Messages sent and messages received vary, from the benign to the severe. The less history you have with someone, the less you'll be aware of the hidden land mines.

Damage Lite

○ **Message giver says:** "I have information that might help you." This is a low-threat way to approach someone with information. Only the most sensitive person would push back at this approach. But it can happen, depending on the depth of an individual's confidence issues.

● **Message receiver might hear:** "I've been watching you or hearing what you've been saying. I've had a similar experience or know someone who has. What I've learned could help solve the problem you're having."

Medium Maddening

○ **Message giver says:** "I know what you should do." This runs a higher risk of offending someone, particularly someone who fancies him- or herself a smart cookie. "Let me show you how it's done," carries an "I know more than you" message. It takes a reasonably thick skin to receive a message such as this and not react.

● **Message receiver might hear:** "It doesn't matter where you've been or what you've done before, you haven't mastered this skill. Even if you're kind of good at it, you're not as good at it as I am."

○ **Message giver says:** "Do it this way." This runs a high risk of push-back from just about anyone, including a few over-confident amoebas. Even an emotionally mature person needs to take a few deep breaths and turn up the corners of his or her mouth in a Buddha smile to serenely survive a directive such as this.

● **Message receiver might hear:** "Don't try to think. If you try to figure this out, you will just mess it up. Other people have already worked out how this should be done. Just follow directions."

○ **Message giver says:** "You can't do anything right." By the time we reach this point on the continuum, advice has long since turned to criticizing. The action or behavior ceases to be as much an issue as the advisee's overall capability. Blaming behavior, not the person, is where some choose to draw the line. Criticizing the person is definitely past the point of diminishing returns. Them's gittin' to be fightin' words, and we best forget about getting anything productive done.

- **Message receiver might hear:** "You have no business trying to do anything more complicated than tying your shoes. In fact, they invented Velcro for people like you." Pointing this out is bound to be taken as a direct assault on the advisee's character (intelligence, education, maturity, pedigree, etc.). In other words, criticizing in all its toxicity. "Why do you even bother to try?" is a rhetorically critical question. Even if the question is not spoken aloud, criticizing always carries similar character-assassinating implications. Possible unspoken message: "You're an idiot."

Permanent Damage

○ **Message giver says:** "Stay away from me!" If someone has been consistently told he or she can do nothing right, everything they do screws things up for other people, and/or their very existence is a burden on others, he or she might feel they have no business being alive. Sound harsh? There are people all around us every day who feel this way about themselves. It's hard to know who they are. Some people are given these and equally debilitating messages from earliest childhood when they're still impressionable enough to believe them.

- **Message receiver might hear:** "You're worse than an idiot. I don't know a word for it. But if there is a word, you're it. Not only are you incapable of doing anything right, you're a drag to have around."

The best communication pairing is a positive message and a positive, willing reception. In the worst possible scenario, a positive message can be interpreted like the "permanent damage" message. Sometimes people are that damaged, and there's nothing we can do about it except to keep quiet. Once the message or the reception is clouded or clogged with a hidden agenda, feelings begin to contradict the words. At least harsh words and harsh feelings are consistent. Which message is genuine vs. loaded? It's hard to be sure. The best we can do is send messages that are as positive and sincere as possible.

Roger's Serenity

A good friend and mentor, Roger, has an adolescent son. He's a great kid; smart, hard-working, and courteous. Even so, the adolescent says and does things that occasionally fire Roger's rockets. Roger has learned to remain serene, however, and keeps himself under control rather than reaching out with advice, criticizing, or an iron fist to control his son. In spite of the fact he's dealing with a teenager, a time when a jury of his peers would never convict him for wholesale use of controlling advice or criticizing to maintain his sanity, Roger sits down with his son, loves him, and listens.

The boy knows his father sets and maintains boundaries. Roger is a consistent and steady parent. He asks his son what's going on and patiently listens to what his son tells him. No criticizing or advice. The most beautiful part comes when the boy *asks* his dad for advice.

This is a ticket home. Get out of jail free. Shirley can only dream of someone setting the table like that. What does Roger do? He shares stories of his life and times as they relate to his son's dilemma. Then, instead of advising or criticizing, Roger lays a paternal hand on his son's shoulder and says, "You'll sort this out. I have confidence in you."

His son always *does* sort it out. What an incredible feeling it must be when his enthusiastic son seeks Roger out to share the solution he's come up with. Roger beams when he tells me about it. The bond, based on Roger's respect for his son, is one of the strongest I've ever seen between a parent and a child.

The strongest bonds I've seen between employers and employees, husbands and wives, parents and children, siblings, coworkers, and bass fishermen are similarly based on respect for other people's abilities to figure out their own problems. As a pre-recovery co-beaver, I was too quick to jump in with advice and solutions. The view from my metal folding chair in the basement of the Methodist church reveals how my exuberant "helpfulness" sometimes robbed people of their opportunity to self-actualize. Motivated by my desire to be in control and feel more secure in a relationship, I tripped up the people I was ostensibly trying to "help." Their focus and energy was turned from solving the problem to resisting me. Bad beaver.

Criticizing and Contempt

Recent research on longevity of relationships indicates *contempt* is high on the list of inflammatory attitudes that burn relationships to crisps. Finding contempt and criticism in advice is like finding a dead mouse in the house. You can smell it long before you're able to locate the body. During Idiots Exposed meetings, veteran recovering idiots often declare, "I want to stop hurting others with my advice."

As a neophyte exposed idiot, I remember being shocked at this new way of framing my "gift" of advice. Was I really hurting people with my best intentions? It was an entirely foreign way to look at the act of advice-giving. As an active exposed idiot, I felt my intellectualized problem-solving capabilities were superior to problems anyone else could have. Coming to recognize my inflated self-concept didn't stop me from lapsing from achiever beaver to co-beaver without warning. Now I realize that what I call my intellect has been one of the chief causes of problems in my life.

For as long as I remember, I've believed my benevolent advice would always help people. *If they would only follow my vision for their lives*, I thought, *all would be right with the world*. The patience to let others work out their own problems, while remaining available to them, is the best gift I can give to those I care about.

The point is this: To be happier, with myself and in relationships, my first job is to prioritize and bring order to *my* life. Before I criticize anyone else's character defects, I must be on the spiritual high road. But if I achieve even entry-level spiritual enlightenment, I'll know that criticizing is always potentially negative and damaging. Ergo, spiritual maturity on my part precludes me from criticizing.

Numerous authors speak of love vs. fear. If I want people around me to act out of love, I must be motivated by love more than fear. Love releases me from selfish, self-serving expectations. Being motivated by fear to control another person's choices would be self-serving, even if I could do it. It's a moot point because I can't. Just wanting to do so is fearful. It indicates I'm afraid I won't be able to handle what they might choose. Trying to control other people's thinking and behavior in such a way as to make my life more manageable is, in a word, "idiotic." Fear wins and love loses. I'm the exposed idiot for not lovingly respecting myself and the others in my life.

Sticks and Stones

"Sticks and stones can break my bones, but words will never harm me." Not. Broken bones eventually heal. Words can cripple for life. I've heard it said that it's best to say nothing unless my words will improve on silence. If I say critical things or imply with my advice that I have no confidence in someone's ability to find solutions, silence would have been a better choice. When I enjoin myself not to give unsolicited advice or criticize, I'm not detaching entirely. If I engage others, through active listening, to share what's going on in their lives, my questions can frame and even guide the dialogue. If I listen or watch how a decision is made or a problem is solved without giving advice, I, like Roger, am rewarded with a deeper understanding of my spouse, child, in-laws, coworker, boss, or significant idiot.

Pray for patience, because even an incredible idiot can find answers to life's persistent questions, given enough time and encouragement. Encouragement and criticizing can't exist in the same space and time. Want to turn an idiot into a bigger idiot? Criticize. Want to show an idiot the gateway to being less of an idiot? Encourage. It may take the patience of Job. Just how fond are you of this idiot anyway?

Keys to living with an idiot

⇨ **Consider how the message will be heard.** Building yourself up by diminishing others through contempt will have consequences. Criticizing other people's characters will have consequences. Giving unsolicited advice can have consequences of varying severity. I might feel pumped up for a moment if I treat someone with contempt. But how long will I be satisfied feeling superior to a deflated ego? Criticizing others might make you feel, if only for a moment, righteous (in an unholy way). Giving unsolicited advice in order to control others might make you feel wise and learned. But how good will you feel in the long run when nobody wants to talk to you anymore?

⇨ **Listen and learn.** Become the teacher and learner all in one. Love and listen the way Roger does with his son. It takes time, patience, and consistency. But the rewards are great and you've given your loved one the best you can possibly give. Children need to be taught, best by example, not told.

They need to learn, not be coerced and/or bribed. If they grow up with no entrenched problem-solving skills, you'll end up doing their laundry until they're 42. Those parts within each of us where we still need to learn and grow like children should be treated with the same loving patience that Roger uses with his teenager—whether we're 12 or 112. No contempt to diminish us. No criticizing to block communication. No unsolicited advice to aggravate us.

⇨ **Give feedback instead of advice.** I'm not playing with words here. Unsolicited feedback is the same as advice and will probably stimulate a comment such as, "Who asked you?" Feedback is a response to someone else's actions, not a projection of your own agenda. The key to successfully giving and receiving quality feedback is permission. You need to ask permission before you give feedback and give your permission to receive it (whether others request it or not). The simple act of asking permission extends respect to the other person and *leaves control in his or her hands.* There is no faster way to become unpopular than to show disrespect by challenging someone else's power to make his or her own decisions.

Advice: Grieving the Loss

A friend of mine in Los Angeles has a pedigree Scottish terrier with attitude. Every time I approach the door, the dog goes nuts. "Stop that," my friend scolds (the dog). "You know John."

"Stop that," my friend's wife scolds him (my friend). "That's what he (the dog) was born to do. If you tell him not to bark, you're taking away the only thing he lives for."

I realize, for many readers, to suggest they think twice before offering advice is like taking away something precious and dear to their hearts. Although it's not easy to alter the way you've always been in relationships, it's important to do it anyway. That's not advice. It's an order. But you will probably need help to do it. If you absolutely, positively, cannot restrain yourself from giving advice, you can at least be like the late Ann Landers (who got paid for her advice): Wait until you get a letter asking for it. Research your answers, proofread, submit it to your editor and your attorney. And don't say anything you wouldn't want a million people to read.

When I was studying for my master's degree in marriage and family therapy, it was drilled into us: "Don't give advice." If counseling professionals are advised not to dispense advice, why should a co-beaver? Instead, give people an opportunity to find answers they'll stick with because they discovered them. Let advice columnists give advice. Let radio psychologists who have 90 seconds to address your most pervasive, life-long, psychological vulnerabilities give advice. Let physicians be directive and tell people to exercise, stop smoking, what to eat, when to sleep, and so on.

I'm sharing these thoughts because you or someone who loves you bought this book. Hence, I feel entitled. I've been invited. As a general rule, before giving advice, at least count to 10 and spend the time listening to the person just as you wish your significant other, children, parents, siblings, in-laws, coworkers, bosses, and local politicians would listen to you.

Life Fountains

Criticizing and Amoebas

When it comes to criticizing, giving advice, or showing contempt, amoebas are fairly innocuous creatures. They tend to be more self-critical than critical of others. Most amoebas don't presume to give advice, as if anyone would ask. Amoebas are intelligent enough to realize other people do idiotic things. However, their restraint when it comes to criticizing, advice, and contempt comes more from a desire to remain invisible than good manners.

Amoebas don't tend to criticize others unless they just think it. But unexpressed criticism can swell into resentment. Resentment in the mind of an amoeba can be *dangerous.* If the amoeba harbors a great deal of resentment, you might not know about it until the building blows up. Who would think to check an amoeba for explosives?

I'll delve deeper into resentment and the amoeba in Chapter 10. But you shouldn't assume that the absence of criticizing coming from amoebas means they're happy with everything and everyone. Believing they lack permission to speak out, their silence does not convey information that could help others treat them better. Neither should you assume they absorb unlimited criticism with no emotional price tag attached.

Critical Beavers

Criticizing starts with the same "C" as control. This takes us straight past the bucolic beaver swinging leisurely on the hammock beside the pond, and the ambitious achiever beaver, busily gnawing trees to build a swing set for the little beavs. They are not consumed with the need to control the world around them the way Category II co-beavers are. Their desire to control feeds the perceived need to be critical or give advice.

Criticizing and co-beavers are natural (although unpleasant) companions. As a recovering co-beaver, it's easy for me to explain this cycle. Consider the co-beaver's desire to make life more pleasant for everyone, with the co-beaver at the top of the list. The co-beaver's weapon of choice is control. This means co-beavers want to set the agenda.

If recipients of the co-beaver's generosity don't subscribe to or comply with the co-beaver's agenda, the co-beaver assumes there is something wrong with the recipient. Out comes the criticism. "What's wrong with you?" Translation: "What defect of character inspired you to ignore my inspired instructions?" "What were you thinking?" translates to "Even a pea brain would be smart enough to follow my perfect agenda." A co-beaver might not become quite so articulate until he or she has one glass of chardonnay too many at dinner. But these thoughts are likely to be just beneath the surface.

There is no mistaking the contempt woven into the co-beaver's criticizing. A vicious cycle is unleashed as the adviser redoubles the effort to change the advisee's behavior and the advisee ratchets up resistance to anything the adviser says. Advice is a co-beaver's attempt to forewarn his or her prey. "A word to the wise…" means "Do it my way or else suffer criticism." "Let me give you some advice," means, "If you don't want me to bite a plug out of your leg, get with the program."

Co-beavers set their hopes and dreams on everyone following their agendas. When others don't follow along, co-beavers feel emotionally wounded. Wounded animals have a tendency to snap when approached. Some wounded co-beavers don't wait to be approached. They'll chase down their ungrateful child, spouse, significant idiot, friend, coworker, or in-law, pretending in the heat of the moment their child, spouse, significant idiot, friend, coworker, or in-law is a tree. Other wounded co-beavers collapse in tears. Go figure.

Altruistic Criticizing

If sufficiently aggravated, altruistic Category III Givers might backslide into Category II co-beaver behavior and slap on some criticism. This is extremely uncharacteristic of the altruist, because *altruist* starts with the same "A" as *anticipation* does. Criticizing would only explode from an altruist's mouth if he or she didn't properly anticipate the offending comment or behavior. That's unlikely.

Altruists generally possess the emotional and spiritual maturity to avoid dispensing unsolicited advice, criticizing, or staying with contempt any longer than it takes to choose against it. That same maturity also helps them listen to unsolicited advice, criticism, or contemptuous comments directed at them without being deflated or taking offense. It's no fun for altruists to get blasted, but faith in themselves and their Higher Power shields them from mixing, compounding, and intensifying verbal assaults with self-criticizing. To a true altruist, information gleaned from unsolicited advice, criticism, or contemptuous comments just adds to the big picture and makes other people easier to understand and anticipate.

As I mentioned, contempt and advice-giving coming *from* the altruist are even rarer because the anticipatory altruist is acutely aware of the negative nature contained in contempt and advice-giving. The altruist's self-image doesn't hinge on others following his or her roadmap for life. By not making satisfaction or fulfillment contingent on the attitudes or behavior of others, the altruist does not leave him- or herself emotionally vulnerable or intentionally cause others pain.

Black Holes

Criticizing and Garden Slugs

I recently overheard a garden slug announce his intention to get involved in a worthy cause as soon as he could find one he could participate in from the sofa. Unfortunately, criticizing, contempt, and advice-giving can be practiced from a sofa. Nevertheless, Category I Taker garden slugs are slow to criticize or give advice because effort is required. As such, anyone living with a garden slug is not likely to be a target of criticism and/or contempt. As long as sandwiches and beer keep arriving at the sofa or recliner in a timely manner, garden slug caretakers won't hear much advice. The slug might point out where you missed a spot while vacuuming, but that's just him or her trying to be helpful.

Criticizing and showing contempt to characters on television is another matter. Garden slugs become quite animated when advising Donald Trump whom he should fire or who should be voted off the island. We all choose our priorities. Being critical of a professional athlete's performance or showing contempt for a presidential candidate during a televised debate are among the highest callings the garden slug can imagine. After the debate, she or he is all but worn out.

I recommend against treating garden slugs with contempt, criticizing them, or giving advice for all of the usual reasons. Advice, criticism, and contempt serve no worthwhile purpose. Even if they did, self-righteous energy would be wasted on someone who finds no vice in immobility. Besides, garden slugs are experts at situational hearing loss.

Criticizing and Jaguars

As with blaming, Category II Taker jaguars are most sensitive to being criticized when they are self-convicted. If jaguars are already aware of their misdeeds, to remind them of the same is likely to set off a snarling cat. Because jaguars are so often paired off with co-beavers, there are a lot of snarling cats out there. Jaguars react adversely to criticism, contempt, and advice from anyone.

If jaguars are not guilty of that which they are accused, they'll blow it off. More specifically, they'll blow off the accuser. This is actually not a bad behavior. None of us should encourage criticizing, advice-giving, or being treated with contempt by passively tolerating it. Jaguars tend to be rude about it, though, which only gives the critical person more ammunition and (presumably) justifiable cause to criticize. Round and round it goes.

Jaguars can be devastating critics. Although advice-giving is not a jaguar's style, he or she will use criticism and contempt to manipulate and get what he or she wants. Jaguars use criticism and contempt to divert attention from jaguar indiscretions. The tactic is effective because jaguars can criticize others with surgical precision. They can be clever, strategically using criticism and contempt as they circle for the kill. They don't waste critical remarks on low-vulnerability aspects of other's personalities. They criticize where we're most insecure or, heaven forbid, have an open wound. Jaguars can smell blood.

Criticizing and Whirling Vortexes

Whirling vortexes often treat others with contempt when they feel other people have failed them. If you don't worship at the altar of a whirling vortex, the vortex is likely to assail your character with unprecedented vitriol. Whirling vortexes feel their needs are so immediate and urgent that you should expect contempt and criticizing if you don't fulfill their desires at all times.

The fastest way to re-ingratiate yourself to a whirling vortex is to convince him you're working to get him what he wants. He'll immediately forget any criticism or contempt and sing your praises. Because Category III Taker vortexes live in the moment, you're never more than a moment away from being showered with praise, if your offering is good enough. Of course, you're never more than a moment away from being stung by their criticizing and contempt if you aren't careful where you're stepping. Pay attention. Choose battles wisely.

If vortexes think they'll get what they want at the other end, they'll listen to advice all day long. Whirling vortexes often seduce co-beavers, in particular, when they listen attentively to advice without pushing back. They'll nod their head, look you in the eye as if they're hearing—which they're not—and even agree with what you're saying. As soon as they get a clue they *won't* get what they're hoping for, listening is over and wind begins to howl.

Keys to living with an idiot

⇨ **Ask, "Is it them or is it me?"** Criticizing is best addressed when you stop to ask yourself what the problem is. Your default setting can lead you to *assume* the other person is the problem rather than that you haven't anticipated what others' behavior might be. Yes, the other person or persons might say or do aggravating things. But is the distress you're feeling a result of what they're doing, or how you're reacting? Just posing this question at the first impulse to criticize positions you to think differently about the situation or relationship. Better yet, posing the question suggests you have power to choose differently.

⇨ **Tell the other person what's bugging you.** "When you gut your trout on the carpet in front of the television set, it creates a big mess, and I feel nauseated." Although there really are some women who must point this out to husbands, uncles, father-in-laws, and sons, my example is extreme. Often, though, words and/or behaviors that ignite critical afterburners, such as gutting fish in the den, can be corrected if you only respectfully point them out to the offending party. Solution-based suggestions, such as watching television in the garage while gutting the fish, steer the conversation away from criticizing and toward getting the clowns and their stupid fish out of the house. Offensive words and behaviors are sometimes not intended to aggravate you. They might be insensitive, uncaring, and idiotic, but not necessarily meant as offensive weapons. Honestly owning and articulating your feelings about the unintentionally offensive words or behaviors is the best way to stop them.

⇨ **Never stop asking.** Okay, the words and/or behaviors *are* intended to offend you. What now? Ask what's wrong. If you can't get to a non-threatening level of conversation in your relationship with a spouse, significant other, child, parent, in-law, friend, coworker, or hockey player, you might need professional intervention. "What's wrong?" is the right follow-up question. "What's wrong with *you*?" is an attack. "Nothing's wrong," is the typical passive-aggressive, denial-laden response. Anticipate it. Remain focused on how to emerge from the encounter unscathed. Criticizing others (scathing them) is not the answer. Criticizing is a counterattack. If you've honestly articulated what bothers you and the other person keeps doing it, there is something more than meets the eye. Asking, "What's wrong?" gives them a chance to tell you. Ask. Wait. Perhaps ask again. But wait until they feel safe enough to tell you. Never stop asking yourself, "What's my contribution to this friction?" It's *their* pain that's causing them to lash out. We probably have nothing to do with it except to be the safest and most available target.

Complimenting

One of the most immediate solutions to the relational sin of criticizing is complimenting. Like so many things we know to be helpful and healthy in our lives, it sounds simple, but can be hard to do. When

I say that criticizing is a default setting, I mean it's a behavior and mind-set many people have been conditioned for from childhood. It was modeled by masters of criticism throughout our formative years, and many of us have spent decades perfecting our own unique versions.

Responding to the devastating effect criticizing has on children, some counselors have adopted a clinical technique called Parent-Interaction Therapy to raise awareness in parents. Parents sit down daily with a child at a fun task. Within the designated five-minute *playtime*, parents must praise the child 10 times. More than just saying, "Good job," they are instructed to identify what the child is being praised for. Within that same five minutes, parents are to drop out all criticism, commands, and suggestions. There is much more to it, but the point of intentionally scripting positive reinforcements and eliminating negative messages is clear.

Sound simple? It's incredibly difficult for adults who are conditioned to criticize rather than to compliment. For a parent who criticizes a young child or makes unsolicited suggestions to an adult child, the answer to "Is it them (with a problem) or is it me?" is *me*. Suggestions are suspect, especially when dealing with children, because they imply demands, which are really not suggestions at all. Asking another adult, "May I make a suggestion?" keeps a suggestion a suggestion.

The most popular words in parenting books these days—in the self-help or the clinical section of the bookstore—are the "P" words. For children beyond infancy, "P" stands for positive, playful, and, most importantly, praise. Imagine children walking around with little sandwich boards that read: "Will work for attention." The powerful reward of attention, properly used, can pay huge dividends to parents and society.

In order to use positive attention to get positive behavior, parents need to work against their natural tendency to pay the most attention to negative behavior. A young female inmate, attending a parenting class in prison, made succinct entries in her journal about how the only way she could get her parents attention as a little girl was to get in trouble at school or on the streets. The rest of her plight speaks for itself.

Negative behavior must be appropriately addressed. But if negative attention is *all* children receive, negative attention is what they'll work hardest to get. When getting their parents' goat is the only thing children can depend on them for, they become highly skilled at triggering their parents' goat-like qualities. Is it any wonder they grow up to be idiots? The behaviors you want to see increase should be the ones you'll grace with attention and compliments.

Same Space, Same Time

The exercise with the children is sophisticated in its simplicity and guarantees positive results if followed faithfully. The counselors have put the laws of natural physics to work in solving a psychological problem. Psychologically speaking, criticizing and complimenting can't exist in the same space any more than oil and water can occupy the same space. If you want to displace oil, add water. If you want to displace water, add oil. Simple as that. The problem is that people are predisposed to water or oil, depending upon their unique nature vs. nurture equation. Whether your disposition is a result of environment, genetics, or some combination of both, the instinctive element can only be displaced with another element.

Criticizing and complimenting work the same way. If I can contain the impulse to criticize long enough to inject a compliment instead, the criticizing is displaced. Criticizing is only displaced for the period I'm being complimentary, but the displacement, as in the counseling exercise, is complete. More than simply blocking time and space, there are additional benefits to choosing complimenting over criticizing.

Criticizing is negative. Advice, no matter how well intended, can provoke negative interpretations. Gratuitous, undeserved, and insincere compliments can be the slimiest type of criticizing. A genuine compliment can only be associated with a positive thought. Choosing to give a compliment requires you to think of something positive about someone else. "Gee, honey, nobody can catch more trout than you. I thought of a terrific place for you to gut them."

That sets a nicer stage than, "You stupid moron..., etc." The fact is, 99 out of 100 human beings, a few high-functioning mammals, and most trout agree that your "Honey" gutting the fish in the den *is* a completely insensitive imbecile. The only one who wishes you'd leave well enough alone is your cat. No matter, criticizing isn't the answer.

Send the temptation to criticize along with "Honey" and the cat to the fish-gutting place. Solutions with alternatives offer help and hope; criticizing doesn't. Cutting back on or getting rid of criticizing is not as effective as intentionally finding something to compliment.

Finding negativity in others and commenting on it (that is, criticizing) dampens people's lives. Complimenting others is a refreshing gift to yourself as well as others as you expel negativity.

Life Fountains

Complimenting an Amoeba

Amoebas are self-critics. Hardly anything you can say to them bears more contempt than what they've already said to themselves. This makes them clean slates for compliments. Anything positive you say to them is all new. Amoebic Category I Givers do many wonderful things for people, which give you ample ammunition with which to fire away with compliments.

Compliments will lift an anemic amoeba's spirits as they will anyone else's. But compliments, as nice as they are, aren't likely to lift an amoeba into Category II beaver or altruist status. After receiving compliments, amoebas smile shyly, nod their heads appreciatively, and disappear as fast as they can. Once in a while an amoeba can get so intoxicated on compliments that she or he will hang around long after others have expected them to disappear. Hence the rhetorical question, "Are you still here?"

Amoebas are quick to give compliments. Why not? They give away everything else. Most people don't usually take amoeba compliments as a great gift, considering how eager amoebas are to please. This is unfair to amoebas. They could just stay quiet and who would know the difference? I'm pleased when the amoeba in me speaks up. However, when I do speak up, it's usually not the amoeba in me speaking.

If you've ever been down and out, your emotional well-being hanging by a thread, lonely, frustrated, and confused—only to notice a gentle hand on your shoulder and an equally gentle voice saying, "Don't worry. I know you'll work this out," it's probably an amoeba. Otherwise we would have seen him or her coming. I've had just such an experience, and it's like being touched by an angel. I, for one, appreciate amoebas and their never-say-die willingness to lend a hand.

Beaver Compliments

As Category II Givers, bucolic and ambitious achiever beavers take compliments kindly. Compliment them and you're likely to hear,

"Thank you, I'm pleased with that myself." Co-beavers will try to dismiss the compliment by saying, "Oh, this old thing?" Or, "No, it's nothing, really."

One of the hardest things for recovering co-beavers to learn is how to accept a compliment without brushing it aside or diminishing it. Even if they just cured cancer, achieved world peace, *and* found the weapons of mass destruction, a direct compliment will make their palms sweat. Even though the co-beaver ostensibly *lives* for appreciation, receiving direct compliments forces co-beavers' poor self-esteem to the surface. If you want to compliment a co-beaver, compliment the job or whatever tasks the co-beaver has done—not the beaver directly.

A compliment issued by a bucolic or achiever beaver is genuine and probably well deserved. Bucolic and achiever beavers are sensitive enough to offer compliments when an emotional boost is needed. A compliment from a co-beaver, even when it is well deserved, might have strings attached.

Co-beavers are caring enough to give genuine compliments. But they're just insecure enough to attach an expectation that complimenting will elicit a compliment, or at least an acknowledgement, in return. If a compliment issued by a co-beaver garners nothing in return, up pops resentment. Co-beavers are the only Life Fountain life-forms that can get depressed by giving compliments.

Altruistic Compliments

Altruistic Category III Givers are naturally complimentary. Altruists purposefully seek the positive perspective in all situations and are usually the first to spot a silver lining while others see only the dark cloud. This is not naive or goody-goody behavior. There is positive energy and opportunity in all things. Altruists find comfort in the Chinese symbol for danger, which also means *opportunity*.

Altruists understand that complimenting is a great way to pass along positive energy. They are skilled compliment-givers, aware of the uplifting effect complimenting will have on a person's mood or attitude. Even when asked for a critique or advice, the altruist seeks to build people up with information rather than make them feel like they just went through a meat grinder.

Black Holes

Complimenting Garden Slugs

If you're holding your breath waiting for a Category I Taker to issue a compliment, you must remember to wear something blue to match your face. It will be a long time. Other than an occasional, "Thanks, honey," without the eyes leaving the television screen, it just doesn't occur to breathing sofa cushions that anything you might do deserves a compliment. If a garden slug has a few jaguar chromosomes and thinks complimenting will get the pizza and beer delivered faster, you might get one. But garden slugs are never in much of a hurry.

Garden slugs don't usually respond to compliments, either. If you're attempting some sort of behavior modification with complimenting, it won't work on garden slugs. Your most impressive compliments will generate little more than a, "That's nice," in return. They might even be suspicious of a compliment if they thought about it long enough. What's to compliment? Garden slugs keep their brains jammed between channels to the point that complimenting and criticizing become indistinguishable. Your sharpest criticism is likely to also generate a, "That's nice."

Complimenting Jaguars

Jaguars lap up compliments. They are cats, after all, and love being petted—when they *want* to be petted. Keeping jaguars happy and content is the best way to keep them from straying, at least until they get bored. Complimenting builds positive atmospheres and jaguars like positive atmospheres.

When jaguars turn on the compliments, they're usually up to something. The problem is that many of us, especially co-beavers, are compliment-starved. We're so thrilled to receive attention, much less compliments, from jaguars, we ignore any type of reality that might creep in and spoil the party.

The Whirling Compliment

Category III Taker vortexes take manipulative complimenting to a higher level. Jaguars are good at making attention-deprived people feel loved. Whirling vortexes can make amoebas feel like they're whirling.

Whirling vortexes are so caught up in the moment that they might believe an amoeba is another vortex...for a moment.

Altruists get their feet on the ground as quickly as possible if they feel themselves starting to spin. They know that's not the state they want to be in. Amoebas and beavers will pull up their landing gear and soar with the eagles until the whirling stops and they fall from the sky. It can be fun while it lasts, or until there is a pile of beavers on the ground with headaches.

Because whirling vortexes are not grounded, any type of comment, including compliments, will only reflect the vortex's reality of the moment. If you can anticipate and keep vortexes' comments and complimenting in perspective, you'll be less likely to wind up in a mound of beavers and amoebas. You can take a cue from altruists and not get upset with whirling vortexes. You can just accept them for what they are and not attach long-term meaning to comments made in the heat of the moment.

Complimenting whirling vortexes has a temporary effect, shorter in duration than with jaguars. Whirling vortexes are whirling under their own power, and little you do will speed them up or slow them down. Granted, upsetting them will make them blow harder and hotter. However, complimenting is not likely to do that.

Keys to living with an idiot

⇨ **Stay in the correct frame.** If you can keep things in perspective and consider the source of compliments or criticisms, you shouldn't be led astray. If you stay in reality, not giving in to fears and self-doubts, you won't be tempted to control with criticizing *or* complimenting. Sincere compliments uplift both the giver and the receiver. Insincere compliments can be taken as veiled criticisms. When your intent is to deceive, you can deflate your own mood. Complimenting, in context, is a building block for a more positive relationship, even with an idiot.

⇨ **Compliment the effort.** Although compliments are positive energy, beware of complimenting people directly. If they have low self-esteem, they'll feel a need to contradict the compliment and set the record straight. Complimenting the effort, the report card, the way the yard looks, the meal, and so on, will not invite self-doubting persons, most likely amoebas and co-beavers, to push back. If you compliment the efforts and accomplishments of jaguars and vortexes instead of the jaguar or vortex directly, still no harm done.

⇨ **Share stories.** Oprah Winfrey does not confront her guests with "You" statements. Instead, she shares her experiences, usually beginning her comment with, "In my experience...." By sharing personal experiences, you're not criticizing others. This gives them the opportunity to find useful information from your idio-t-syncracies. Storytelling is a powerful tool that keeps the pressures and sensitivities of the moment out of the way. People retain the power to opt out of your story if they're not comfortable there. The worst that can happen is the listener dismisses your story as irrelevant. That's a lot less caustic than putting them on the defensive. Advice hits people like a paint ball; messy, but not fatal. Criticizing and contempt run over people like a truck. A good way to compliment someone is to tell a story of a similar situation. In a word, empathize. It's better to give people positive images with which to associate. "I heard of a beaver once who built an enormous dam, like the one you just built, and it made the biggest pond for miles around." "It's not easy earning all *A*s and *B*s." "Many people will benefit from the research you're doing." Jaguars and vortexes like pedestals. Garden slugs could care less. You can anticipate and guide your significant idiot to where the positive power flows. Will they tap into it? No one knows. But *you* know you did the best you could

Chapter Summary

Uninvited criticism wastes time and blocks communication by putting people on the defensive. Expressing contempt for others can aggravate their already damaged self-esteem. Even if it seems to elevate your mood for the moment, you'll probably end up lonely at the end of the day. Contempt, like criticism, can fuel a vicious cycle of attack-counterattack, punch-counterpunch, and accusation-counteraccusation. Unsolicited advice, at its best, is a role of the dice to see if anyone takes offense. Knowing someone well reduces the risk. At its worst, unsolicited advice can be a sneaky and spineless way to criticize. If it is, it will probably be taken that way, too.

Acting with contempt, criticizing, and advice-giving contain negative energy. Compliments contain positive energy. Compliments and positive energy displace criticizing and negative energy. Complimenting and criticizing can't occupy the same space and time in the universe. It's not enough to eliminate criticism and contempt from your life. The resulting vacuum must be filled with a positive alternative or things will just go from bad to worse.

The good news is that you and I can intentionally inject more compliments and positive perspective in our lives. It will lift our spirits and the spirits of those around us. It's something we have control over. It requires continuous effort and can't be done once and expected to last forever. No spouse ever kept romantic flames kindled by saying, "I told you I loved you when we were married. When I change my mind, I'll let you know." Criticizing and a negative outlook might have been part of our socialization, but re-framing is remobilizing and empowering. Negative or positive, criticizing or complimenting, it's our choice.

It's the old bigger-hammer-to-drive-the-square-peg-through-the-round-hole mentality. It takes the re-framing perspective of honest self-examination, a recovery program, a support group, professional intervention, or counsel from another trusted source to realize how hurtful advice-giving can be.

To-do list:

- ☑ Consider how the message will be heard.
- ☑ Listen and learn.
- ☑ Give feedback instead of advice.
- ☑ Ask yourself, "Is it them or is it me?"
- ☑ Tell the other person what's bugging you.
- ☑ Never stop asking.
- ☑ Stay in the correct frame.
- ☑ Compliment the effort.
- ☑ Share stories.

Chapter 8

The Fourth Relational Sin and Solution: Denying vs. Accepting

HAVE YOU EVER HELD A BEACH BALL UNDER WATER? It's fun to let go and watch it erupt through the surface and then float effortlessly. The beach ball belongs on top of the water. It's a bubble. Forcing it under water, into an unnatural state, creates tension. The beach ball exerts pressure against any force that tries to hold it under water. It continues exerting pressure as long as it's held under there against its will, or until it is deflated and the air inside escapes to the surface in a million bubbles.

Denial is an unnatural state for human beings. Knowing something is true, even at an unconscious level, and pretending it is untrue is like holding a beach ball under water. The natural state of truth is out in the open for all to see. The truth will apply pressure as it attempts to erupt through the surface. Saying, "I'm not mad," when you are. "Oh, how nice," when you're disappointed. The pressure won't go away as long as it's held under the surface and kept away from its natural state.

Virtually everyone denies the truth at one time or another, to greater or lesser degrees—some more than others, some hardly at all. Some people spend much of their precious time and energy holding beach balls under water. Some people do little else. Idiots, being the clueless creatures they are in their pre-recovery state, won't engage much in denial because they're not much good at assessing what's true to begin with. They can walk right past a swimming pool, see someone struggling to hold several beach balls under water and say, "That looks like fun. Can I try?"

145

Shirley Denies Denying

"I'm not in denial," Shirley insists. "I don't know why everyone brings that up."

"Does it feel like something inside of you wants to come out?" I query.

"Like what?"

"Like how you feel about the way your daughter-in-law does things?"

"There's nothing wrong with how I feel about my daughter-in-law."

"How do you feel about her?"

"Fine," Shirley pushes back.

"Fine?" I persist. "Are there times when she's more fine than other times?"

"Of course," Shirley says, seeming relieved at the wiggle room I just offered her.

"When do you feel the best about her?"

"When she's following my advice," Shirley confesses. "I know I'm not supposed to give advice. But when I have no choice and she follows it, we get along fine."

"Would she say you're getting along fine at that point?"

"I'm sure she would. You know what they say."

"What do they say?"

"When mama's happy, everybody's happy."

"I always thought they said, 'When mama ain't happy, ain't nobody happy.'"

"It's the same thing, isn't it?"

"Not necessarily. Keeping you from being unhappy is placating. Placating probably doesn't make your son and daughter-in-law happy. It just maintains the fragile peace."

"We'll have peace as long as they treat me with respect."

"And do what you think they should do."

"Of course."

"I'll bet you could be even happier."

Shirley straightens up a little and leans forward. "Really?"

"How would you feel if your son and daughter-in-law did exactly what you wanted them to do without your even telling them?"

Shirley's eyes light up. "How can that happen?"

"Let go of each ball you're holding under water."

Shirley's shoulders slump. "Let go of my what?"

"Have you ever talked openly to your son and daughter-in-law about how you feel? What you want from them? What they can expect from you?"

"No," she says indignantly. "They'd never listen."

"Do you mean they might disagree with you?"

"Perhaps. What difference does it make?"

"I'm beginning to see why you keep the truth about your feelings and expectations under water."

"Surely you don't expect me to come right out and tell them how uncomfortable I am with the way she does things."

"Why not?"

"Because they couldn't handle my true feelings," she admits.

"Can you handle your true feelings?"

"Of course I can."

"Then why can't they?"

"Well," she hesitates. "They just can't."

"Wanna find out?"

Shirley tilts her head and turns slightly until she's looking at me from a suspicious angle. "How can I find out?"

"Let go of the beach ball."

Her shoulders collapse and the air rushes out of her lungs. "What is it with you and this beach ball?"

"I like to wear out my own metaphors. It's simple, but scary. Invite your son and daughter-in-law to discuss how you truly feel about them and their relationship to you. Own your feelings, use 'I' statements, and restrict your end of the conversation to your feelings. No advice. No criticism. No contempt. Can you do it?"

"What would that accomplish?" she asks, exhausted by the mere thought of such a conversation.

"The truth about your relationship will come to the surface and you won't need to spend all your energy holding it under water," I say eagerly. "Plus, you'll give them permission to be honest with you and let their beach balls pop to the surface."

Shirley recoils in shock. "They're holding beach balls under water when it comes to me? Are you serious?"

Denying: The Un-truth

I already taught you my denial song in Chapter 4. Using the same melody ("Let It Snow") you can join me in the lying song:

Oh, there's little to gain from lying,

So, what's the use in trying?

Unless you want your nose to grow,

Let it go, let it go, let it go.

Shirley felt in control as long as she was the one holding beach balls under water. As soon as she realized everybody was holding beach balls under water, some with her name on them, allowing hers to surface became a more enticing proposition. In an ideal world, we could all let our beach balls go and deal openly with our true feelings; first to ourselves, then to others. But denying is *fear in action*. Fear is a powerful motivator and can stymie much good from happening. Overcoming fear, or at least pushing it back long enough to allow true feelings to emerge, is a conscious, deliberate act.

The big psychological lie is that feelings don't exist, when they do. Or if we ignore them, they'll go away. To engage in denial is to lie to yourself and others about how you feel. It's a defense mechanism against the mother of all fears: rejection. "If others find out how I really feel," you reason, "they'll reject me." The other side of that coin is the belief that I don't want to know how others feel about me, unless it's good news. In case it's not, I'll just pretend.

See how pleasant living with idiots can be by comparison? You should count your blessings before dumping your significant idiot and running out to find a more dramatic and exciting partner. As clueless creatures, real idiots don't live lies. They live in ignorant bliss. To let one of my own beach balls pop to the surface: I envy the truly clueless. I envy their low blood pressure, lack of stress, how easily they fall asleep, and how refreshed they wake up in the morning.

Energy spent perpetuating lies and holding beach balls under water is energy no longer available to build happy, healthy relationships.

As you grow older, you have less energy to hold beach balls down, and it begins to take its toll. You begin having nightmares that a beach ball will accidentally get loose and pop to the surface. The sooner you let the beach balls pop up and deal with them, the sooner you can redirect your energy back toward more fulfilling activities. Waiting until the twilight years to finally let the beach balls go is like the guy who clings to the windowsill all night long only to find out at dawn his feet were inches from the ground.

If you're willing to reveal what's beneath your surface, your best choice of friends, partners, coworkers, bosses, or in-laws will be those willing to do the same. One honest person does not an honest relationship make. When you are the only one willing to be honest, then you should do it with discretion and finesse. In other words, don't haphazardly spill your innermost feelings and vulnerabilities at the feet of people who will pick them up and beat you over the head with them. You can be honest without being a fool about it.

Beach Ball Compatibility

If there is any one thing that points to long-term compatibility, it's honest disclosure. Have you ever seen a relationship of any kind enhanced in the long run by denying? None of my experience as a counselor for marriage and family therapy, in group work, or any research I've seen recommends denying as a healthy relational factor. Denial can create strong bonds when everyone is hiding from the same ugly truths. But the bonds in such cases are really shackles, and no one's happy. No one is free. They're chained together by fear.

Even deeply submerged denial can be reversed. That's why recovery is called recovery. It implies a return to a time before it was thought denying was necessary. It's never too late to re-frame the context and foundation upon which the relationship is based. Many people I've worked with have found new energy and rekindled youthful feelings of romance and naughtier things by paring their relationships back to the core and building again in a no-denial zone.

Some are too cynical to try. That's always sad. For many, the fear is too great and they are buried with their beach balls. Some choose to idiosyncratically vacate relationship after relationship to avoid dealing with their beach balls. Ever wonder why some people are addicted to the honeymoon? I define the honeymoon as a highly energized period during which beach ball hiding is easy because no one's looking. If life could only be lived completely above the surface. If only cosmetic surgery could beautify what's on the inside. Contrarily, beautifying the inside through honest disclosure beautifies the outside countenance without surgery. It will even make idiots more attractive.

Life Fountains

Amoeba Denying

When amoebas struggle with difficult and painful truths about themselves, they sigh, "So, what else is new?" Their expectations for themselves and their relationships are so low, there is little point in denying the obvious. This doesn't mean amoebas don't dream of more vibrant and fulfilling relationships; they're resigned to living the bland and insipid lives they're used to. Television ratings depend on them having no lives.

In my amoeba moments, I appreciate how little use amoebas have for denial. They are smart enough to manipulate the truth. They have enough energy. They just don't see much point. There might be some appeal to imagining they are more important to their significant others, anybody for that matter, than they really are. But that's more a wild fantasy than a denial issue. No matter how much you try to pump up an amoeba, the most excitement you're likely to get will sound like, "Oh, okay. That's nice. Thank you."

Beaver Beach Balls

Category II Giver beavers love beach balls. Bucolic and achiever beavers swat them back and forth at the beach with their big, flat tales like oversized Ping-Pong balls. This is especially amusing to the little beavs.

To co-beavers, beach balls are more serious business. They hold as many as possible underneath the surface of the pond. Co-beavers are trying to control everyone and everything around them without appearing to control everything and everyone around them. Denying is a way of life. It begins when a bucolic beaver waddles past the pond and asks the co-beaver, "Whatcha got under the water there?"

"Nothing." It goes downhill from there. Of course, "Nothing," is a trite answer. Any experienced co-beaver will do better than that.

After all, they've had lots of practice. "Just flattening the bottom of the pond," is a better answer. The unsuspecting bucolic beaver might nod his or her head and say, "Uh-huh. A beaver's work is never done," and keep on waddling.

As a recovering idiot who spent more time as a co-beaver than an amoeba or altruist, I can testify that denying is part and parcel of codependency. I couldn't admit to myself what I was doing most of the time, because I didn't *realize* what I was doing most of the time. Even when directly and accurately accused of being a passive-aggressive control freak, I denied, denied, denied. Looking back, I'd say 75 percent of my denying involved thinking and behavior I truly wasn't aware of and 25 percent of my denying were outright fibs.

Trying to rescue people seemed so heroic. Yet, my true intention was to increase my accounts receivable column. Paying all the bills in a relationship made me feel important. But it's more honest to say it made me feel worthy to be there at all. Not feeling worthy to be in a relationship elevated the role of denial to new heights.

Most all of us have principles we've been aware of our whole life, but never get the hang of *applying* them. Principle: As a child of my Higher Power, I have value—just like everyone else. For that reason alone, I deserve respect and dignity—just like everyone else. I recognized this for others, but stopped short of applying it to me. The Idiots Exposed 12-step program finally helped me put the lifelong principles of faith and reliance on the God of my understanding into action.

As I mentioned in Chapter 2, there are dozens of programs—12-step as well as others. Mine is a program for overcoming control issues. I'm not recommending everyone rush out and join a program. But trying to get a handle on these issues and improve in isolation is a much tougher road. Accountability to peers in a fellowship of equals is like a weigh-in at Weight Watchers.

Years ago, letting beach balls pop to the surface in front of others would have scared the bejeebers out of a co-beaver such as me. Now disclosure gives me more serenity and strengthens me emotionally more than my three post-graduate degrees. It also puts wheels on what I learned in ways I didn't know were possible. Personal growth programs are the intersection of intellect *and* spirit.

The more I began to believe in my own value, without self-embellishment or enhancement, the less I needed denial in my life.

Woo-hoo. Saying good-bye to the dance of denial has been liberating to say the least, although I'm still vulnerable to backsliding. It takes time and effort to apply new thinking and behaviors on a daily basis, but, over time, I become better grounded and less likely to slip.

It's particularly difficult for co-beavers to deal with denial in others because we recognize it and appreciate how invested others are in their denying. As the regulars in the Methodist church basement on Thursday nights say, "If you can spot it, you've got it." Spotting denial in others helps us become more aware of it in ourselves.

Altruistic Denying

In a word: doubtful. Altruistic Category III Givers are too aware of the downside potential of denial to engage in it themselves. Because they are anticipatory, big-picture thinkers, altruists have a hard time justifying denial in themselves or anyone else. If they discover they're engaged in unconscious denying, altruists will be the first to examine the cause and seek help to deal with it. Altruists are most likely to be committed to speaking and acting out of love. Engaging in denying would be contradictory. Truth, not falsehood, is the foundation for an altruist's belief system.

Altruists tend not to be frustrated by denial in others. Like so many things, they anticipate it. Altruists understand why people engage in defensive behavior, even if they themselves rarely do. When they encounter denial in others, Category III Givers extend themselves to give, as you might expect, the denier an opportunity to express the truth in a safe environment. Altruists understand denying increases proportionately with the perceived hostility of the situation.

Black Holes

Denying and the Garden Slug

It's difficult to deny a couch potato's existence. If guests spend enough time in view of the den, they'll wonder, "Is that sofa cushion breathing?" Can't deny it. Try to ignore it, maybe. Deny it? Difficult. A tuckered out amoeba, beaver, altruist, jaguar, or whirling vortex can display sluggish symptoms after collapsing in exhaustion. But they'll be on their feet again eventually. Spouses, significant others, siblings, children, parents, in-laws, friends, and coworkers may try to deny that a garden slug is lazy to the bone. But sooner or later they must accept it.

Some spouses, siblings, children, or mother-in-laws of garden slugs make excuses for their slugs out of embarrassment. "Floyd has a bad back." "Florence suffers from fainting spells." "Henry works the grave-yard shift." "The doctor told Edith to stay off her feet." "Barney is paralyzed from the armpits down."

Garden slugs are a fact of life. If you wind up taking care of one, you must beware of the three-tiered denial trap. On the first level, you'll be tempted to rationalize that waiting hand and foot on an in-animate object is normal. This denying blocks guilt and embarrass-ment for your role in the situation. On the second tier, you'll deny feelings of disappointment or regret in casting yourself in such a role. Third, you might go so far as to deny you have options to deal with the garden slug, such as not catering meals anymore.

The most extreme garden slugs will completely deny the ability to get up, get a job, or get a life. Admitting they have such abilities im-plies they have consciously chosen against using them. They'll usually cop the same excuses their embarrassed caretaker's claim. The en-abling cycle is complete. Garden slugs believe in their heart of hearts that being waited on hand and foot is normal. No need for denying there.

Garden slugs deny the fact they became developmentally arrested before childhood individuation was complete; before they found out that participating is fun. As long as they're cared for, why bother? If others stepping and fetching for them feels like l-o-v-e to them, and feels the same to the step-and-fetchers, nothing will change.

Denying and the Jaguar

Jaguars are never at fault. They'll deny anything that pins the rap on them. As highly skilled manipulators, jaguars not only deny re-sponsibility for things they do and say, they attach the blame to some-one or something else. "We can't take a family vacation. I'm too busy making business contacts on the golf course." They are so fast and agile, you might find yourself blamed for something before you're aware there's anything wrong. It all started with the jaguar's instinc-tive denial of responsibility for anything that might stick to his or her sleek fur.

Some people associated with jaguars deny the jaguar *is* a jaguar. The jaguar is so proficient at manipulating information to evade responsibility that it's easy to join in his or her denying. Even if you acknowledge you're involved with a Category II Taker jaguar, accepting the truth about his or her behavior can be a bitter pill to swallow. Supporting a jaguar's version of the truth, thereby denying reality, often postpones and intensifies the eventual bump in the road.

Jaguars can be genuinely happy and forthcoming with good news. They enjoy good times with their friends, families, coworkers, and others. Denial creeps in when they heedlessly cross lines that hurt others, such as having more simultaneous intimate relationships than are socially acceptable in Vermont (as dictated by the "Vermont is for lovers" bumper sticker). They might push the boundaries of professional ethics a bit farther than is, say, ethical. If denial hasn't surfaced before, it comes at full speed when they're caught or even suspected.

Many jaguars want to have a happy home life and everything else, too. Their skill with denying can keep things intact at home long after jaguars slip their paws into other cookie jars. Strong attraction to jaguars, especially among amoebas and beavers, can fuel denial about the jaguar's true behavior on the part of many spouses, significant others, siblings, children, parents, in-laws, friends, coworkers, and even bosses.

Whirling Denial

A whirling vortex is hardly going to stop whirling long enough to sit down for a conversation with you about how his or her behavior is affecting someone else. Rather than taking time to be specific and surgical with his or her denying, a whirling vortex might just blow it off with, "I don't know what you're talking about," when confronted about something he or she said or did. Whatever "it" is gets blown back in the accuser's face. A whirling vortex's usual approach to dealing with responsibility could be called blanket denial.

A whirling vortex might surprise you with a brazen, "Yeah, so what if I did?" Whirling vortexes are so caught up in the moment they don't look at the big-picture implications of what they say or do. Their need for gratification is immediate. If they paused long enough to ponder the impact of their words and actions, they might get a more accurate picture of themselves and how they fit into the scheme of things. But then, reflection is so *not* a whirling vortex.

If someone hooks up with a whirling vortex, they're the ones likely to be in denial. They might even overindulge in denial enough to use the portion the vortex is leaving unused. The double-dose of denial might seem necessary. This is a whirling vortex after all. He or she will be much easier to deal with if their partner doesn't fully acknowledge the true nature of a whirlwind and why they are so attracted.

People are likely to deny being drawn to the drama and histrionics of a whirling vortex to distract them from their own emotional and spiritual needs and/or to fill up emptiness they feel inside. As with the jaguar, if what they're getting from the whirling vortex is supplementing what they perceive to be deficiencies in themselves, they'll do as much, if not more, denying. The dance of denial takes two or more to really become a spectacle.

Keys to living with an idiot

⇨ **Count the beach balls.** How many beach balls are you holding under the water? Until it's brought to your attention, you might not have believed you're hiding anything from sight. If you are an emotionally mature, fully disclosing altruistic Category III Giver, you might be withholding very little. Blessings on your head if that's the case. More likely, the exercise of checking for beach balls is worthwhile. The things you're denying are the things that frighten you most. So, it's natural to avoid looking at them, or admitting they exist. But if you're going to re-frame the way you relate to the idiots in your life, you need to minimize distraction. The energy and scheming required to keep beach balls under water directly reduce the energy and focus you need to develop new skills and habits. I'm not saying to let all the beach balls pop to the surface before you or those around you are ready to deal with the consequences. At this stage, it's enough just to acknowledge they exist and the amount you're dealing with.

⇨ **Note how often you fib.** Most of us recoil a little at the suggestion that we lie. I shade the truth to fit situations where I don't want to come off abrasive or where I've judged that cold hard facts will be more useful if softened. It's not that we intentionally mislead, but choosing what to say, and when and to whom we say it is manipulating information. We all make editorial choices and call it discretion. The time I need to get a grip on what I'm doing and why I'm doing it is when I'm tempted to mislead by embellishing or withholding information. If I say I'm protecting someone else, chances are I'm protecting *myself.* Perhaps I'm protecting myself from the ever-frightening possibility of confrontation. Maybe I'm trying to keep people from being upset with me. I might even be hiding from my own feelings. By making a conscious note of how frequently I'm tempted to mislead, I can get a sense of how desperately I'm trying to work around relational situations rather than work through them.

⇨ **Separate denial; your own from others'.** Denial is all around you. Before you begin dealing with it effectively, you must determine which denial is yours and which denial belongs to someone else. In most cases it's easy. The part about recognizing denial in others, that is. We all know how to cinch up the corner of our mouths, nod knowingly, and then shake our heads slightly in disapproval. Cinch, nod, shake. Cinch, nod, shake. That's the international sign for noticing denial in others. Sometimes it involves folding the arms prior to the righteous cinch, nod, shake. The initial reaction to having your own denying exposed is the wide-eyed, head cocked back, "Me?" This causes your trusted adviser to fold, cinch, nod, and shake. If you recognize and accept your denying, you'll bury your forehead in the palm of your hands and shake your head back and forth. There's that pesky question again: "Is it them, or is it me?" If it's me, I can do something about it. If it's them, I can contemplate my best response, if a response is called for at all.

Accepting

One of the most powerful solutions to living with the idiots in your life is accepting reality. I repeat, one of the most powerful solutions to living with the idiots in your life is accepting reality. Accepting the truth about who you really are and the people with whom you have relationships puts you on a solid foundation from which to build a better relationship. If you really want to know how to live with an idiot, you'll want to learn how to accept idio-t-syncracies and stop denying them. If the ultimate goal is to live a happier and more fulfilling life with your significant idiot, you'll need to operate from a basis of reality, not denial.

To accept someone else's behavior doesn't necessarily mean you approve of it. Accepting someone else's behavior doesn't even mean you're willing to be subjected to it. Acceptance, as I'm using the term, means acknowledging that something exists, that it is real, and you need to decide if, when, and how you intend to deal with it.

If acceptance were easy, people would accept many things they'd prefer to deny. Think about something pleasant in your life. No problem accepting that image, right? Trying to consciously think of unpleasant things is more difficult. People can do it to a point. The things you push further from your consciousness, even to the point of holding them under water like the beach ball, range from annoying to unthinkable.

As long as you're denying or repressing reality, there will be tension in your life. Sometimes people manufacture their own reality and try to displace the real deal. At some level, however, they know *their* reality is not the *real* reality. They know that, despite their fervent denials, there is a truth they are not accepting. The result can be emotional confusion and chaos.

Speaking for myself, it can get pretty chattery inside my head when I'm deliberating a decision based on denial. Some of my more mature thoughts recommend dealing with the situation the way it truly is. "What if this happens or that happens," my less disciplined thoughts argue. "Then everything will magically turn out great." Fine. It's still best to deal with things realistically and let the magical stuff, if it happens, be icing on the cake.

Surrendering to reality and truth doesn't mean giving up hope. It means giving up false hope. Once you surrender to the reality of your predicaments, you'll be positioned to pursue your hopes more effectively. Surrender is a big pill to swallow. It's a test of faith. You must really, truly believe that there are better days on the other side. Otherwise, why not forget the pill and hang on to what hasn't been working? It doesn't make sense, that's why.

Self-Acceptance

It's one thing to accept the reality of a situation or certain truths about other people. It's another thing to accept truths about yourself you would prefer to keep below the surface. The more serious you are about changing some aspect of your life, such as learning how to live with an idiot, the more likely it is you will seek help. Help might come in the form of private counseling, a support group, an actual 12-step recovery group, or extensive personal study and reflection. With luck and good planning, the tightest and most intimate support group will be yourself and the idiots closest to you.

When the bubble is pierced and you begin accepting what others have known about you, and/or things *nobody* knew about you (especially you), it can throw off your equilibrium. Contact and support from other people will help restore your balance. I recommend seeking it out. When I joined a recovery group and my beach balls started popping up all over the place, I couldn't have made any sense (or good use) out of the new information without the wisdom and shared experiences of others.

Others are what they are because of the choices they make. That's not so difficult to see. It's more difficult for me to see, much less accept, that I am who I am because of the choices I make. At any moment in time, all of us have the ability to make amoeba choices, beaver choices, and altruistic Category III Giver choices. Despite the type and category in which we spend most of our time, we can experience moments in other types and categories, which enhances our capacity for empathy. Hopefully, it will also help us maintain perspective on ourselves.

If we include acceptance of what it's like to be in someone else's shoes, even temporarily, we can make much better informed relationship choices. Better relationship choices lead to more pleasing relationships. If I know my significant other hates broccoli, I'm not going to serve it. There are plenty of other vegetables to choose from.

If I can't stand discussing religion or politics, I hope my significant other, friends, in-laws, coworkers, and others will respect that. If they want to have a warm and fuzzy relationship with me, they will.

It is more important, by far, that all of us accept *ourselves* for who we really are. People with an empathic capacity to understand what it's like to walk in our shoes will be the best guides, counselors, peer supporters, and mentors. Never underestimate the help an empathic buddy can provide. Never underestimate how helpful we can be to others who are experiencing similar struggles.

Life Fountains

Amoeba Acceptance

Acceptance seems to come naturally to amoebas, although it can appear more like resignation. What looks like amoeba acceptance might even be amoeba acquiescence. An amoeba is not usually going to be invested enough in what he or she will get out of a relationship to get angry when the rewards are few and far between. So, choosing to accept how things truly are is not that much of a challenge to amoebas. Their expectations are limited to begin with.

Nevertheless, abdicating your roles and responsibilities in relationships is not the same as accepting something less than you hoped for. Life tends to ebb and flow, even for an amoeba. Sometimes you get more than you expect, and at other times, less. If you feel as though you always get less than you expect, expectations are over-calibrated. If you expect very little, as in the case of the amoeba, make that under-calibrated.

Sometimes it's difficult to accept an amoeba's passivity, especially if you're the amoeba's friend, relative, coworker, or therapist. You want to pump her up, cheer her on, and push her through the door of assertiveness. But that would be more to comfort yourself than to help the amoeba. You might feel better, but the amoeba might just be annoyed. If you're ever in an intimate relationship with an amoeba, I hope you'll accept the natural passivity of this single-cell creature and build from there.

Accepting Like a Beaver

The biggest single difference between co-beavers and other beavers is acceptance. A bucolic beaver's easygoing personality is grounded in a solid self-image. He or she might not be the brightest beaver that ever gnawed a tree or even the best beaver to look at, but the bucolic beaver takes it all in stride. Bucolic beavers accept their strengths as well as their limitations. That's why they're bucolically laid-back and easygoing.

I have easygoing, self-confident friends, business associates, family members, and clients who fit nicely into the bucolic beaver category. They're reliable, steady, dependable, and not at all hard to accept for who they are. I can say the same thing for the ambitious achiever beavers I know. They tend to have loftier goals and more energy to pursue them. Not hard to accept them either.

Neither bucolic beavers nor achiever beavers have as much trouble accepting me as I once had accepting myself. As a recovering idiot, also recovering from co-beaver-ism, I'm learning and applying all kinds of principles that are making enormous differences in my life. Essential natures never go away entirely, and I'm not sure I would want them to. For example, I accept that I'm good at listening to and helping people. Now that I accept my co-beaver tendency to control situations and outcomes, I can intentionally and effectively back off when I'm tempted to *listen to control.*

Accepting my true nature, and the fears of abandonment and failure that once drove my efforts to control other people, gives me a stronger sense of effective control over the decisions I make. Co-beavers have a lot of good qualities, which make them quite likeable (dare I say loveable), as long as they keep their intentions honest. Acceptance and genuine surrender to who I really am, and, more importantly, who I am capable of becoming, positions me to enjoy happier, more fulfilling relationships with virtually everybody.

Co-beavers who cling to their controlling ways might feel safer and more secure in those familiar waters. But holding beach balls under water is hard work. It doesn't get any easier as they get older, and not everybody is fooled. I remember what it was like to be holding beach balls under the water when an altruistic Category III Giver walked by and casually said, "Nice beach ball."

Altruist Acceptance

Altruistic Category III Givers can't achieve the type of emotional and spiritual maturity they achieve without accepting the reality in situations, the truth about others, and the truth about themselves. An altruist won't saunter by the beaver pond and say, "Nice beach ball," unless she or he is aware that (a) I have at least one under the water, and (b) I can handle knowing someone else knows.

Altruists know that acceptance is incredibly liberating. If you can completely let go of denial, whatever caused you to deny reality in the first place will eventually dissipate. "Let it go, let it go, let it go." Easy to sing; sometimes very hard to do. When you deny that the clueless creatures you deal with in various forms day in and day out are clueless, how can you let it go? How can you make their cluelessness less abrasive and agitating?

Altruists also understand and appreciate how difficult it is to let go of something that's become a way of life, or at least a familiar fixture. Accepting that clueless persons have little awareness of how their words and actions affect others makes it easier to anticipate their behavior and reduce the resulting anger and resentment. Emotionally and spiritually mature people seem to get along with most everyone, clueless or not.

When I make speeches or do seminars, the first people to laugh and embrace their inner idiots are the most solidly grounded people in the group. The people most likely to be offended (there's always someone) are those who have other, more intense self-doubts and misgivings. Altruistic Category III Givers have more sincere self-confidence.

Altruistic Givers laugh easily at their own shortcomings, feigned or real. Altruists are also the most accepting. Because they see the biggest picture among all Giver types, the altruists are capable of demonstrating the broadest acceptance. The difficulty the rest of us have fully accepting altruists indicates we still have a beach ball or two under the water.

Black Holes

Accepting Garden Slugs

Sometimes an amoeba just wants to be helpful. Who is more helpless than a garden slug? When a Category I Taker garden slug and a Category I Giver amoeba can accept each other for what they are, it can be a halfway decent relationship. It's doubtful an amoeba will wait on a garden slug hand and foot and think he or she is serving a grandiose purpose. On the other hand, a garden slug thinks that being waited on hand and foot *is* a high calling—for whoever is doing the serving.

Next to amoebas, beavers are most likely to serve breathing sofa cushions. However, they're much less apt to like it. Bucolic and achiever beavers, like the amoeba, will accept couch potatoes for what they are. What they won't do is put up with them for very long. Co-beavers are seemingly the only ones from the dam-building Category II Giver family willing to tolerate garden slugs.

I don't think the co-beaver accepts the slug for what he or she is. Co-beavers get stuck on slugs for two reasons. First, co-beavers are kings and queens of d'Nile and might believe, at least superficially, the garden slug is destined to fly off the couch as a sleek jaguar sometime between the late news and Jay Leno. Second, a codependent's worst nightmare is to be abandoned. What are the chances a well-fed and watered couch potato is going anywhere?

Garden slugs don't seem to have a problem accepting their plight in life, if it can be called a plight. There are times when I envy garden slugs the life of apparent leisure they lead. My friend Roger (with the adolescent son) constantly reminds me that we really don't know what's going on with other people. Even when we think we do—perhaps *especially* when we think we do—we probably don't. How can we be sure the garden slug doesn't exert a tremendous amount of effort remaining sluggish? Who's to say how difficult it is for them to tough it out on the couch day in and day out? In the end, perhaps the healthiest choice is for us to accept slugs in all their infamy, throw a blanket over them, and go to bed.

Accepting Jaguars

Jaguars are natural predators. As you see them stalking their prey, gracefully, stealthfully, they are something to be admired. Then in one bound, muscle and grace combine to pounce. The attack is over almost before it starts. Jaguars accept their superior speed, power, and keen abilities. They rarely, however, own responsibility for the carnage they can leave behind.

If you want to enjoy a relationship with a jaguar, it's up to you to accept what she or he is and anticipate accordingly. Jaguars accept you for what *you* are: slower, less agile, and less calculating than the big cats. Pre-recovery co-beavers, who are often in relationships with jaguars, can be crafty and calculating as they try to control situations and the jaguar him- or herself. Co-beavers might even pull it off if it weren't for the jaguar's superior strength, speed, and agility.

At the first sign of getting trapped, shackled, or contained in any way, the jaguar is off like a bolt of lightning. Accepting the jaguar's volatility is difficult for anyone intent on keeping the jaguar close to home. A healthy form of denying, if there is such a thing, might be to hook up with an achiever beaver and pretend he or she is a jaguar. Things will be much more pleasant around the lodge.

Whirling Acceptance

Category III Taker vortexes leave the issue of acceptance to you. For as much as they understand who they are, whirling vortexes accept who they are in stride. They can't imagine being anything but what they are. Why not accept it? They figure keeping up with them is your problem. Because so many folks are willing to chase the twisters, at least for a little while, whirling vortexes have little need to face realities about long-term relationships.

Whirling vortexes are so used to other people bailing them out, they have little need to face the reality of the situations they're in. They know they blow, but not *why*. If you plan to have a relationship with a whirling vortex that won't leave you tattered, you must accept the nature of the atmospheric disturbance and its need to keep whirling. That acceptance must lead to anticipation of what it's like to live with a hurricane.

On a kinder, gentler note, accepting a whirling vortex for what he or she is can be like accepting a garden slug. This is a good-natured book. I would never suggest such a thing except to illustrate a point. If you were to accidentally wire each of a garden slug's toes to a lamp cord and plug it into the wall, you could make an impressive whirling vortex—until your sympathies kick in and you unplug. Just imagine you are the whirling vortex and you *can't* unplug. I, for one, accept that whirling vortexes don't lead easy lives, despite how many people they wear out in the process.

Keys to living with an idiot

⇨ **Accept who you are.** It starts with you. By now you should be used to me saying that. I was halfway through the daily readings in my Idiots Exposed program for the second time before I accepted that the business of recovery wasn't going to start with my spouse, significant other, siblings, parents, children, in-laws, friends, or business associates. Accepting who you truly are is a process that often requires outside help. You need help to be objective about your behavior and intentions. You also need help to keep you honest and provide support when you're tempted to fall back on old thinking and behavior that didn't work well for you before. It's important to have someone walk by on a regular basis and say, "Nice beach ball."

⇨ **Accept who they are.** This can also be a challenge because accepting who other people really are reflects back on those who chose to have relationships with them. That would be you again. Accepting the realities in other people and situations doesn't mean judging, as I'll deal with in Chapter 9. Neither does it mean assuming. It means being as realistic as possible with the information you have available. All that's left is to accept whatever he or she happens to be. That's the only solid basis from which you can make decisions about how to relate, if you choose to relate at all. Sometimes it's the final acceptance of who someone is that makes it clear there is no healthy way for you to relate to them, except from a distance. Painful. But sometimes the least of all the painful choices.

⇨ **Accept who you are together.** There's *who you are*. There's *who they are*. And there's *who you are together*. When two or more people get together, a composite personality is formed. I deal with this "third personality" when I consult with leadership teams in organizations. The same principles apply to families and organizations of all kinds. The combination of character qualities in any group produces an overriding personality different than the sum of the individual personalities. Early on in my marriage and family therapy program, I learned that no two siblings are born into the same family. Every time another person is added or removed from a group, the group grows or shrinks. You can see that with the naked eye. What you can't see is the new composite personality created each time. But it's there. How often have you heard someone say, "They're both good people, they're just not good together"? A statement like that leaves me a little suspect of the diagnosis. But the point about two or more people forming an overriding personality is right on. You need to accept the fact that composite personalities are formed and you need to deal with them, just as you need to deal with individuals.

Chapter Summary

How many beach balls can you hold under water? For how long? I tried to use the beach ball metaphor in a seminar, but I couldn't bring a tank of water into the room that was large enough to submerge beach balls. So, I went to Plan B: Ping-Pong balls. I asked a fellow in the group to help me. I put Ping-Pong balls, one by one, into a large glass bowl full of water.

I asked him to hold all of them under with one hand, which he did. I hadn't planned on that. I was trying to demonstrate that it couldn't be done. I hadn't properly anticipated how many Ping-Pong balls I would need, or the size of my helper's hand. So it is in real life. Sometimes our most ingenious demonstrations go awry. Yet, he demonstrated something I didn't expect. Some people can hold more beach balls under water than we might think. Sometimes the secret is never revealed.

It's amazing how some folks can expend all of that energy and focus for a lifetime. But they can and do. It just shows how important it is to them. It could be the only way they know how to handle confusion and contradiction in their lives. Maybe it's the only way to avoid accepting things that are difficult to accept. Maybe they never read a book called *How to Live with an Idiot.*

Even a recovering idiot like me has a pretty good idea that accepting people and things as they are, without judgment, is necessary in a quality relationship. We don't have to like people to accept who they are. We don't have to like situations to accept reality. When I became a recovering co-beaver, I discovered lots of things I didn't like about myself—things I had been denying. That brought me to a decision point.

Accepting unpleasant things about me is my first order of business. To grow, develop, and find happiness as a person, and thereby become a better friend, partner, coworker, boss, or bowler, I need to deflate the beach balls I'm holding under the water, put them away, or give them to the beavers to swat around. I need the energy for more gratifying things.

To-do list:

- ☑ Count the beach balls.
- ☑ Note how often we fib.
- ☑ Separate denial; ours from others'.
- ☑ Accept who you are.
- ☑ Accept who they are.
- ☑ Accept who you are together.

Chapter 9

The Fifth Relational Sin and Solution: Judging vs. Forgiving

IT TOOK ME A LONG TIME TO LEARN that an accusing finger pointed at somebody else ("Judge not...") is poised just above three more accusing fingers pointed back at me ("...lest you be judged"). The significant idiots in your life make it awfully tempting to judge. But if we were supposed to sit in judgment of one another, we would have been born wearing robes. Maybe there is a reason we were born naked.

Because idiots are essentially clueless creatures, they usually pick the worst times to judge others—not that there's any *good* time to judge others. This only results in the idiots being judged more harshly. One idiot laughing and pointing at the "Kick Me" sign taped on another idiot's back doesn't impress anybody if he has toilet paper stuck to his own shoe. Idiot number two disqualifies himself.

There is no justification for judgment—as in distain and condescension. People willingly submit to judgment in legal matters and chili cook-offs. On Judgment Day the choice whether to submit will be taken out of our hands. When it comes to human character, your Higher Power has the monopoly. Unless the God of your understanding delegates judgment to you, you need to accept others for what their behavior indicates, and respond appropriately. If someone runs at me waving a butcher knife, I might *judge* her to be a dangerous threat to my health and welfare. Technically, however, I'm assessing potential violence and anticipating possible blood loss, neither of which appeal to me. My list of appropriate responses may include pretending I'm a jaguar and running like the wind.

Climb Down

Remember the line from the song on page 16, "Oh, judging won't make folks like you"? There are good reasons to let go of judging. I think back on the veteran recovering idiot who sat in the Methodist church basement and said, "My God-given talents and abilities took me to good places my character defects wouldn't let me stay." The character defect that wedged him loose from those good places and sent him tumbling off the Idiots Exposed wagon, was judgment.

The second line in the song, "In fact they might despise you," can mean more than vicious glares. If people feel you are judging them, they might take action to bring you to a level lower than the one you judged them to be on. It's a lot smarter not to climb on their heads to be above them to start with. Judgment conjures images of elevation. People don't like being "looked down upon," "talked down to," "considered beneath us," "made to feel small."

All of these thoughts infer you've climbed a hill, some steps, a ladder, a pedestal, something that puts you above others, so to speak. Relationships, even with idiots, are always more copacetic when they are level. That's why recovery groups are always a fellowship of equals. To cause someone to feel, or always be positioned to feel, defensive is a major reason relationships become unleveled. Insecurity is another. These are all reactions to judgment. And nose-diving like an amoeba doesn't make the problem go away.

People often attempt to elevate themselves to render judgment on those they feel *inferior* to. This is a problem where there is perceived inequality. Someone less obsessed with comparing him- or herself with others might walk by and ask, "What are you doing up there?"

What would you say? "I'm up here to judge you in case you condescend to me." That must mean you expect him or her to climb onto something taller than your platform. You would then need to climb higher still, and so on, until it all gets pretty silly. Judging is about as silly as the toilet-paper-stuck-on-the-shoe pointing at the "Kick Me" sign. But the feelings that motivate it are serious.

Shirley Feels Judged for Judging

"Nearly everybody I know thinks I'm judgmental," Shirley moans.

"And that would be judging on their part," I assure her.

"Exactly."

"Do you feel victimized by their judgment?"

"Yes."

"Still, they must feel as if you judge them or they wouldn't say such things."

"It's all in their imagination," she protests.

"Is their judgment of you all in *your* imagination?"

"Of course not."

"How do you know they feel that way?"

"I just know. A person can tell."

"I agree."

"That they're judging me...?"

"That a person can tell when he or she is being judged."

"I'm not following you."

"Has anyone come right out and told you that you're judgmental?"

Shirley thinks for a moment.

"No."

"How do you know then?"

"I can see it in their eyes."

"How could you convince them you're not?"

"I suppose this has something to do with how I talk to my daughter-in-law," she says sourly.

"How has she been taking the compliments?"

Shirley cocks her head slightly. "Quite well, actually."

"What would happen if you complimented those people who you feel are judging you?"

"They might smirk."

I blink my eyes a couple times. "What makes you think that?"

"That's how they are. Always looking down their nose at me."

"Why not live dangerously? Give them the compliment treatment and see what happens."

"What if I can't think of anything to say?"

"What do you usually say?"

"I guess I usually make a comment about what we're planning to do, what we just ordered for dinner, what they're wearing."

"Do you plan what you're going to say ahead of time, the way you now do with your daughter-in-law?"

She purses her lips. "No, I just say whatever pops into my head."

Judging as a Natural Defense

When I'm tempted to say judgmental things I, like Shirley, tend not to think. Judgmental comments are virtually automatic. When I'm feeling insecure or condescended to, I have judgmental comments preloaded and ready to deliver on a moment's notice. Intentionally saying something else, preferably positive, requires premeditation.

I'm making remarkable progress. I *do* say positive things in most situations where I formerly would have said something judgmental. The positive comments, if a comment is called for at all, feel much better to me, and are taken better by the other person. All it takes is considering my comments before making them. Anticipating, when possible, helps keep me from being caught off guard.

Dealing with my hair-trigger judgmental tendencies wasn't possible until I put my trust in people who could help me recognize the tendencies and ask probing questions, such as, "Why are you doing that, John?" The answers are almost always the same. I'm inclined to make judgmental remarks when I'm defending myself. What I've learned is: the best defense isn't always a good offense; sometimes it's reflective silence.

With the objective help of friends, skilled helpers, family members, priests, pastors, rabbis, and fellow group members, we can realize most of the condescension we're so sensitive about is in our own heads. The more we accept who we truly are and who other people are, the less prone we'll be to fictionalizing. Many of us can still puff ourselves up with synthetic self-confidence at will. Getting judgmental used to be my default setting. But now I can take a deep co-beaver breath, act more like an altruistic Category III Giver, and re-frame the condescension into something I can deal with.

Life Fountains

Judging and the Amoeba

Amoebas are inverse judges. Whereas most of us look for something or someone to climb on to elevate ourselves, amoebas might as well say, "Don't bother. I'll just squat down." Amoebas don't tend to judge others because they condescend to themselves. Others condescending to them seems normal. When amoebas are looked down upon, they don't get defensive. They say, "Sorry." At least they don't say, "Thank you."

What could amoebas climb up on to achieve elevation anyway? They'd probably just slip off and end up back in the vicinity of the doormat—or under it. You have to love amoebas. For single-cell invertebrates, they get a lot of work done. They're quiet about it, too. Maybe that's why others don't tend to judge them. Most people ignore amoebas and let them go about their chores. This seems to suit amoebas. When I do, or say, something embarrassing, I slip into an amoeba moment, and crawl under the carpet; being ignored is the best of all possible outcomes.

Beaver Judgment

Category II Giver beavers deal with judgment as differently as they do other relational sins. Bucolic beavers and achiever beavers are secure in their pelts and don't experience much self-doubt. Without insecurity to feed illusions of self-righteousness, they don't need to use judgment as a defense. Laid-back bucolic beavers and friendly-but-ambitious achiever beavers don't feel a need to judge others. Live and let live. Gnaw or don't gnaw. They leave it up to you.

Always the most energetic of the beaver family, co-beavers make up for the benign natures of the bucolic and achiever beavers. Co-beavers believe if they make a good enough dam, a good enough pond, and a good enough lodge, all will be right with the world. If all is not right with the world, they will (a) take the responsibility on themselves, (b) blame others for not cooperating in the co-beaver's master plan, or (c) take responsibility on themselves *and* blame others for not cooperating in their master plan.

This is all very confusing and leaves co-beavers feeling conflicted. Yet co-beavers wouldn't have such grandiose expectations in the first place if they weren't compensating for something. Their need to control reveals insecurity, which can cause them to sense contempt, even if no one else is around.

But beavers don't climb trees, so it's difficult for co-beavers to achieve adequate elevation to be judgmental. The result can be resentment. Beavers are burrowing rodents and are more inclined to tunnel into the stream bank, muttering under their breath. As tempted as they are to judge, co-beavers truly come into their own in Chapter 10 on resenting.

Altruists and Judging

Altruistic Category III Givers aren't as vulnerable to problems of low self-confidence as amoebas or co-beavers. Altruists aren't overconfident or even falsely confident. Their big-picture thinking and patient understanding of people and situations keeps things in perspective. They appreciate that all Life Fountains and Black Holes are doing what they can with the knowledge and skills they currently possess. Altruists feel no compulsion to judge.

Even when altruists themselves are harshly judged, they tend to take it in stride. They are skilled re-framers and know how to anticipate. If anyone can appreciate the good nature in an idiot, it's an altruist. Idio-t-syncracies pose no threat to an altruistic Category III Giver. Neither does judgment. Accepting themselves and others, in their roles in relationships, buffers altruists from the temptation to judge.

Black Holes

Judging Garden Slugs

Garden slugs make easy targets for judgment. It's almost too tempting to pass up. Their nonengaging demeanors can provide a blank canvas on which to paint all kinds of recriminations. The most common judgments passed on breathing sofa cushions include laziness, shiftlessness, excess body fat, and chronic slumber. More intensive judgments include not listening, not talking, and not caring.

Slugs don't seem to be wounded by such judgments. They switch channels or roll over and snooze on. The good news is they'd rather pass than judge those who judge them. That, at least, reduces the judgment problem by half. Still, it would be nice to see some response out of a slug. On second thought, no response is better than meeting judgment with judgment. As strange as it sounds, garden slugs set a good example for people by not allowing themselves to be wounded by judgment.

One of the things that keeps people from becoming garden slugs, at least full-time, is judgment. Speaking for myself, it's not the judgment of others that keeps me off the couch. It's my own self-judgment. I have trouble relaxing in the middle of the day, even when my schedule allows. Somehow, garden slugs have overcome self-judgment. They've also overcome the drive to perform, exercise, or do windows.

My hat's off to them on the nonjudgment part. Because judgment is never a good practice, to not be victimized by it and to abstain from practicing it earns the garden slugs a gold star. Now, if they would just get off the couch and do something for a change....

Judging Jaguars

You can pass all kinds of judgments on jaguars. But it will be super difficult to make them stick. Highly maneuverable jaguars use their superior acceleration to confuse judge and jury. Jaguars are sensitive to being judged because the judging, although inappropriate, is probably accurate. Jaguars don't like being snared by the truth. In the end, judging jaguars backfires on the judge. I've known many who've tried to judge jaguars and wound up miserable for their efforts. Hopefully, they learned from the experience.

Jaguars' ranging behavior is often annoying to beavers or amoebas they have relationships with. Jaguars are not home as much as their partners or children would like. Consequently, they are often judged as uncaring and distant. Anticipating jaguars' proclivity to care first and foremost for themselves, based on historical behavior, is different than judging them to be defective in character.

Jaguars are what they are, and, by taking care of themselves first, they can be better and stronger in extending a hand to others. That's a sound personal growth principle. Many jaguars provide very well for their broods from the spoils of their successes. It's the emotional distance stuff that gets them in trouble.

I had a jaguar couple in marriage counseling several years ago. It was obvious how they simultaneously excited and aggravated each other. They looked great together; a million-dollar couple from all appearances. But they were both predatory. Each one wanted the other to stay home and tend to the children while he or she prowled. Each judged the other one as uncaring and unfaithful for the precise behavior the judge engaged in. I tried to help them accept the jaguar in each other. Passing judgment on one another, especially in their case, was self-indictment.

Vortex Judgment

Whirling vortexes have one-track minds. They are exclusively focused on getting their immediate needs met. If you're on their radar screens, it's because you have something to offer in that regard. Vortexes don't take time to pass judgment on others. They make instant decisions whether or not you're valuable to them in the moment. If you are, they don't care about any defect in character you might have. Whatever you have to offer is all that matters.

Vortexes accept anything of value to them without judging the presenter. That's why people with low self-esteem, like many co-beavers and amoebas, bring offerings to their feet. No matter how severely others judge themselves, the whirling vortex won't ignore, or judge, a gift-giver. The givers feel, by accepting what is offered, the vortex is accepting them just as they are. The ones bearing gifts might get a wild ride to spice up their otherwise dull and colorless lives. The wiser ones figure out the true nature of the trade-off and run to greener, more bucolic pastures. Those addicted to the drama keep coming back for more.

Pompous and pious people get little satisfaction from judging whirling vortexes. They judge with great vim and vigor, mind you. But their judgments have little or no effect on the vortexes and, therefore, bring little satisfaction to the judge. That's an interesting aspect of judgment. In Shirley's case, her judgments were intended to produce a sense of being convicted in the one judged. I'm not quite sure how that's supposed to work. But in my experience, if the judged one shows no concern, the one doing the judging feels slighted.

Keys to living with an idiot

⇨ **Check altitude.** When others point out that you've been judgmental, you shouldn't freak out. Consider the source, and be open to the possibility they're right. They could be the ones feeling judged. If you notice a tendency on your part to be judgmental, or if others have pointed it out, you can consider your elevation. Have you climbed up to a high place in order to condescend? Are you standing on your tippy toes? Are you up there because you feel the need to defend yourself from condescension you feel from others? Unless you're a bird, perching in high places is a sign you're reacting. If you're a beaver, up in the small limbs of a tree instead of on the ground, gnawing it down, you need to seek help.

⇨ **Climb down.** Whatever is causing your impulse to judge, you won't find it on top of a telephone pole. You must climb down and figure it out. Garden slugs don't need to move to blow off judgment from others. Why should you? First of all, you need to figure out if there really is judgment going on or if you're misinterpreting some other signal. Self-judgment can be triggered by lots of things—old parental programming, embarrassing experiences in your past, or hyper-religiosity. Even if you are being judged by people who should know better, the time to consider your best response is when your feet are planted firmly on the ground.

⇨ **Laugh it off.** Most of us are probably more sensitive, with a better sense of humor than a garden slug. Why else would we be in the middle of this book together? Let's put that good humor and good sense to work becoming more resilient to the slings and arrows others might send our way. Let's not give them the satisfaction of seeing us squirm. Climbing on top of something or someone to meet judging with judgment is a sure sign that they got under our pelts. Humor is a great deflector shield. I don't mean gratuitous laughter in the face of those judging you. I mean finding something truly humorous in the situation; hopefully, in a good-natured way. Imagine that the person judging you is a duck or a goose. Honk. Whatever works.

Forgiving

Forgiveness is your best defense. It isn't a tool to change others. Forgiveness is the key to unlocking your own serenity. When someone offends you, intentionally or unintentionally, retaliation only makes things worse. But that's the first place my mind used to go. Then I learned, the hard way, how retaliation for my retaliation significantly escalated the conflict. To be angered by something offensive is natural. To begin passing judgment relinquishes control to the offender. If they meant to cause you pain, and you hold on to it, you're aiding and abetting them. When you re-frame your view in order to forgive, you liberate yourself from sleep-depriving judgment that doesn't keep the other person up at night anyway. Like most of these techniques, forgiving, when you prefer to rip somebody's lungs out, is not easy.

Remember how compliments displaced criticism? Forgiveness and judgment can't exist in the same space or time. This is helpful to remember when you're tempted to label forgiveness as too fluffy and friendly for the likes of whoever slimed you. Forgiveness is practical. If for no other reason, you should consider it in order to block judgment or retaliation, neither of which will make you feel better in the long run anyway.

You shouldn't avoid forgiveness because you think you might fall prey to the judge again. Let it go quickly and re-frame. By laughing it off or, better yet, forgiving the offender, you disarm them. That's the best hedge against future assaults. Rewarded behavior is repeated behavior. Squirming in pain encourages a sadist. Taking the satisfaction out of something is the best way to make it stop. To forgive is to let go and let it float away. Holding on drags you down.

Sometimes, forgiving and forgetting are the way to go. But forgiving isn't always forgetting. At the other extreme, co-beavers are passionate scorekeepers. At any moment in time they can quote exactly how many gestures of love and support they have dispensed and how many have been reciprocated. This is not true forgiveness. It's accounting. It's silly to forget a painful situation or relationship only to walk into the same spinning propeller again and again. Such "forgetfulness" looks more like denial to me.

As a recovering co-beaver, I've learned to etch painful experiences in my personal logbook and let go of the pain and resentment. I want to grow wiser, not develop amnesia. Besides, the idiot part of me wasn't all that aware anything was wrong. Retaining the lessons I've learned is a good thing. When I hang on to pain, however, I set myself up to act irrationally or just be depressed. "Let it go, let it go, let it go." Log the experience for future reference, but don't stay in it any longer than necessary.

Holding on to pain and resentment is being stuck. Forgiveness starts things moving again. Holding on to pain imprisons you. Forgiveness sets you free. Staying in what the Idiots Exposed regulars call the "ugly spot" leads to wallowing in self-pity. That really encourages those who are out to get you. If there really are people out to get you, you're doing their work for them. In the same way forgiveness displaces judgment, it gets us unstuck. With the burden of judgment lifted, we can take the next right step toward a healthier place from which to operate.

Self-Forgiveness

For many people, forgiving the trespasses others commit toward them is easier than forgiving themselves. I can recall times too numerous to count when nobody meant me harm, yet I interpreted their words and/or actions as judgmental. I let things bother me for weeks, months, and years that were nothing more than misunderstandings.

The predisposition to judging yourself is sometimes referred to as the *critical voice of an internalized parent.* That's probably about right. It seems to be a three-generational process for many families. Many people tell me how their parents suffered at the hands of the grandparents and passed on the favor. Now the parents are grandparents and have figured out how hurtful that was. They've decided to support the current parents in their campaign to provide a distinctly different home environment in terms of love and acceptance of the children. Of course, they now run the risk of spoiled brats. But if you must err one way or the other....

Life Fountains

Amoeba Forgiveness

Amoebas are often mistreated. Unless they are given permission to harbor a grudge, they won't hold on to it. This results in forgiveness by default. Just as well. What is an amoeba going to do to an offender anyway? If you're thinking, "What about the silent-but-deadly types who allow resentment to build up until they blow up a building or shoot up a school yard?" Thanks for bringing that up. It's rare, but even amoebas can freak out.

Those folks are not real amoebas anyway. They're a splinter strain of angry beavers. Beavers naturally dam things up. If they don't find an acceptable emotional outlet, the dam can burst. Even co-beavers act out in less catastrophic ways as a rule. Amoebas sort of let things pass through their single-cell bodies and change shape as necessary to minimize friction. I'd call it forgiveness with a capital "F" if it weren't for the fact that amoebas just come by it naturally.

Forgiving Like a Beaver

Bucolic and ambitious achiever beavers are quick to forgive others, and they don't seem to be overly punitive with themselves. Their ability to forgive comes from not taking much offense to begin with. Although bucolic beavers and achiever beavers go about things at different speeds, they're still likely to barbecue together on the weekend. Either one of them might accidentally knock over the other one's beer. Beaver tails are unwieldy after all. If that happens, you'll probably hear, "Sorry. No offense." "None taken." That's the end of it. No big deal.

Leave it to co-beavers to complicate things. It's not easy for busy co-beavers to make everything right with the world and keep score at the same time. But that doesn't stop them from trying. As if making everything right with the world and keeping score at the same time isn't complicated enough, co-beavers can get their lower lip stuck out over minor offenses. It's difficult for a beaver to pooch out a lower lip past those big incisors, but co-beavers have plenty of practice.

Recovering co-beavers who have sought help with their incredible, self-inflicted burdens, find forgiveness one of their best friends. The relief forgiveness brings to the forgiver is so instant, they must be careful not to hold a grudge against themselves for not learning the value of forgiveness sooner. Co-beavers are usually the critters most in need of forgiving and being forgiven. They can spin like a miniature whirling vortex when they get caught up in the judging-begets-more-judging cycle.

Letting go of judgment takes a weight off your shoulders. Making the choice to forgive and let go rather than clinging tightly to resentment, helps shed the heavy load. Co-beavers can do it. It doesn't come as naturally to them as it does to bucolic or achiever beavers. But when they do, co-beavers learn to relax a little and wear a twin-incisor grin.

Altruistic Forgiveness

Altruistic Category III Givers can appear to come by forgiving behavior naturally, just as amoebas do. But Category III Givers actually make the choice to forgive. Like the achiever and bucolic beavers, altruists are not instinctively judgmental. However, altruists reflect on the big picture and understand the good and the bad in it. They know the benefits of forgiveness and they see the extent of the sometimes cruel intentions of the offenders.

Altruists forgive anyway. The advantages of forgiveness so outweigh the disadvantages, there is no contest. To altruistic Category III Givers, forgiveness is more than a practical solution that displaces judgment and disarms attackers. It's a principle to live by. I find the example my Higher Power sets by forgiving me is a good road map for me to follow.

Altruists hope as much as anyone else that their forgiveness will be reciprocated. But if it's not, they still forgive. If there is any single reason the God of my understanding wants me to graduate into a full-blown Category III Giver, it's probably to become a more proficient forgiver.

Black Holes

Forgiving Garden Slugs

Sometimes an amoeba can really get sore at a nonresponsive couch potato, but it doesn't last for long. The amoeba won't forgive as much as he or she will just give up. It's more of the same for these two. The garden slug might be a teenager, in-law, spouse, or other significant idiot. Amoebas tend to slough off irritation with these various nuisances.

Co-beavers won't be so patient, especially if the breathing sofa cushion is an adolescent, in-law, or worse, an adolescent in-law. What co-beavers need to realize is all that nagging only makes the slug turn over and go back to sleep. Forgiveness, in this case, begins with acceptance. The garden slug isn't doing *nothing* to aggravate the co-beaver or anyone else (double negative intentional), he or she is just doing what comes naturally.

The slug is doing what slugs do best, and the irritated party needs to reflect on how things came to be in such a state. If original expectations for the garden slug's bright future haven't panned out, go to Plan B. First, check your expectations. Based on past performance, the slug is living up to his. Accept that you invested in flawed expectations. Accepting your role in the scenario paves the way to forgive the slug for underachieving. Finally, ask the slug's forgiveness as you carry your bags out the door.

If leaving is too extreme, you can lovingly explain the new rules you plan to live by, which don't include waiting on a garden slug hand

and foot. No need to ask forgiveness for terminating sofa-side service. As any recovering co-beaver knows, you should ask forgiveness for doing it in the first place.

Forgiving Jaguars

Jaguars are hard to forgive. If they can't convince you of their innocence, their in-your-face-what-are-you-going-to-do-about-it attitude leaves little room for discussion. Remembering that we're all doing the best with what we have to work with, one has to wonder why jaguars feel the need for independence and possessiveness at the same time. Whatever the motivation, it's up to you to decide how you're going to deal with it. Jaguars know how *they* want to deal with it.

Forgiving a jaguar and letting go of the hostilities his or her behavior might have generated is a tall order. But what good is hanging on to them? Show a jaguar a scorecard and she or he will ignore it, slink away, or chew it up and spit it out. Jaguars have to lose just about everything in their lives before they seek help or get into a recovery program. They're certainly not idiots when it comes to getting what they want.

With the rarest exception, beautiful, sleek, and powerful jaguars can form new relationships with ease. They don't have the patience to work through problems. Forgiving is usually a function of the jaguar's friends, family, pets, coworkers, or whomever. Because forgiveness is such a liberating experience for the forgiver, that's good news for friends, family, pets, coworkers, or whomever.

Whirling Forgiveness

Category III Taker vortexes bring forgiveness to new heights. The vortexes themselves forgive any past indiscretion or offense as long as the offender doesn't show up empty-handed. Showing up with empty hands, even if you've never offended a whirling vortex, could be considered an indiscretion. Whirling vortexes know what they want and can assign instant value to it. They also know the value of zero.

It becomes easier to forgive whirling vortexes when you consider the deep, mysterious discomfort that sets them to whirling. Not that you should feel sorry for them. That will only play into the enabling behavior you want to avoid. You can identify with vortexes when you consider how emotional discomfort motivates people to do things they later regret.

How much a vortex regrets self-destructive behavior is hard to say. When the discomfort becomes sufficient, the vortex will get some help. It happens. Meanwhile, you can consider forgiveness as a way to liberate yourself from a destructive relationship, if that's how far it goes. Aspiring to be more like the altruistic Category III Giver, you can forgive whirling Category III Takers because it's the right thing to do.

Keys to living with an idiot

⇨ **Forgive yourself.** Let's not be hypocrites. It won't work. I've stumbled over this mistake many times. I have the stubbed toes and bruised shins to prove it. Trying to be a wonderfully forgiving person without forgiving myself was fraudulent. If I'm not willing to first forgive myself, my "forgiveness" of others is just a ploy to make them like me. I might not be consciously aware of my maneuver, but when I'm not *really* forgiving, I'm not letting go either. When I don't let go of this stuff, I receive no relief, and the acid builds up inside. Forgiving *me* is much harder than forgiving others. It's hard to do without the support of others to encourage me. Without help, I'm apt to snatch back the guilt as soon as I let it go. This is the kind of lesson friends, family, professional helpers, and other metal-chair dwellers help teach.

⇨ **Forgive others.** Easier than forgiving yourself—but still no picnic. I'm a third-, possibly fourth-generation scorekeeper. I grew up keeping tabs. On many occasions, when I felt the balance sheet was unfairly tipped against me, I protested instead of finding an equitable way to balance things out. My protestations, some of them resembling tantrums, give the new me a vivid backdrop of what a life without forgiveness looks like. Now, if I'm tempted to think someone owes me, I'll consider what my role was in getting things out of whack. It's usually not hard to see where I went too far and gave too much in hopes of buying friendship, favors, influence, or whatever. If somebody took from me, it's probably because I was too willing to give. That doesn't make what they did right. But it sets the stage for me to forgive myself, forgive the other party, and learn to use more discretion in the future.

⇨ **Know you are forgivable.** This is where many people get hung up. You've been convinced by someone or a lot of people that there's something wrong with you, and that no one will forgive you. Ultimately, you're responsible for buying in to the notion. But if that's all you have to work with, you need a replacement notion before you can get rid of the stinkin' thinkin'. If you give it some thought, how could God not love an innocent little amoeba? There's nothing more endearing than an eager beaver—even a tuckered-out, frazzled, frenetic co-beaver. Who can't honor the honorable behavior of an altruistic Category III Giver? It takes a little more divine assistance to love a garden slug, a dangerous-but-beautiful jaguar, or a major atmospheric disturbance. But if our Higher Power can love us all, the least we can do is give it our best effort—starting with ourselves.

Chapter Summary

To have a happier, healthier relationship with the significant idiot and others in your life, you must resist the temptation to judge. It might seem as if they are inviting you to judge them, idiots especially, but you must resist. Judging won't make folks like you. It won't make you like yourself, either. It might make you feel momentarily smug and superior. But how many smug and superior people do you like?

If the temptation runs deep in you, the way it runs deep in me, this is no small attitude adjustment. It starts with assessing the whole concept of judgment. If you can find something good about it, write and tell me. Otherwise, let's support each other's efforts to outgrow judgment. Let God do God's work and we'll do our own.

The antidote I suggest for judgment is forgiveness. Please don't be cute and say we must first judge people guilty in order to forgive them. This isn't a presidential pardon we're talking about. This is a letting go of the offense because there is no value in holding on to it.

Forgive yourself. Forgive others. Let it go. Tear up the scorecard. Try to remember people are doing the best they can with what they have to work with. If someone is not living up to your standards, it will be easier to forgive if you accept he or she is working with limited resources, your expectations are unrealistic, or both.

To-do list:

- ☑ Check altitude.
- ☑ Climb down.
- ☑ Laugh it off.
- ☑ Forgive ourselves.
- ☑ Forgive others.
- ☑ Know you are forgivable.

Chapter 10

The Sixth Relational Sin and Solution: Resenting vs. Appreciating

Just when I thought holding beach balls under water was tough, one of my mentors told me his favorite parable about resentment. He described how a guy standing neck-deep in a pond wanted to get out, but he was holding a huge rock. The rock weighed so much, all the man could do was stand there, stuck in the pond.

A bucolic beaver popped her head out of the water nearby. "That's a big rock you have under there," she said. "How much does it weigh?"

"I don't know," the man groaned, barely able to get his arms around the boulder. "I can't reach my scorecard anymore."

The beaver started gliding through the water in a slow circle around the man. "What's a scorecard?"

"That's how I keep track of the people who treat me unfairly."

"Why do you do that?"

"So I'll know how big a rock to hold."

"Why are you holding such a big one?"

"Lots of people have been unfair to me for a long time."

"You hold a rock because people are unfair to you?"

"It beats the alternative."

"Which is?"

"I'd have to tell them."

The beaver reversed herself and started swimming in the opposite direction, propelled by graceful sweeps of her flat tail. "You mean the people who treated you unfairly don't know it?"

"Hard to say, some might, some might not."

"That doesn't make sense," said the beaver. "Why don't you just tell them how you feel?"

"I'd have to get out of the pond, and this rock is so heavy, I can't move."

The beaver stopped swimming in a circle and paddled in place. "That's simple," said the beaver.

"Simple...?"

"Let go of the rock."

"I can't do that," the man said, astonished.

"Why not?" the beaver asked. "If you ever want to pick it up again, it'll be right where you left it."

His eyes grew wide. But the bucolic beaver couldn't tell if he liked her idea or it scared him. My mentor only told me the part about the man holding the rock. His story ended with an ordinary guy walking by and suggesting the man drop his rock. I cast the bucolic beaver in the role of the passerby to increase the fur factor. The rock, of course, is resentment. It is the aggregate of all the wrongs we feel have been done to us.

The primary purpose of the scorecard I suggested tearing up in Chapter 9 is to keep track of resentments. It starts with making a judgment that someone did you wrong. The disillusionment, accurate or inaccurate, gets stored as resentment. Before I found my way into Idiots Exposed, I didn't want an ounce of resentment to slip past me. The heavier my rock, the more self-righteous I felt holding on to it.

Letting go of resentment rocks is as hard, if not harder, than letting go of unsolicited criticizing and advising. I was in my program a year before I admitted harboring resentment. I'm encouraged by the fact that people who aggressively work the IE program have reduced their rocks to the point they can carry them in their pockets or purses.

If harboring resentment against those you know or imagine have disappointed or mislead you is your customary way of handling anger and disappointment, you're likely to have a long scorecard. I refused for the longest time to accept that life is not fair. Although I counseled people about what an unreasonable expectation that was, I clung to my fantasy that everyone would reciprocate the wonderful things I did for them.

When that didn't happen, I hoped *most* people would reciprocate. Then, I wished for some. A few. One. The game was to control what others did for me by doing for them. I found folks ready, willing, and able to accept my generosity. But they seldom signed on for the reciprocity bit. I hungered for people I could control, for their benefit and mine, of course. To earn their friendship and affection through my good works would make me powerful, I thought, a power for truth, justice, and the American way.

Lots of people were doing wonderful things for *me*. My family. Friends. Business associates. They weren't reciprocating. They were just graciously doing kind things the way family and friends do. They were acting out of love. I did the same for them. I'm lucky to be surrounded by a loving family, quality friends, and stand-up business people. But family and close friends didn't count in my conquest for control. For that I had to range beyond familiar circles.

Poor, misguided, beaver. Everything I needed for emotional happiness was readily available. Although I ignored it, there was even a 12-step cure for my grandiosity. Looking back, I can see how I turned my back on new relationships because the person didn't *need* me. There was no challenge in a happy, healthy person. If I couldn't find people who truly needed me, I pretended they did. Yet every time my mission to rescue an unhappy person (real or imagined) failed, which was every time, my resentment rock got heavier. My valiant attempts to play the great rescuer annoyed people who don't want or need to be rescued.

The Odor of Resentment

The words of the the Thursday night regulars still haunt me, "Expectations are just resentments waiting to happen." I established expectations time after time, without consulting anyone. Nevertheless, I expected other people to fulfill them. I thought I was exercising beneficent power by setting the outcome. I ended up giving all my power to those who could fulfill or ignore my arbitrary expectations.

An article in the *Journal of Personality and Social Psychology* (May 2004) describes an indicator of longevity in relationships: low expectations. Seriously. It makes sense. Lofty, and probably unrealistic, expectations are hard to fulfill. Unfulfilled expectations result in heavy rocks.

Because I didn't explain the expectations they were to fulfill, it was pure chance if things turned out as I wanted. I wanted to win the lotto without buying a ticket. They were supposed to read my mind and then follow my agenda. For me to tell them outright would void the game. It was a recipe for failure from the start. No wonder my list of resentments grew.

Resentment is born out of a sense of unfairness and injustice—injustice against us—real or imagined. Resentment is also the residue of failed expectations. The expectations are part of our internal agenda. We don't bounce our desires and longings off other people for fear they'll say we're expecting too much. They might be right.

Resentment is stored internally, right next to our agendas. Although it's internal, resenting makes everyone around us uncomfortable. If we're not blabbing negative thoughts to anyone who will listen, we're giving the people we resent most an icy reception, or keeping our distance, all the while denying anything's wrong.

Friedrich Nietzsche said nothing on Earth will consume us more than the passion of resentment. *Consume* is a good choice of words. As acidic resentment begins to eat away at us, we consume ourselves from the inside out. The decomposing expectations within us emit an odor that's impossible to hide. No matter how civil and polite we act, anyone with the least bit of sensitivity will catch a whiff. Mouthwash won't help.

Rocks and Trees

I knew a couple who relocated to another city for professional reasons. Their beautiful brick house sat empty in a soft real estate market for more than six months. The house didn't even show during that time. When a Realtor finally took prospective buyers inside, she found a tree branch had grown through the kitchen window. Window panes were shattered and, although the cable TV was disconnected, tree-climbing critters were enjoying full access to the house anyway.

Although throwing a rock through the window would have been a quicker way to break it, the tree branch, flexing itself over several months, was just as effective. That's how it is with resenting others. It grows slowly within us until it is so strong it breaks through our sensibilities. Tree roots take time to push up concrete sidewalks. But they do. Resentment, working slowly and silently, is just as powerful.

Long before I started attending Idiots Exposed meetings, I prayed for God to "...remove the root of resentment from my heart." I didn't have a clue what I was asking. I didn't think I had real resentment in my heart. Just a seedling? Maybe? Giant sequoia is more like it. It was difficult to admit that something could infect me and grow so utterly out of control without my knowing it. "Lord," I should have prayed, "please, send the Forest Service."

Let's let go of our rocks. Let them sink to the bottom and let's walk out of the pond like the Creature from the Black Lagoon. Unlike the Creature, we'll be smiling. Let's clear the timber growing inside of us. Start with the saplings and work our way up to the old growth resentments. It's a long, arduous process. After years I'm still in the midst of it. But with vigilant effort, I no longer fear a jungle of resentment will grow inside me with tangled branches, roots, and vines. I can see blue sky overhead and feel sunshine on my face. Hallelujah.

Happiness and Resenting

I had a real *a-ha* moment a short time after I started attending IE meetings. While jogging one morning, I suddenly realized it would be impossible to reach higher levels of happiness *and* hang on to resentment. The thought came to me in that wee, small voice of wisdom my Higher Power sends when I need a nudge.

The insights the wee, small voice whispers in my ear are always simple to grasp. But they are incredibly profound. Illuminating. Life-changing. I inverted the thought and wondered how I ever came to believe resenting would make me happy. Who told me that? Nobody raised a hand. It made no sense. Even though I could rekindle the self-righteous emotions associated with resentment, I couldn't recall when or why, if ever, it made sense to me. The bottom line: resenting was not a conscious choice.

Not allowing resentment to contaminate my relationships with significant others, significant idiots, pets, in-laws, business associates, or politicians is a conscious decision. If there's anyone deserving of resentment, it's a professional politician. But even the people of the political class can be accepted for who they are. What they *are* is fodder for another book, perhaps *How to Vote for an Idiot*. Happiness must be consciously chosen. Letting go of resentment must also be an overt choice. Complacency, vis-à-vis resentment, is a green light for hostilities to accumulate, anger to simmer, resentment to thrive.

Denying anger doesn't make it go away. Choosing something other than anger can displace it. Claiming you're not angry, when you are, suggests you don't feel entitled to be upset. Perhaps getting outwardly upset in the past has resulted in outright punishment. Maybe your childhood protests were ignored. No matter who took it or how it was taken away, you lost permission to express your dissatisfaction.

Shirley's Shovel

"I'm not mad."

"Yes, you are."

"No, I'm not."

"Your face is beet red."

"It's hot in here."

"When my face gets beet red, it's because I'm agitated."

"That's you."

"Yes it is."

"I don't get mad."

"Really?"

"I get even."

"How mad at me are you, Shirley?"

"Don't worry."

"Thanks."

"I have a lot bigger scores to settle."

"You're serious, aren't you?"

"Do I look like I'm kidding?"

"Do you want to talk about it?"

"What's to talk about? I give and give and nobody gives back."

"Is that why you give? To *get back*?"

Shirley doesn't swing her purse at me as I anticipated she might. "I'm not sure," she says with sudden calmness. "But I can't stop giving."

"Why not?"

"How would they get what they need?"

"Money?" I ask.

"No."

"Food?"

"No."

"Shelter?"

"I'm not going to say it."

"Advice?"

"I call it wisdom."

"What does it feel like when they don't act on your *wisdom*?"

"I feel ignored."

"What does *ignored* feel like?"

"It hurts."

"What does *hurt* feel like?"

"Anger. Burning."

"What do you do with the anger, Shirley?"

"Keep it to myself. I guess I swallow it."

"Do they ever see you angry?"

"I won't give them the satisfaction."

"Would it make them happy to see you upset?"

"Oh," she sighs. "Probably not."

"But you keep it inside anyway?"

"I bury it where no one will know it exists."

"Are they comfortable around you?"

"When we're in the room together the temperature drops 10 degrees."

"You need to bury it deeper, Shirley. They can still smell it."

Shirley wants me to agree with her. She wants a friend to reinforce and justify her position. She wants confirmation and corroboration that she's treated unfairly. If I give it to her, I'm the one guilty of treating her unfairly. I'm familiar with how seductive the role of victim can be. Victimhood can be like a badge of honor you earned with sweat, blood, and tears. I know what it looks like. I also know how unfulfilling it is. I'll listen to Shirley. I'll engage her as a friend, as far as she allows. But I won't enable her resentment.

Self-Inflicted Wound

Shirley's resentment, like anybody else's, is self-inflicted. Your own expectations. Your own disappointment. Every fiber in my co-beaver body wants to make her feel good. My knee-jerk response would be to agree with everything she says. She'd thank me for being so understanding and consider me one of her best friends. I *am* one of her best friends. That's why I stay true to the program. Resenting won't get my vote, no matter how vigorously Shirley urges me to cast it.

Life Fountains

Amoeba Resentment

If anybody has a right to build resentment, it's the amoeba. But this is not about rights. The ACLU (American Civil Liberties Union) will protect the amoeba's "right" to be resentful. That's probably why ACLU lawyers always seem angry. I'd rather help the amoeba be happy. Amoebas might be happier than we realize. They don't show much emotion, one way or the other. They might also be more resentful than we realize.

It all depends upon the amoeba's sense of justice. If she or he feels deserving of more attention, affection, and/or recognition than she or he is receiving, there could be a rock involved. To be treated like an amoeba triggers *my* resentment meter. But I'm looking at it from a co-beaver perspective. Amoeba's who recognize the telltale signs of resentment might want to start the purging process.

Like any of the rest of us, if an amoeba makes sarcastic remarks, there's probably something eating away beneath the surface. If the amoeba is passive-aggressive, same thing. If the amoeba is more sullen and sulking than dry toast, all clues point toward resentment issues to be dealt with. Resenting is no healthier for a quiet, single-cell creature than it is for any of us.

It's rare for Giver or Taker types to be resentful of amoebas. Garden slugs might blame the amoeba's constant stepping and fetching for their own inability to get off the sofa. But even the slug knows that's a lame excuse. The rest of us tend to accept amoebas as the benign characters they are. Even in my near-daily amoeba moments, I could get upset with myself. Instead, I've learned to say, "Okay, John. Enough of that."

Beaver Resentment

A bucolic beaver gliding past a co-beaver in the pond notices the co-beaver panting and struggling to stay afloat. "What's wrong?" asks the bucolic beaver.

"Nothing," says the co-beaver.

"Aw, come on. Beavers don't swim like that."

"It's nothing, really."

The bucolic beaver pokes her head under the water and pops back up again. "Nice rock you're holding."

"Is not."

"Not a rock?"

"Not *nice.*"

"I saw a human in the pond this morning holding a big rock," says the bucolic beaver.

"What did he do?"

"He let go of it."

The co-beaver releases the rock with a sigh and immediately begins gliding through the water in classic beaver fashion. "That's much better," she says. "Thanks."

"Glad to help." As the bucolic beaver swims away, she thinks, *That was too easy. The human had a much harder time letting go of his rock. Oh, well. No sense worrying about things I can't control.*

The next morning, the bucolic beaver is gliding through the pond again when she hears a commotion from the other side of the beaver dam. She slips to the edge and peers over. There's the co-beaver furiously scooping mud from the creek bed with her flat tail and slapping it hard against the base of the mud and twig dam.

"I don't know," *slap,* "what I have to do," *slap,* "to get a little respect around here," *slap.* "After all I do," *slap,* "you'd think the least they could do is say *thank you,*" *slap, slap, slap.*

The bucolic beaver slips away in silence. She can tell the co-beaver is in a mood and doesn't need any advice. The co-beaver dropped her rock all right. But she didn't *let go* of her resentment. It reemerged in a different form. As a recovering co-beaver, I recall with the clarity of hindsight how, when my initial attempts to solve everyone's problems failed, I continued trying with increased vigor and volume. When I couldn't get my square peg through the round hole, I got a bigger hammer.

Co-beavers wrote the book on resenting. They start with unrealistic expectations. Disappointment follows. Finally, resentment. After each expectation-disappointment-resentment cycle is complete, the co-beaver starts over at the top. My perennial question to the person in the mirror applies, "When have you ever known unrealistic expectations to be fulfilled? Never? And you keep trying because...?"

Altruistic Resentment

Altruistic Category III Givers defy gravity. They do wonderful things for others and don't have expectations. The very thought of this gives co-beavers a headache. It just doesn't compute. How can the co-beaver give his or her time and/or resources away without expecting something good in return? Isn't that the essence of enlightened self-interest?

Enlightened self-interest is just that: *self*-interest. If others benefit by what I do to take care of myself, that's icing on the cake. But the giving is still contingent, to a degree, on *getting*. A commercial company that does community service rarely does so without public recognition. In deference to those who do community service anonymously, there is a lot of anonymous altruism going on.

The goody-goody notion that altruists do expectation-free good works because they're angels in disguise is wrong. It's even a little snippy. Altruists don't think they're better than anyone else. They *do* operate on a slightly different plane of understanding. Altruistic Category III Givers are aware of the inherent danger in expectations and avoid them accordingly. It's common sense. It doesn't take a genius to realize that the best way to avoid burning your hand is to keep it out of the fire. The best way to stay rock-free is to not pick them up.

Altruists also understand the devastating toll resentment takes. They stay clear in order to see clearly. It makes no sense to get intentionally involved. I sometimes wonder if true altruists have lodge meetings where they sit around and chuckle at those of us who burden ourselves with resentment after resentment, compounding like the national debt. It would be like watching *America's Funniest Home Videos*. Resentment-addicts must look that silly to someone who's figured out how beneficial it is to face and fix problems rather than doing a slow boil over them.

Black Holes

Resenting Garden Slugs

Garden slugs are the authors of *un*enlightened self-interest. They get waited on hand and foot without posting a sign over the couch

reading, "This slug cared for and cleaned up after by (fill in the blank)."
The caretaker might put up a sign reading, "This slug resented by (fill
in the blank)." Better yet, they could combine their effort and post a
sign reading, "This slug cared for, cleaned up after, and resented by
(fill in the blank)." That keeps the whole thing in perspective.

There would be no resentment involved except for expectations.
The caregiver could wait hand and foot on the breathing sofa cushion
without resenting it one bit, as long as there are no expectations. Talk
about unreasonable. When, exactly, was this garden slug full of en-
thusiasm to leap out of bed each morning and take on the world? If
it's been five years or more, cancel your subscription to *Expectations
Monthly*.

Another way to cure resentment is to do nothing. Where there is
no expectation of a response, no response is necessary. The preferred
method is to replace unreasonable expectations with reasonable expectations. Otherwise, you'll end up doing nothing at all. You might
as well tell the garden slug to scoot over, you're joining the club.

Resentment and the Jaguar

Jaguars are Teflon-coated when it comes to resentment. You
can resent the snot out of them and they just don't care. Yet in a
refreshingly bright spot (in an otherwise checkered emotional re-
sume), jaguars figure resentment is *your* problem. Indeed it is. The
jaguar's behavior doesn't cause resentment. Your expectations lead
to resentment.

Before I let jaguars off the hook entirely, what about those promises? Jaguars often tell you what you want to hear. They might even
fully *intend* to live up to their promises. Even so, what's the jaguar's
track record? Has he or she given you sufficient cause to expect follow-
through? Or enough cause to keep the eternal flame of hope burning?
It could be both. It happens.

I'm not making excuses for naughty jaguars, mind you. But they
can be as confused as anyone else. I believe family and home life are
important to most jaguars, just not at the expense of their freedom to
roam, hunt, and sleep in trees. If expectations continue to be unfulfilled in a relationship with a jaguar, it's a good idea to revisit issues
such as acceptance and anticipation. If what you're receiving from the
jaguar is sufficient to tolerate the other aspects of the relationship, you

can accept the compromise and drop the rock. You will be happier for it. The jaguar probably won't notice.

Whirling Resentment

Resentment doesn't build up inside of whirling vortexes. As soon as they feel it, they purge it. They expect everything, all the time. If they get it, they're happy. If not, they'll fling you aside and look to the next provider. As with the jaguar, it's a healthy moment in an unhealthy situation. The jaguar has a specific expectation that someone will usually fulfill. All vortexes need do is whirl around expectantly until they blow across someone.

Vortexes are not interested in relationships as much as in getting their needs met. You set yourself up for disappointment when you attempt to control relationships so as to get *your* needs met. To vortexes, relationships are disposable. It's not the vortex's fault if you have unfulfilled expectations that lead to resenting.

Having said that, I should add that whirling vortexes are promise-makers of the highest order. Although they tend to believe they'll be able to fulfill their promises, they don't really have an operational sense of the future beyond, say, the next 30 minutes. You need to learn over time, accept, and anticipate. Fool me once, shame on you. Fool me twice, shame on me. Fool me a thousand times and who's the idiot?

Keys to living with an idiot

⇨ **Release the rock.** Another one of those sounds-simple-but-it's-not situations. The rock analogy is appropriate because the sheer weight of resentment weighs you down. You expend all your energy lugging a heavy weight. Add denial, and it's no wonder you get worn out. Holding beach balls under water and holding a big rock at the same time is a super-human task. Co-beavers, who are especially likely to try both tasks at once, are capable of super-human feats. It would be nice if the super-human feat accomplished something worthwhile for the beaver. The longer you clutch the rock, the harder it becomes to let it go.

⇨ **Get rid of the odor.** Resentment is acid stomach. Leave it untreated long enough and the next thing you know, bad breath. If unaddressed resentment were as obvious as bad breath, friends and family members would demand you deal with it. As it is, resenting just delivers enough odor to make people uncomfortable and wonder where it's coming from. They won't even know what it is, much less be able to identify the source. They'll know they're uncomfortable. If you want people to enjoy being around you, you must eliminate the odor. To eliminate the odor, you must clean out the resentment. The Idiots Exposed mantra I mentioned before: "Harboring resentment is like drinking a cup of poison and waiting for the other person to die," makes no sense under any circumstances. It does you no good, and them no harm. Good riddance.

⇨ **Say farewell to victimhood.** Victims are not happy people. My hesitation to admit I held a resentment rock, much less let go of it, was connected to my self-image. I saw myself as a victim of others' refusal to meet my expectations. In more grandiose terms, I felt like a martyr. I really didn't qualify as a martyr. A true martyr dies. I lived to suffer. "Oh, woe is me," is the language of a victim. Releasing resentment is a big deal if it's been the steam in your boiler for a long time. I'm lucky. I finally got tired of hearing myself complain. Now I choose to talk about all the things I'm grateful for. I'm still liable to resent without thinking, because it's my default setting. So, I now think before I speak and ponder, "Is this an improvement on silence?" People enjoy being around me much more.

Relational Solutions: Appreciating

All the relational sins I'm describing are difficult to give up because they become so ingrained. Changing attitudes and behaviors is not a stroll in the park for anybody. Different people struggle more with some than others. That's why it helps to have something positive with which to replace the negative. The positive piece then occupies the space where the negative was.

But the positive does not give the same emotional payoff. You need to make conscious choices over and over about the emotional roller coaster you ride during behavioral transitions. Unless you decide the discomfort and uncertainty of working against your negative conditioning is worth it—unless you re-frame to *appreciate* what the effort will bring about—the change won't stick.

Appreciation is a most effective attitude for displacing unhappiness. My fellow recovering idiots call it the "attitude of gratitude." Using compliments to displace criticism is most effective at the time the compliment is expressed. Appreciation is effective when you're alone, thinking about the things you resent. You can apply as much appreciation medication as you want. You might start with little, bitty appreciative thoughts.

Suppose your significant idiot, spouse, teenager, or live-in in-law dings the fender pulling into the garage. Instead of seething about it, you could say to yourself, "At least he or she didn't drive the car off the freeway overpass, crashing through the windshield of a school bus full of handicapped children from the inner city on their way to church camp on Rotary Club scholarships."

When you consider you didn't lose someone you care about, no catastrophic loss of life took place, widespread suffering of innocent families was avoided, and you didn't end up on the 6 o'clock news as the owners of the vehicle, that dinged fender isn't so bad. But I digress. Resentment is more likely to result from us feeling we're treated unfairly.

Suppose a teenage boy dings the fender and gets grounded for a year while he pays off the repairs by mowing lawns or working at Burger Town. His teenage sister dings the fender and the worst punishment she receives is to drive Dad's Porsche while her Beetle is in the shop.

Resentment. If the boy tries really hard to think of what a great sister she is otherwise, he might displace some of that resentment. Realistically, that's not going to happen. He will plot his revenge for the next 20 years. In his mid-30s, when he has a darling daughter, he might get it, and begin to appreciate his sister. Then the resenting will finally subside. We hope.

For those of us already in our mid-30s and beyond, it's high time we polished up our appreciation skills. By purposefully re-framing another person in the context of appreciation, we take control over resentment. To a recovering control freak, finding out there are positive ways to be in control is like finding money in the laundry. If I don't pick up the habit of appreciation, resentment will stay in control. It's my decision to think in appreciative terms instead of holding grudges. It's also my call to express my appreciation when and how I want.

Life Fountains

Appreciating Amoebas

Amoebas blush when told how much others appreciate what they do. That's part of the fun in complimenting them, although they'll only take so many compliments before they find an excuse to slip out of sight. Although the expressions of appreciation might be graciously received for a while, amoebas still have that nagging self-image issue. Too much of a good thing and they'll be tossed into a full-blown identity crisis.

Amoebas are good for practicing on. Practice is good, whether you're just rehearsing appreciation in your thoughts or you're actually remarking on how much you appreciate something or someone. It's more difficult to appreciate someone who's making life difficult— such as any of the Black Holes and/or certain beavers, who shall remain nameless. Warming up with an innocuous amoeba can get the ball rolling. When there's some momentum built up, you can drop in a few names and a positive observation or two.

If you listen to amoebas closely, you'll hear them making many appreciative remarks. Amoebas are extremely appreciative when they're treated nicely. Despite their shaky self-esteem, they're not masochists. One thing I appreciate most about amoebas is the example they set. There's a lot to be said for conscious servanthood. Granted, altruists choose to serve, while most amoebas feel they have no choice. They can still be okay with it, which proves you can be positive about yourself without conquering the world; just quietly taking care of it.

Beaver Appreciation

An appreciative attitude helps keep bucolic and achiever beavers on an even keel. Hard workers themselves, they are naturally inclined to appreciate things done for them. They don't hesitate to express their appreciation. They nod their heads graciously when someone sends an appreciative remark in their direction. It's all consistent with the laid-back, no-offense-intended/none-taken demeanor of these easy-to-get-along-with Category II Givers.

Co-beavers wake up in an appreciative frame of mind. Their *think positive* approach propels them out of bed each morning. "Today I'll finally be appreciated." But as the little beavs leave the lodge without eating their breakfast, the spouse or significant beaver waddles out with no kiss, and so on, the co-beaver starts to think, "Same song, different day." The co-beaver's waking optimism starts to fade. Optimism turns to disappointment. Disappointment turns to hurt feelings. Hurt feelings turn to resentment. It starts where all resentment starts, with expectations. By mid-morning, the co-beaver is at the base of the dam, slapping mud over yesterday's mud.

If the co-beaver wakes up and puts on an attitude of appreciation for the others in his or her life, the little beavs' and significant other's behavior won't come as such a disappointment. "Okay, we're not Ozzie and Harriet beavers. But we're *good* beavers. Things could be worse." The co-beaver might want to build up some momentum by thinking appreciative thoughts about the amoebas that live next door and then segue directly into positive thoughts about the beaver clan.

Showing appreciation to co-beavers is what the fur-bearing mud-slappers live for. I'm not recommending the use of appreciation as manipulation. But co-beavers are sometimes manipulated by others who are aware of their hunger for approval and connectedness. If a co-beaver is suddenly smothered in appreciation, where there was little before, he or she might do well to pause and wonder, "What's wrong with this picture? Could it be this flatterer wants something?"

When co-beavers are driving others bonkers (even co-beavers sometimes find fellow co-beavers a bit much), there is still a lot to appreciate. Co-beavers are incredibly giving and hard-working, even if their motivations are less than optimal. The difference between a busy-but-critical, advice-giving co-beaver and a busy-but-copacetic achiever beaver might be as little as a few degrees of expectation.

Altruistic Appreciation

Altruistic Category III Givers appreciate appreciation on two levels. The first and most obvious aspect of appreciation is its displacement factor. Altruists fully understand how appreciation knocks resentment out of its slot and keeps it out as long as the appreciation persists. The second and more subtle benefit is how appreciation softens the hearts of those who habitually assume the worst. For those whose relational experiences have been mostly negative, it's difficult to be around someone to whom it appears positive relationships come easily. To them it feels like rubbing salt into an open wound.

I appreciate the wisdom and patience altruists demonstrate in the choices they make. Others glance over at altruists and see what appears to be luck in relationships. Closer examination reveals that the quality relationships result from discretion, not luck. Thomas Edison said, "Genius is 1 percent inspiration and 99 percent perspiration." When it comes to altruists and the healthy relationships they keep, I say it's more like 50 percent consideration and 50 percent appreciation. Even if my math is off, you must admit, consideration and appreciation never ticked anybody off.

Black Holes

Appreciating Garden Slugs

They're always around to keep you company. You can't complain about that. How does appreciation help the garden slug? By helping the rest of us snarl less, I suppose. It might appear on the surface that appreciation is of little value when dealing with a garden slug. It's hard to tell how much a slug appreciates a more cordial and relaxed atmosphere at feeding time. But we'll feel better, and that's what this book is about.

When I'm right with my Higher Power and doing right by me, I'm okay to pass it on. Not every idiot in my life is a breathing sofa cushion. Not everyone in my life is an idiot. Who is and who is not becomes less important as I become more appreciative. The more comfortable and appreciative I become with my situation, the better off everyone is.

If gaining confidence in yourself means letting garden slugs feed themselves, they might prefer you pick up a rock. Oh well. Every slug for himself. Your employees, boss, spouse, children, parents, friends, in-laws, siblings, and significant idiots of all kinds will have a more authentic, loving, and genuinely caring employee, boss, spouse, child, parent, friend, in-law, sibling, or significant idiot as soon as you learn the art of appreciation.

Appreciating Jaguars

People initially appreciate jaguars for the sleek and beautiful animals they are. But they tend to attribute other characteristics to the jaguar as well. If a relationship with a jaguar becomes troubling over time, it's probably due, in part, to those *other* characteristics. This is caused by forming unrealistic expectations. Looking at your insufferably attractive creature, you inevitably project your own agenda.

"Jaguars are incredible to behold. They're wild and exciting animals," you might think during courtship. "But *my* jaguar is different. Mine is *also* going to be home at 5:30 sharp every night, cut the grass on Saturday mornings, and read to the kids at bedtime." Are you having as much trouble with this picture as I am?

There is much to appreciate about jaguars in terms of power, agility, and ability. They can be good providers, and truly value a good-looking, well-cared-for family. It's not hard to appreciate what jaguars have to offer. Jaguars also appreciate what *you* have to offer. As long as expectations are realistic and you're willing to accept each other's limitations, appreciation can play a valuable role in maintaining your sanity around jaguars. First things first. Sanity today. Serenity tomorrow.

Whirling Appreciation

It's easy to appreciate the entertainment value of a whirling vortex. Those with realistic expectations are least susceptible to getting blown away. But letting your expectations get away from you is easy around whirling vortexes. They live in and for the moment, and you can easily get caught up in their moments. Depending on how bored you are in your own pelt, you might even throw yourself into the moment, not caring what the following moment might bring.

Whirling vortexes appreciate anything that helps propel their hurricane-force winds. Their appreciation is real in the moment, but it only lasts a moment. If you are attention-starved, that moment can be intoxicating as the vortex swirls around *you*. You are better off to accept the way Tab A (attention) fits into Slot B (need for attention). It's real. It's basic. You can appreciate how simple and direct the exchange is. Spending time around a whirling vortex makes one appreciate the peacefulness of a beaver pond.

Keys to living with an idiot

⇨ **Appreciate your Higher Power.** Keep the God of your understanding at the top of your list. Part of being appreciative is being humble. I'm sure God appreciates your obedience, gratitude, and the way you come to love your neighbors as you love yourself. I say that as if it's a piece of cake on your part, which it's not. But appreciating what your Creator does for you should be easy. If you resent not getting everything you want or think you deserve, you may get mad at God (it happens). Whenever I find myself slipping into that downward spiral of resenting, I know I'm not looking with appreciation at what's there for me. Before I try to identify things in myself or others to appreciate, I figuratively or literally get on my knees. If I can't get into an attitude of gratitude with my Higher Power, I'll never be able to appreciate myself or anybody else. So, that's where I go first.

⇨ **Appreciate yourself.** After your Higher Power comes you. This was a hard recovery principle to grasp. I was raised in the German Lutheran tradition to count others as better than me. My needs came last, and all that. I now understand this to mean that serving God is my first order of business, and I do that primarily by serving others. As the altruists show us, we need the ability to give before we can give. We need to be in a position to help before we can help. We must be of sound mind and body before we can let someone else lean on us, or extend a hand to pull someone else up. We're fearfully and wonderfully made. As they say, "God didn't make no junk." Appreciation of ourselves, and all we're capable of, extends our appreciation of God.

⇨ **Appreciate others.** The three naturally go together. Awareness of and appreciation for your Higher Power makes it possible to appreciate yourself as a unique creation. Without developing appreciation at these first two levels, I don't believe anyone can truly appreciate other people for who they are, rather than the roles in which they are cast. If you believe yourself to be a unique creation of God, you must believe others are, too. If you believe your Higher Power loves you unconditionally, it follows that others are welcome in the same relationship. To appreciate other people is to bring peace to yourself. That, in turn, hoses down the flames of resentment and hostility. You can only fight the fire on your side of the street, but that's enough to keep your own house from burning down. Appreciation, if it is genuine, will make living with idiots much easier through greater appreciation of your own inner idiot. Your Higher Power, of course, has no inner idiot. But God gives us the sense of humor to keep idiots in perspective.

Chapter Summary

How many rocks am I carrying? I can carry quite a few. Not that I should want to do that again. Opening my arms and letting go of a big boulder is easy to do physically, but not having something in my arms to cling to scares me. Oh, me of little faith. One of the encouraging things about recovery programs and support groups is getting to see the bottom of ponds, swimming pools, and other bodies of water covered with rocks people have let go of. Another benefit is the opportunity to make practical application of faith in a Higher Power. Do I need the rock of resentment or do I need to trust my Higher Power? Resentment or trust? Hm-m-m-m.

Resentment stinks. Appreciation airs the place out. Resentment makes other people uncomfortable, even if they aren't the ones you resent. Appreciation makes you feel more open and positive, and the effect can open others. Even if you don't share your appreciation of others openly, your frame of mind is refreshing.

Appreciation is a grand circle. For me, it starts by appreciating a Higher Power who gets bigger every time I park my posterior in one of those metal folding chairs. Appreciation for my Higher Power is followed by appreciation for who I am as a creation of my Higher Power. Finally, I appreciate others as God's creations. If we can't get beyond that point, the exercise is still worth the investment. It takes amoebas, beavers, altruists, garden slugs, jaguars, and whirling vortexes to make the world go round. Actually, the world goes around all by itself. We're all along for the ride.

To-do list:

- ☑ Release the rock.
- ☑ Get rid of the odor.
- ☑ Say farewell to victimhood.
- ☑ Appreciate your Higher Power.
- ☑ Appreciate yourself.
- ☑ Appreciate others.

Chapter 11

The Seventh Relational Sin and Solution: Shaming vs. Affirming

THE BEST DEFINITION I'VE HEARD FOR SHAME comes out of the distinction between shame and guilt. To me, guilt is a feeling of regret or remorse for something I did. In amoeba-speak, you could say, "Guilt means *I'm sorry* for something I did." (That statement is essentially true for anyone. "Sorry," is just a natural utterance for amoebas.) Spouses, significant others, children, parents, siblings, in-laws, coworkers, and idiots everywhere can feel guilt and be sorry for unpleasant things they did to you. Wouldn't that be nice? You, too, can feel guilt and be sorry for hurtful things you did to spouses, significant others, children, parents, siblings, in-laws, coworkers, and idiots.

Shaming is more than being critical of someone's behavior, it's an assault on someone's character. That's a horse of a different color. Shaming (perhaps I should call it *shame-ism*) means causing the feeling of shame. As children, we're completely vulnerable to being shamed by adults because adults define the terms and conditions. As we become adults, we become responsible for fending off attempts by others to shame us. Although we might not always succeed, we aim to be shame-busters just the same.

Shaming is a universally unpleasant experience. It's possible for spouses, significant others, children, parents, siblings, in-laws, coworkers, and idiots everywhere to feel shame for who they are. If you, intentionally or unintentionally, cause them to feel shamed, you *should* feel guilty.

I've had thoughts of revenge, getting even, payback, and you-name-it at different times in my fertile imagination. All I *really* wanted the offending party to say was, "Okay, I'm sorry. I did you wrong. My bad. Here's your money back." I never wanted him to feel shame for who he is. In fact, once he owned up to his evil deeds, I forgave him, and didn't wish any malfeasance to befall him. Of course, in real life, people seldom own up, and I rarely get my money back. An idiot and his money never seem to grow old together.

No Defense for Shaming

Some will argue that shame can be a good thing, and that it can serve a practical purpose. I'll agree that shaming someone can alter his or her behavior, particularly in childhood, but at what cost? It's good for people to have a sense of humility; to accept not being perfect. When it comes to shaming, however, the cure is probably worse than the disease.

To shame children for bed-wetting is to attack their characters over something they can't control. It's much better to anticipate that phase of growing up, speak of it in terms of normal behavior, reduce liquid intake before bedtime, and set the alarm clock. To tell children they should be ashamed of themselves in such situations sets them up to carry shame around with them for years to come.

Some spouses attempt to shame their partners into getting with the program. "Shirley's husband takes out the garbage without her having to ask him." If the partner being shamed has carried a shameful image of self from childhood, he or she will probably think, "You sound just like Mom and/or Dad." The shaming will probably just drive a bigger wedge in the relationship. Sounding like a shaming parent won't promote intimacy or cooperation.

The argument in *favor* of shaming is built on teaching children to avoid saying or doing things to bring shame upon themselves or others. I disagree. Parents can disapprove of their children's inappropriate behavior without attacking their characters. The point of the lesson is to build up who they are and urge them not to give their integrity away. If parents take their integrity away early on, what do they have to operate with later on?

Shaming needs to be avoided. How can victims of a shame-based upbringing establish and maintain healthy boundaries in personal and professional relationships if they don't feel they're worth anything? Many people act like idiots because they don't have enough self-worth to expect more of themselves. "What's the point?" they mutter. It's easier to be clueless. Reversing the effects of shaming later in life is almost as difficult as separating the yolks from the whites after the eggs have been scrambled.

Falsely Accused

Holding people responsible for what they do is different than laying a guilt trip on them. If they were raised to be responsible for things outside of their responsibility, they might lay a guilt trip on themselves. You don't need to encourage them to take on guilt for things they have nothing to do with. When Roger lets his son talk through his confusion and frustration, the boy will usually come out the other side realizing there's no reason to take on the mantle of guilt. Responsibility for his choices, yes. Certainly no need for shame.

You can learn to remind yourself that some things are *not* your fault, and you should let them go. It takes patience and practice to make progress, but it can be done. The same goes when you're dealing with your significant idiot. If something is not his or her fault, "Let it go, let it go, let it go." If it is your significant idiot's fault, hold him or her responsible for fixing the car, cleaning up the fish guts, or whatever, but no shaming is necessary.

Shamees tend to pair up in relationships with shamers because the language is familiar. It's not until the shamee discovers other languages can be spoken in relationships that he or she seeks to change. The chances of the relationship becoming multilingual are slim, unless shamer and shamee both seek out a translator in the form of a counselor or an organized group. Parlez-vous "affirmation"?

Shirley's Shame

"I don't shame people," Shirley says.

"I'm glad to hear that."

"I'll admit I'm a rabid advice-giver," she continues in a sudden mood to confess. She notices my eyes growing a little wider. "It's true. I won't argue."

"Who's arguing?"

"In conversations with my son and daughter-in-law," she goes on, "I can hear myself starting to sound like my mother."

"Me, too."

"You sound like your mother?"

"My father, actually. It's taken me a long time to recognize that."

"What does that feel like for you?" she asks.

"I feel tricked. I swore I'd never become a rage-aholic and one day I found myself screaming at someone at the top of my lungs. It was like an out-of-body experience. I couldn't believe that was me, but it was."

"Me, too," Shirley says.

"So, all the anger, blaming, criticism, denial, judging, and resentment issues we've talked about were carryovers from your mother?"

"Many of them."

"My character defects weren't all that original, either."

Shirley's eyebrows raise a little.

"Okay," I say. "Maybe I got more creative with some of my relational sins than my father was with his."

Shirley smiles. "Me, too."

"I've committed every one of my seven relational sins, Shirley. And 70 more I didn't list. Thank goodness my Higher Power has that 70-times-seven forgiveness rule."

"My mother was a shamer," Shirley adds. "That's what I heard myself doing."

"We're breaking the cycle, Shirley. We've stopped shaming others or ourselves. We can pat ourselves on the back for that. But if you're like me, the end of the tunnel is still a long way off."

"I'm changing how I appreciate and compliment my son and daughter-in-law. I think they like it. They haven't *said* anything, but they *did* ask to take me out to dinner."

"I think that's saying *plenty.*"

"We'll see," Shirley says with a curious blend of anticipation and skepticism. "We'll see."

Once again, Shirley ended up teaching me a few things about myself. That's how good conversation and honest self-disclosure works. The truth eventually comes out, and it's not so horrible after all. Hearing other people share their experiences triggers recollections of experiences I've had. Knowing I'm not alone makes it easier to re-frame my life portrait.

Shirley was right that shaming should be taboo. The less I do it, the better I feel, and it becomes easier to avoid over time. I'll get it right if I live long enough. The great thing is, I can celebrate every little part I get right along the way. As we remind ourselves on Thursday nights, "It's about progress, not perfection."

Life Fountains

Shame and the Amoeba

Amoebas are likely to say, "I'm sorry for who I am," not only because "sorry" is the core of their vocabulary, but because they probably really *are* sorry for who they are. In many cases, that's precisely why they're amoebas. It's hard to say how much of an amoeba's personality and behavior is driven by low self-esteem and how much is just choosing the course of least resistance through life. Either way, their mantra could be "Find the lowest level I can and then lay down."

That could be shame talking. It could also be extreme timidity. Although many amoebas have been intensely shamed throughout their lives, you'll seldom, if ever, hear an amoeba shaming someone else. There are some personalities that carry shame forward, and some, like Shirley, who don't. Whenever I hear someone attempting to shame their child or some other significant person, especially innocent amoebas, it sounds as if a voice other than their own is coming out to shame *them*. It's eerie. At least amoebas have opted out of all that.

Beavers and Shame

Co-beavers absorb responsibility like a sponge. They often feel guilty for things that were not their responsibility to begin with. They can also feel shame that has nothing to do with anything the beaver ever did, but has been passed on to them just the same. Shaming is the worst extreme in co-beaver controlling behavior. Co-beavers are members of the Life Fountain Giver family. They have to be pretty emotionally damaged before they will resort to such demeaning tactics. But if that's all they know, who's to say? Beaver-see, beaver-do.

Habitual shaming is so unpleasant that a critical, advice-spewing co-beaver is an easy pill to swallow by comparison. Fortunately, there is usually a bucolic or achiever beaver nearby and shamees can get at least a glimpse of alternative ways of behaving. Attempts to shame a bucolic or achiever beaver usually bead up and roll off their pelts like water, the same way criticism and unwelcome advice do.

Altruists and Shame

Legend has it that someone in a support group accused the facilitator of "pushing his buttons." As the story goes, the facilitator calmly replied, "And who installed your buttons?" It always comes back to *you*. That's not the answer most of us like to hear. That's not the medicine most of us want to take. Altruistic Category III Givers understand that a person who has been conditioned to play the role of shamee is like an open wound that can be easily and unintentionally irritated. An innocuous comment, harmless to non-shamees, can be like a drop of lemon juice or grain of salt, causing an intense sting.

When altruists encounter someone reacting strongly to apparently benign comments, they quickly put two and two together. Altruists use their emotional maturity to recognize when emotions don't match situations. When that happens, they know there are major influences outside of the present moment and present situation driving this person's behavior. When someone launches into a shaming frenzy, it's time to be quiet and listen. Altruistic Category III Givers know they're not responsible for what the shamer is ranting about. Afterward, altruists go home and take a shower.

Black Holes

Garden Slug Shame

Garden slugs fall into the category of people who have no shame. Specifically, they don't appear to have any sense of shame. If they do, they keep it well hidden. I don't want to veer off into addictive behaviors, but where there is a lot of shame being felt, a lot of pain is being medicated in a variety of self-destructive ways. Breathing sofa cushions are not typically skin and bones. Their medication might consist of too much comfort food and too little exercise.

Shaming a garden slug into more energetic and productive behavior is not likely to work. To shame someone who has internalized a lot of shame usually just confirms what they already believe about themselves. If they've suffocated the shame under caloric intake or some other comforting consumption, nothing you do will bring it to the surface.

I'm glad shaming doesn't work on garden slugs, because I don't advocate shaming under any circumstances. It's too bad the shameless slug has no compunction about lying in front of the TV in his underwear and socks when your bridge club is about to show up. But that's for you to anticipate and plan for.

At least the slug won't intentionally try to shame you in front of company, or anytime, for that matter. It would take too much energy. Slugs might act like they're dying of malnutrition if you stop delivering pizza sofa-side. This is a clumsy attempt on their part to appeal to your sense of decency and humanity. Do with that what you like.

Shame and the Jaguar

Jaguars have a sense of shame. Otherwise they wouldn't exert so much effort to avoid it. Assuming all cats hate water, shame is like rain to the jaguars. If they get caught outside when it starts to sprinkle, they'll try to run between the drops until they get to a dry place. Afterward, they'll immediately groom their damp fur.

The cunning cats know you have an Achilles's heel called shame, and they're not afraid to use it against you. One of the most effective manipulative tactics in a jaguar's arsenal is the shame you carry inside. Those who are lucky enough not to have internalized shame are immune to this type of manipulation. Those who have built an effective immune system to shame are likewise protected. It's those among us who have yet to address shame and the power it has in our lives that need to find an antidote if we want to keep company with jaguars.

If you try to shame a jaguar, the big cat is going to snarl and bare its teeth. If you attack with enough velocity, the jaguar will bolt, as if caught in a downpour. I'm again pleased that shaming is so ineffective with jaguars. If it were the right thing to do in any relationship, it would probably be generalized to other relationships. Best just to leave shaming out of the mix with anyone, anywhere.

Shame and the Whirling Vortex

Whirling vortexes are often voted by their classmates as *most likely to remain shameless*. They think anything they do to please themselves in the moment is a noble cause. If confronted later with evidence of a shameful act, the vortex might (a) deny having done it, despite the videotape and sworn affidavits; (b) admit to doing it with a, "What was I supposed to do?" thrown in for good measure; or (c) ignore the accusation, saying, "You wanna go for a ride in the new Jaguar my ex bought me?"

Just because they remain shameless doesn't mean whirling vortexes are without shame. They are usually self-loathing at their cores. But they spin fast and furiously to stay one step ahead of bad feelings. They instinctively know, if they slow down or stop, the shame and self-criticism will overtake them. Refusal to slow down is a defensive measure that provides protection.

With their constant whirling, vortexes seldom slow down long enough to consider whether or not you and I have any internalized shame. In the rare event they try and use shame as a device to get what they want out of us, they dredge up things that make them feel ashamed. If a vortex says, "You're a rotten excuse for a (spouse, sibling, significant other, child, parent, boss, coworker, in-law, bowler, or fill in the blank)," he or she is probably quoting his or her own childhood shamers.

Of course, anyone who attempts to shame another is probably using his or her shamer's language. Isn't dealing with a whirling vortex enough of a challenge to leave shame out of it? Isn't *any* relationship enough of a challenge to leave shame out of it?

Keys to living with an idiot

⇨　**Separate guilt from shame.** Don't get these two mixed up. Guilt has its place. A sense of shame has its place. Guilt is a function of behavior, and can help you avoid repeating wrong behavior. Shame is condemnation of character. Trying to make others feel guilty is not a relationship-enhancing thing to do. Trying to make others feel ashamed is a relationship killer—like quietly doing something you asked the other person to do without saying a word about it. The main reason to separate guilt from shame is to know how the two are affecting you. I can resolve to adjust my behavior so as to avoid future guilt. Adjusting who I am as a person so as to escape shame is a taller order. You have enough issues to deal with just getting through the day without complicating matters.

⇨ **Deal with your own and leave the rest.** Guilt becomes harmful when it is inappropriate. It becomes inappropriate when you feel badly about things that aren't really bad or negative, and/or when you assume responsibility for things you had nothing to do with. You can, and should, deal with your own sense of guilt. Let the rest go. Shame, except as a social, ethical, and moral boundary, is a character assassin. Shame is passed on from someone carrying internalized shame like a contagious virus ready to be transmitted by casual contact. If you are acting out in shameful ways, bringing shame on yourself and those connected to you, the shame is on your head. If you're only being made to feel the shame for someone else's unresolved shame-based experiences, it's time to start putting distance between you and shame that doesn't belong to you.

⇨ **Displace shame.** The rule bears repeating: never take anything away from someone without offering something better to replace it. This supports the concept of displacement filling the void left by removal of undesirable behavior. Affirmation is my suggestion for displacing shame. In my experience, when I surrender the temptation to berate others, the God of my understanding affirms me with peace *beyond* my understanding.

Affirming

To affirm is to uphold, as in honoring a belief. It's almost a cliché to use spoken affirmations to change thinking and behavior. There's "I Believe in You" (sung into a mirror) from the Broadway musical *How to Succeed in Business Without Really Trying*. There's Al Franken's famous *Saturday Night Live* character Stuart Smalley, who utters his daily affirmation (said into a mirror), "I'm good enough, I'm smart enough, and doggonit, people like me." Christians stand together during worship services and recite the Apostles' Creed, an affirmation of faith in the God of *their* understanding.

Although we seldom give it much thought, and discuss it even less, what belief system do we operate from? All of us need to identify our core beliefs regarding how we should live and continually affirm them. Without beliefs about what's right, what's wrong, what's healthy, what's not, what's good, what's evil, we have nothing to affirm. Using core beliefs to affirm people builds character. Using them to shame people destroys character. Like appreciation, affirming is something we do within ourselves *and* outside of ourselves.

There are books loaded with suggested affirmations. Many people, secular and believing alike, adopt the biblical number 40. Choosing something they want to change in their lives, they say an affirmation 40 times a day for 40 days until it becomes ingrained. My experience in saying affirmations is that they help connect the affirmation with a conscious effort to displace nonproductive thoughts. However, just *saying* something affirming, over and over again, without any action associated with it, doesn't displace unwanted *behavior*; at least not for long. Expressing affirming thoughts in word *and* deed will get it done faster and better.

"Hold on, John. I'm not the idiot here. I'm just trying to learn how to live with one."

"Gotcha covered on that, Shirley. That could be your affirmation."

"I'm not the idiot here?"

"Yes. That's what needs affirming."

Shirley thinks for a moment. "I need to live the way I want to live *in spite* of my significant idiot."

"Kind of like the way you're now allowing your son and daughter-in-law to live their own lives."

"Yes. Once I realized I was trying to control them, I looked more deeply into what might be making me unhappy. I realized I was giving up what *I* wanted to do to make my husband happy."

"He never asked you to give anything up, right?"

"There was just this understanding that I lived by."

"Have you found something about him you can appreciate?"

"Once I focused on him, I found a lot about him I appreciate."

"A compliment now and then...?"

"Works like a charm," she says. "But sometimes, in my weak moments, I feel like I'm becoming invisible again."

"Why?"

"It's a throwback to the childhood shame stuff."

"How do you get out of it?"

"I tell myself, *it's okay to do what Shirley wants.* Everything will be fine."

"Sounds affirming to me, in a practical way."

"It is. I have some of my favorite verses and other truisms, from people such as Benjamin Franklin and Helen Keller, on my refrigerator and kitchen bulletin board for those moments when I need loftier inspiration."

"It sounds like you're focused on taking care of *you*, Shirley."

"I'm getting better at it every day."

"As far as I know, that's still the best way to live with an idiot."

Life Fountains

Affirming Amoebas

Speaking of Stuart Smalley, there is a suspicious amount of amoeba-like behavior there. I particularly like the stay-in-bed-and-eat-Fig-Newtons-all-day way of comforting himself when he feels inadequate to the challenges of daily living. Talk about making yourself invisible. It wasn't so long ago I couldn't have stayed in bed all day if I'd had a leg amputated that morning. My self-worth was tied too closely to accomplishment. I had amoeba-like moments. But I couldn't pull it off for an entire day.

It would be interesting to bug an amoeba's house and listen for any affirmations that might be said. I'll wager we'd hear a lot of sighs and, "Oh, well. This, too, shall not pass." Amoebas tend to have the invisibility thing down to a science. Saying affirmations like, "I'm going to work out, become strong, and beautiful to behold," would just make an amoeba faint.

Still, I like to affirm everyone I come into contact with—it helps displace negative grousing. I don't mean spreading compliments around like Johnny Appleseed. I believe in consistent affirmation of my beliefs. To not offer affirmation to others would undo that. The result is: affirming others through expressions of appreciation—such as listening, nodding, and complimenting—underscores my appreciation of the things I choose to do. I especially love to affirm amoebas, just to watch them squirm.

Beaver Affirmation

Shirley could be the matron saint of co-beavers everywhere. Being a busy beaver is a good and natural thing, as long as the beaver is busy doing positive beaver things. The achiever beaver is a good example. With a positive attitude and outlook, these busy beavers are building for the future in a way that makes all fur-bearers proud. Co-beavers, if still entangled in their vicious cycle of expectations and resentments, are equally busy. But weighed down by resentment and revenge, they never make any progress and usually feel like they're slipping farther behind.

Once a co-beaver breaks through to the understanding, as Shirley did, affirmation becomes a wedge against backsliding. Shirley is a highly productive co-beaver by definition. So am I. A good recovery group, good friends and mentors, and new skills and habits brought all that about. Affirmations for ourselves and others reinforce us and keep us on track. You can't affirm others until you have something to affirm. That belief becomes a beacon.

Beavers believe streams should be dammed. Not all farmers share their belief, but God planted that idea in their heads, nonetheless. It's a beacon. A road map for a beaver's day. The bucolic beaver's laid-back work habits and the achiever and co-beaver's more frenetic approach notwithstanding, the beaver agenda stands. Every tree gnawed down, every dam and lodge built is an affirmation of what they believe.

You also know what you need to do. Sometimes you feel lost, alone, and without a clue. But how long does it take with a trusted adviser before you realize you knew what to do all along? If living with an idiot cramps your style, you can make maintaining your style a priority. The idiot will just have to deal with it. If your style is *not* to live with an idiot, you know you have options. You're not going to reinvent the idiot. At least, not without divine intervention. While knowing and doing are two different things, affirming your belief helps *knowing* become *doing*.

Affirming Altruists

Altruistic Category III Givers look like they have it all together. For the most part they do. The more mature and "together" people are, the more they're willing to admit they need to continuously affirm what they believe. They do this by surrounding themselves with mature and "together" people. They reflect on what they think and do, and ponder if there are better ways. Did they miss something?

At the end of the day, the constancy of their lives and the strength of their relationships affirm they're operating with a healthy belief system. Doing the right thing, the next right thing, and the next, requires faith in their belief system. The belief system becomes second nature with consistency over time. Although altruists appear to be lucky, their luck is no accident. It's a strong belief system, affirmed daily.

Black Holes

Affirming Garden Slugs

Affirm what? That life is better when well rested? Believe it or not, breathing sofa cushions have beliefs, such as that one. As long as it keeps working out for them, garden slugs get all the affirmation they want. Even though you didn't make garden slugs the way they are, waiting on them hand and foot doesn't exactly discourage them. Enabling slugs neither helps or hurts them. They are who they are.

The question is: "What is it doing to me?" Is waiting on garden slugs affirming what you believe? If you keep doing it, the answer must be yes. If you truly believe that waiting hand and foot on garden slugs is inconsistent with a Higher Power's purpose for your life, don't do it. That's where the proverbial question, "What choice do I have?" originates. The proverbial answer is, "There are always alternatives."

When you verbally affirm a belief and then contradict yourself with your actions, you disaffirm the good you've done. Actions speak louder than words. Words won't displace actions. Actions displace actions. New habits and skills can displace self-destructive habits. The dilemma of the garden slug is a good test. Continuing nonproductive behavior might not hurt anyone. But who does it help? If you feel you're stuck with an idiot, with no way out, you must believe you have no choice. If you didn't believe that, your affirming actions would open up other alternatives.

Jaguar Affirmations

Jaguars affirm themselves constantly. They identify what they want, work hard to get it, and usually do achieve it. You could say their belief system is flawed, if you were the judging type. As it is, their belief system is just jaguar. If you run afoul of it, that's your business. The fact jaguars believe they are sleek, powerful, insufferably attractive creatures comes as no surprise. People tend to see them that way, too. People act accordingly, and so does the rest of the world.

People's attraction to jaguars affirms their natural narcissism. Over time, what does it affirm about you? That you deserve to be in a relationship with a sleek, powerful, and insufferably attractive creature? That you deserve to be in a relationship with another party who sucks up most of the attention? That you deserve to be as sleek, powerful, and insufferably attractive as the jaguar?

It's hard to say what's being affirmed in a jaguar relationship. If you are in one, and you're unhappy, it can mean you have changed what you believe about yourself and others. The ball is in your court, though. You always have the power to choose. You're free to do anything you want. But you're responsible for everything you do.

If you want to make a relationship with a jaguar work for you, the same rules apply. You must decide what you believe and then affirm it with your actions. You owe it to yourself to live in the relationship according to what you believe. The jaguar has every right to reject your beliefs, and vice versa. (That's why it's nice to work out these little details *before* you commit.) When it comes to relationships, when in doubt, don't.

Affirmation and Whirling Vortexes

Whirling vortexes get the impression that their behavior affirms their belief in instant gratification. Unlike jaguars, who hunt and provide for themselves and their broods, vortexes tend to live on the generosity of others. In terms of affirmation, it's the caretaking and providing others do that affirms the vortex's belief system. Wind back the tape to the lowly amoeba, who affirms his or her own self-depreciating role as a sort of self-fulfilling prophecy. The whirling vortex's self-inflating role is affirmed by the admiration of others.

The focus then turns to you. If you're in a relationship with a whirling vortex, what's being affirmed about your beliefs? To bring the shaming vs. affirming issue full circle, the concept of affirmation confirms what you truly believe about yourself. Affirmation can only act as a displacement for shame if you choose against shaming—yourself or others. If your actions affirm the presence of internalized shame, it's time to re-frame what you believe about yourself. If giving everything and getting little except blown away in return works for you, you will stay with a vortex. If not, you will look for what you need and how to go about getting it.

Keys to living with an idiot

⇨ **Believe in something.** As the country song says, "...or you'll fall for anything." Sometimes people resist commitment to strong beliefs for fear they will be labeled. Sometimes they resist because they don't want to invest in a belief system that might collapse like a house of cards. Sometimes people don't feel they deserve to be a part of something bigger than themselves. If someone is sufficiently arrogant, that person might feel he or she has no need to be part of something bigger than him- or herself. I've had my moments in that spotlight. I can't emphasize how important it is for all of us to lock in on a belief system that designates a way of living. I mean consciously consider, decide, and lock in. Here's a news flash: *we already have.* Every action we take is evidence of what we believe about living. If we're unhappy with how we're living (Dr. Phil might say, "It's not working for us"), it's time to get serious about examining our beliefs.

⇨ **Use affirmation as confirmation.** Once you consciously decide how you want to live, you then identify the beliefs that reinforce that lifestyle. In other words, what must you do to live that way? In any situation there can be doubt about whether you're doing something progressive or slipping back into old thinking and behavior. I've found that asking a simple question can clear things up in a hurry. "Is what I'm doing right now affirming what I claim to believe?" If not, I might not really believe what I say I do. Or I might not have the skills and habits to pull it off. That's what books, counselors, pastors, rabbis, support and recovery groups, and prayer are for. The answers are out there, and they're closer than you might think. It's up to you to find them.

⇨ **Affirm yourself and others.** Cynics like to point out that people don't make a difference in the world. "Stick your hand in a bucket of water," they say. "Pull it out and see the impression you left." That might be true in a bucket of water, but not in human relationships. Either negatively or positively, people make an impression. Name a parent, teacher, spouse, significant other, child, in-law, coworker, or boss who didn't weave at least *one* fiber into your personal tapestry. Even idiots alter the system with their words and actions. To be meaningful, an expression of affirmation needs to include words or actions; ideally words *and* actions. Smiles and hugs are actions. Continuously affirming what you believe through actions is essential to making positive changes stick. Affirming the good you see in others, through your actions, strengthens their resolve as well as confirms your own.

Chapter Summary

Like the appreciation trilogy in Chapter 10—appreciating your Higher Power, yourself, and others—the shame-reducing affirming process begins with you. You need to acknowledge and appreciate a relationship with the God of your understanding before you can genuinely appreciate yourself and others. It's important to remember that you can abstain from shaming children and adults, and still shame yourself or allow yourself to remain stuck there. You must believe the God of your understanding doesn't intend for you to live in shame, and will help you liberate yourself from the debilitating effects of shaming others.

To deal effectively with others, many of whom act like complete idiots, you must be able to recognize the signs of shame in them and avoid pouring salt into their wounds. Overreacting to minor aggravations, self-deprecation to the point of self-devaluation, hesitation to meet others eyeball-to-eyeball, and reluctance to stand up for basic entitlements (such as respectful treatment and dignity) are some of the most obvious signs of toxic shame.

You need to identify your belief system and commit to it, no matter what your parents, teachers, spouse, significant other, children, in-laws, coworkers, or bosses think. How you relate to them and the value of those relationships is a big part of your belief system. Things such as, "Working is good." "Paying my mortgage or rent on time is good." "Taking responsibility to make my part of these relationships positive and appropriate is *good.*"

Finally, your words and actions must affirm your beliefs. If there is a disconnect between your words and action and your espoused beliefs, your beliefs are probably wobbly at best. Actions speak louder than words. Behavior over time says most of all. If your actions affirm the beliefs you espouse, dissonance will die down and, with the help of your Higher Power, you can live with whomever you please and get along just fine.

To-do list:

☑ Separate guilt from shame.

☑ Deal with your own and leave the rest.

☑ Displace shame.

☑ Believe in something.

☑ Use affirmation as confirmation.

☑ Affirm yourself and others.

PART III

GOD, ME, AND
THE IDIOTS...
IN THAT ORDER

Chapter 12

Changing Me
Changes Everything

AMOEBAS AND BEAVERS AND SLUGS, OH MY! This whole living-with-an-idiot-thing is the classic good news/bad news scenario. The bad news is that idiots are going to be idiots. There's nothing to be done about that, except, perchance, if the idiots decide to reflect upon the behavior of others that seems to bring balance and happiness to their lives. I wouldn't hold my breath. At Idiots Exposed, we reflect upon the strength and courage gained from trust in a Power greater than ourselves. This allows us to breathe easier.

Some clueless creatures eventually wrap their feeble brains around the concept, pack their shaving kits, a change of underwear, and set off on the long road to recovery. If you're one of the lucky ones, your idiot spouse, sibling, significant other, child, parent, coworker, or boss will be spotted along that road. If you see us, wave. We'll wave back.

The good news is that you can feel better about living with an idiot—whether your clueless friends ever get a clue or not. The new awareness you've created can make the intolerable tolerable, the agonizing entertaining, and the inexcusable—well, that will probably still be inexcusable. While there are limits to everything, it doesn't have to be crazy-making anymore. You can move forward day by day, entertained by charting new ways to navigate old waters, instead of being tossed around by old storms.

Prisms

Each of us looks at others through a personal prism. Many people probably started reading this book hoping it would contain magic words to turn their garden slug into an achiever beaver, an amoeba into a jaguar, or a whirling vortex into a bucolic jaguar (if such a thing even exists). More likely, they're reading this book because the prism they once peered through made a slug look like a jaguar, a co-beaver look like an amoeba, an amoeba look like a bucolic beaver, or a whirling vortex look like an altruistic Category III Giver. Over time, as the prism lost its power to bend light and distort, the real picture became all too clear.

Other people see us through their prisms, too. While our prisms were bending light and distorting the way we once saw our spouses, significant others, siblings, parents, children, postal carriers, coworkers, and employees, their prisms were distorting their perceptions of us. We can't alter their prisms, but we can start being who we really *want* to be, and see how that alters our relationships. Let's be truthful. While I'm play-acting to convince others, and possibly myself, I'm something that I'm not, others might be peering through their prisms at me, pretending I'm something I'm not. Beware the idealized images you conjure of others. They will come back to haunt you.

Sometimes people put on what I call *operational armor.* To succeed in a certain role professionally, some people think they need to show as a jaguar on the outside when they're really a bucolic beaver on the inside. Over time, though, beavers in jaguar fur grow weary of keeping up the illusion, and start acting like beavers again, forgetting to remove the fur. They look silly. Jaguars in beaver pelts will eventually betray their identities and start acting like jaguars. In a pelt, with 2-inch incisors, and a flat tail, jaguars look even sillier.

Now that both you and I know more about the idiots we live with, our serene and sanguine life with spouse, significant other, siblings, parents, children, postal carriers, coworkers, and employees will depend on two things: mental preparation and how we express ourselves. The mental preparation can come from meditation, reflection, prayer, reading, opening our soul in trusted company, and/or listening to wise counsel. We will express ourselves through new actions, and new words, and, hopefully, find new results.

It will help us to know the difference between *conveying* information for the sake of informing, and trying to *convince*. There's nothing wrong with trying to be convincing; especially on matters of which we're already convinced. We need to beware of the tendency for convincing to cross the line and become an attempt to *control*. There's a big difference. With awareness of our motives, we can keep from mixing up conveying, convincing, and controlling.

Idiot-Speak

Idiot-speak is a language through which you can effectively express yourself to the important people in your life and, equally important, communicate with your own inner idiot. In other words, find a way to be heard. Seeing people as clearly as possible helps you take care of you, and be authentic with yourself and others. Fur-bearing animals should wear fur and hairless creatures should remain hairless. That starts with seeing yourself and your significant idiots without distortion. No prisms.

Part of learning idiot-speak, or anyone else's unique language for that matter, is paying attention to your idiots' behavior over time. They express themselves through words and actions just like you do. When you anticipate how others are going to behave, you minimize your angry and startled reactions. If you speak in Venution to a Martian, it's no wonder they tune you out. Speaking their language takes planning, but when you do, the amount of our data they manage to download increases exponentially.

Anticipating

"That makes me so mad."

"*Makes* you?"

"Okay, I cho-o-o-ose to get mad. But he does that all the time."

"What led you to believe this time would be any different?"

"Nothing."

"Then why get mad?"

Besides being an antidote for anger, anticipating is also an alternative to assuming. Anticipating prepares you. Assuming can hang you out to dry. I'm not referring to morbid anticipation of the worst in everything and everybody. Anticipation means forethought, planning, and preparing. Assuming, as I'm using the term, means prejudging in a way that doesn't prepare you for a variety of outcomes. Assuming the worst limits what you're prepared for. It's better to anticipate a range of possible outcomes.

The language of sports is one of the easiest and simplest to master. If, say, the garden slug is watching a football game on TV and you need him to take out the garbage, try saying, "During the next *time-out,* I want you to score a *touchdown* at the dumpster." During a televised hockey game, "*Between periods,* I want you to *score a goal* in the dumpster." Between innings, "I want you to *hit one out* of the pantry and into the *center-field* dumpster." "When *time expires,* I want you to *suit up* so we won't be late for the *opening* dinner *buzzer* at the Whimple's tonight." If your child is in ballet or just has an iPod surgically implanted in his or her ear, *dancing* all the way to the dumpster might be a concept they could grasp.

Long ago, you learned the words, phrases, and tone of voice that drives your spouse, significant other, siblings, parents, children, co-workers, and employees up the wall. If you pay as much attention to what gets through to them as what sets them off, you won't have to pull them off the ceiling so often. The act of making a request or expressing a want or a need is not the time to deliver stingers and sarcastic remarks. Mixing messages like that gives the receiver permission to shut down in self-defense.

Anticipating also means dealing with your own *inner* idiot's track record. Not goofy internal alter-egos with red noses and clown make-up. I'm talking about the confused person inside who always manages to get your best intentions tangled in the underbrush of your worst resentments. You need to get your own story straight if you're going to have any chance of being heard. You need to be heard if there's to be any chance of getting what you want. If what I want is to rip a little flesh from my significant idiot with sarcasm, why bother couching it with any other message? I don't recommend ripping flesh under any circumstances. Ergo, I don't recommend sarcasm. Your emotional health and well-being will be better served by effectively addressing the issue that enraged you in the first place. That's the long-term solution. You can help your inner idiot get his or her act together by anticipating future behavior based on past performance.

Re-framing

What is it you want to communicate through idiot-speak? Why do you want to communicate it? In short, *what do you want?* For many of us, asking this question requires enormous re-framing. To know what you want is to know what to ask for, in a language you *and* they will understand. Here's some tough love for your inner idiot: "If we don't ask, how will they know?" While it continues to be a struggle to ask outright for what I want, I accept that not asking is giving up. Like I said before, to play read-my-mind games and hope others will give me what I want is like hoping to win the lottery without buying a ticket.

It's always a good idea to begin a statement with the other person's name if you want to be heard. "Harry, I want...." Harry might respond with, "Oh, yeah, well *I* want...." Harry just gave you some good information. It might not be the immediate and complete gratification you want. But you've started a dialogue with Harry that up until this point, has only been in your head.

Harry (spouse, father, son, boss, whomever) is now likely to reveal his version of the economy of exchange. It might come as a surprise that Mr.-show-no-emotion-whatsoever has been feeling neglected. You, of course, were avoiding him because he seemed so distant; maybe even sullen. The need for re-framing is obvious, and it all started with an "I want" statement. Having the confidence to organize your wants and needs, and then the courage to share them, is huge.

In spite of your best-laid plans, you run the risk of rejection, which assumes the worst. Being prepared for the worst (anticipating) is part of re-framing. "I'm going to decide what I want, and then I'm going to share that information." You must then be prepared to (a) not be heard; (b) be heard, but ignored; (c) be heard and have your suggestion rejected; (d) be heard and responded to with new information about the other person; or (e) get exactly what you want.

If "e" is the only acceptable outcome within your current frame, buckle up. It will be a bumpy ride. More realistically, "d" will initiate that all-important dialogue that can improve the tone and nature of a relationship so dramatically that you'll forget exactly what it was you were holding out for in the first place. You might have an idealized image of what you want in your head. First getting that thought clear in your own head and then transferring it into someone else's head can open up a realm of possibilities you didn't think were available to you.

If the other person(s) doesn't respond as you wish, and distance themselves even more, you then decide how much you want the desired response, and what you're willing to do to get it. You also know the information you shared made them uncomfortable. Even though the outcomes are beyond your control, you took the right steps and began the process of taking care of yourself. That's an empowering feeling. It's up to you to take care of yourself, not wheedle someone else into seeing it your way.

Complimenting

Expressing yourself through compliments flows naturally out of anticipation and re-framing, and enhances idiot-speak. Anticipating and re-framing are internal processes you can engage in anytime and anyplace, without fear of rejection or disapproval. Compliments also start as internal processes because they need to meet two essential criteria: (a) they should be sincere, not manipulative; and (b) they need to be appropriate.

If you can't think of anything positive to say about someone—preferably something they have done—it's best to let silence do the talking. If you're following the mantra of anticipating and not assuming, you'll look for positive change in the behavior as you've experienced it. Something as simple as: They got out of bed that morning. Their socks match. That shirt and tie actually go together. They got to work on time. They went to work. They came home last night. Sometimes you need to begin with the basics. There's going to be positive behavior in there somewhere.

Say to someone, "I loved that term paper you wrote in college on existential motifs in amoeba sexuality," and you'll probably get a strange look. I'll guarantee you'll get a strange look if: (a) college was 25 years ago, (b) you haven't discussed existential motifs in amoeba sexuality in 25 years, (c) the topic is irrelevant to your current discussion, (d) you wake someone out of a dead sleep to tell them, or (e) the person never went to college. In other words, when you start handing out compliments, you want to anticipate what will be meaningful to our significant idiot. Keep compliments appropriate.

Accepting

Acceptance is another of the seven relational solutions that benefits both inside and out. Staying in reality is key to anticipating, re-framing, and complimenting. If you remain in denial about some aspect of yourself or others, chances increase that you'll miscalculate how to express yourself. Accepting who you are positions you to be yourself with others. Accepting the good or bad outcomes of your best efforts keeps you genuine. Accepting others as they are positions you to be authentic with the relationship. How your significant idiot responds to your best efforts to communicate what you want speaks volumes about who *he or she* really is.

We'll keep the "idiot-speak" classification between us. No sense in being unnecessarily incendiary. But it works both ways. The reason Harry suddenly got honest was because you got honest with Harry. Once you became willing to accept his answer, no matter what it was, you had the courage to express what you wanted. Voila. Harry had wants he hadn't expressed before. Why am I not surprised?

Accepting what's on the inside as well as the outside is part of the cycle of surrender. Serenity to accept what we can't change and courage to change what we can has come into the common vernacular straight from 12-step programs. That's what we ask of our Higher Power. Accepting things and people as they are sometimes takes a lot of trust. That's how surrendering plays out to me—trusting way beyond what I'm comfortable with. Learning new ways to express ourselves is similar. Nothing ventured, nothing gained.

Forgiving

If you or I were to walk around telling people we "forgive them," it would sound a little pompous. If they didn't feel they had done anything to offend us, they'd think we're a little worse than pompous. Consistent with the other relational solutions, forgiving starts inside you. But it really doesn't do you, or anyone else, much good until it's expressed. Expressing forgiveness in idiot-speak is not hard. Cooking someone's favorite meal, doing something you know your spouse, significant other, siblings, children, parents, in-laws, income tax preparers, or anyone else will enjoy, are ways to express forgiveness.

If a person doesn't realize they've done anything wrong, you can still forgive them internally. Your presumption that they did something wrong is your own problem. It becomes a bigger problem if you become resentful and passive-aggressive. Internally forgiving a presumed wrong helps *you* find peace, regardless of what the other person thinks. Your significant idiot will, no doubt, appreciate the relaxed and judgment-free atmosphere. Forgiveness clears the air.

Appreciating

Appreciative words and actions also clear the air of the fog of resentment. Appreciation also works its way from inside out. If appreciation begets appreciation from others, terrific. But like the other relational solutions, that's not why you do it. "Giving to get" is the co-beaver behavior many of us are trying to replace with more genuine giving. Like the other relational solutions, appreciation benefits both the appreciator and the appreciatee only if it's the real deal. Any expression of appreciation that doesn't come from the heart assumes the appreciatee is an idiot.

Dangerous assumption. Expressing appreciation needs to be woven together with all the other relational solutions because appreciatees might not be idiots. Perhaps they act clueless in everything else, but in this one thing, they're pure genius.

I shouldn't make appreciation sound like a preventative measure. But every relational solution used to express your wants, desires, and concerns to your spouse, significant other, siblings, children, parents, in-laws, income tax preparers, or the guy who removes the worms from your computer, is, to some degree, preventative. Operating out of relational sins will tick people off sure as the day is long. Who can blame them? When you find things to appreciate about people, and express those things in a language you, and they, can understand, you've done all you can do. The rest is up to them.

Affirming

If I can reach into the future to copy and paste fear into today, the pain will still be out there waiting. Let it wait. Why give over reality to something that hasn't happened yet? If I have time to catastrophize the future, I have time to plan the next right move. If I can worry, I can work. Nothing affirms us more than making the things happen we have the ability to make happen.

Don't get excited and think, "At last he's going to tell me how to program my idiot." I'm still talking about programming *you*. My friend Roger (with the adolescent son) likes to remind me that we all know how to pull ourselves out of emotional ruts, get unstuck, and start moving in the direction we need to go. Even so, I think it's possible to *not* recognize this information within us. Either way, outside help is often necessary to jump-start recovery.

Roger also reminds me that I can't *think* my way out of my rut, no matter how many affirmations I recite. I can affirm myself mentally, to a point. It's certainly better than beating myself up. The secret is in the *doing*. When I express affirmation by doing things I know will bring positive results, even small ones, I feel confident through and through.

Affirming others through action is also more powerful than mere words. The whole employee-recognition industry is based on affirming professionalism through gifts and incentives. It bears repeating, rewarded behavior is repeated behavior. (Hopefully, it's positive.) Rewarding positive behavior is a language even a recovering idiot can understand. Try me and see. Affirmation through action, both giving and receiving, is assurance that we're on the right track.

Let Go of the Outcomes

The reason most of us resist learning idiot-speak to communicate more clearly is because we fear rejection. If speaking another person's language is what it takes to be heard, the important thing is to be heard. After that, we listen, regardless of the response. By prejudging the response, we muzzle ourselves and limit our chances to get what we want. I hate when that happens. The good news is, I can choose to stop worrying about the outcomes and say what I mean.

Changing allows me to be and feel whatever I choose to be and feel. That's idiot-free serenity. Not that the idiot(s) go away, we just don't let them drag us down anymore. Of course, when I first realized and accepted that I allowed others to rain on my parade, I felt a little idiotic. I didn't stay there long, though. I did something to demonstrate to myself how *not* there I am anymore. I started asking myself how much energy I want to spend worrying about things other people are not doing. The answer is painfully simple: none.

For a long time I've focused tremendous energy on things I wanted people to do, but weren't doing. Now I focus energy on doing the things I've decided are the best actions for *me* to take. Action on my part can open opportunities and increase the likelihood of getting the things I want. Whether the rest of the universe cooperates with my plan is out of my hands. It takes planning and awareness of what I want. Knowing what I want is being aware. It's hard to be aware and idiotic at the same time.

Giving up trying to control outcomes you can't control anyway is like letting go of the big boulder you're clutching. Accepting what comes your way without letting it injure you frees you to start moving again. Giving up and accepting can take work, but the freedom is worth the effort. Giving up your attempts to control outcomes doesn't mean allowing yourself to become vulnerable. If I hear a train coming, I'll get off the tracks.

Keys to living with an idiot

⇨ **Decide what you want.** This continues to be a problem for me from time to time. I'm like *Mad* magazine cover boy, Alfred E. Newman, who said something along the lines of, "I don't know what I want, but I'm pretty sure I don't have it." That makes me kind of like a ship without a rudder. A kite without a tail. A vapor without a trail. It's not an easy exercise for some of us to be specific about what we want. To risk admitting to ourselves, much less anyone else, that we want something specific, sets us up to be let down if we don't get it. "I want my significant idiot to become a genius. No, a *good-looking* genius." Back in reality, when a desire for a basic need gnaws away at you like a beaver on a birch tree, it's best to put a name on it. To not think about what you want in order to avoid being let down is to live powerlessly. Making decisions about what you want is empowering, even if you don't get it.

⇨ **Say what you want.** There is only so much you can do for yourself in a relationship and still call it a relationship. If learning another person's language is what it takes for you to hear them, and for them to hear you, so be it. If identifying what you want is essential to making those needs known, so be that, too. Granted, just admitting what you want to yourself is sometimes difficult. Admitting you want *anything* can be difficult. But you know better, and the longer you putz around with it, the longer you'll be waiting. To whatever extent your needs involve another person, you need to tell them.

Sharing your needs with someone else can be infinitely more difficult than admitting a want or desire to yourself. That's why co-beavers hope to hook up with mind readers, and amoebas keep their thoughts to themselves. In the end, you must speak up or forever hold your peace—just beyond your reach.

⇨ **Let go of the outcomes.** Beginning at the end can make all this possible. If you truly let go of your need to control the outcomes, deciding what you want to begin with, and sharing that with the appropriate parties, gets far less intimidating. You know how: "Let it go, let it go, let it go." As long as you hold on to an expectation and nothing less will do, outcomes are bound to be disappointing. If you let your Higher Power deal with outcomes, you can focus on making the right choices. If things keep ending badly in a relationship, there are choices to make. You need to get your inner idiot under control if you hope to make good choices. There's no place for cluelessness where happiness is concerned.

Teeter-Totters

No matter what kind of relationship you're involved in, it takes two to make it work properly. Parent/child, husband/wife, wife/husband, significant (fill in the blank), sibling/sibling, coworkers, co-players, you name it. If only one person is working at it, it can still work, although it won't be balanced by conventional standards. By doing your part, you give relationships every chance to work. But that's *all* you can do. The more you try to do the other person's part, the more unbalanced you become, until the relationship crashes.

Relationships remind me of teeter-totters. You can't make the contraptions work on your own. Not the way they're designed to work, anyway. It takes two. You *could* stand over the fulcrum, with one leg on either side, and try to keep the plank level. But that would take a more agile idiot than myself.

Co-beavers are quite a sight, controlling the teetering and tottering by running furiously back and forth, from one end of the plank to the other. If the co-beaver stops at one end to rest, he or she will go thumping to the ground. If someone decides to jump on the opposite end when the co-beaver isn't looking, the furry critter will be flung into orbit. Beavers and wooden teeter-totter planks don't mix. Not all beavers can resist their natural impulse to gnaw.

In a perfect world, you do your part and the person at the opposite end does his or her part. As a kid, I learned quickly what happens when the kid on the other end of the teeter jumps off. That sudden jolt to the tailbone got my attention.

I've talked about displacement theory and economy of exchange. Both apply to teeter-totter theory. The balance in relationships comes from what's on both sides of the plank. If the other person has boxes of heavy stuff on his or her side, you need boxes of heavy stuff on your side to balance. But the boxes don't need to be filled with bad stuff, such as resentment and hostility. You can displace any bad stuff in your boxes with positive characteristics and attributes. What fills the boxes across the way is the other person's jurisdiction. You can move stuff around on your end of the teeter, but you can't move the other person's stuff.

You can share with the other person the things you appreciate them bringing to the balance. At least workaholics who make a lot of money—make a lot of money. Non-workaholics, who spend a lot of time with the kids, but don't make a lot of money—spend a lot of invaluable time with the kids. The people on the other side of the totter bring something to relationships or the other side of the plank would be empty.

If there's nobody on the other side of your plank, you're no longer worried about how to live with an idiot; unless it's those ever-present *inner* idiots you're coming to know and love. Maybe you chewed off the other end of the plank and broke the other person's tailbone. Maybe they chewed through yours. Successfully living with an idiot can mean re-framing the teeter-totter scenario while the other person is still riding. Then it's up to them to decide if they like the new arrangement and adjust their balance accordingly.

The alternative is to not teeter or totter. Many amoebas make this choice and remain alone, while whirling vortexes are often seen with a whole crowd on the opposite side of their teeters. What do you include on your side to balance the load? Is it positive or negative? Is it good or bad for you? Is it all you know? Is it time to learn some new lessons? Is it time to change? Ultimately, these choices are yours to make.

Moving the Middle

Whether they realize it or admit it to others, people are always seeking balance in life. Even when things seem out of kilter, there is balance. Otherwise they'd walk around lopsided. I've spent as much time walking lopsided as the next person, but eventually I figure out something's wrong and seek balance again. But (and it's a *big* but) if people don't consciously decide what they need to balance their lives, their sly and clever unconscious will balance the load for them. And we usually don't like what happens when we leave it up to our sly and clever unconscious to balance the load. Our sneaky unconscious usually follows the path of least resistance straight to the lowest common denominator.

In relationships, what you don't get from the other party, you try to provide for yourself, consciously or unconsciously. If you're keeping yourself company, the least you can do is be *good* company. Being with an idiot may be better than being alone. Then again, being alone has its good points. It all depends upon how clueless the creature really is and what you're willing to put up with.

Whatever change you try to make, it's going to *move the middle* and shift your balance. Your entire sense of balance will become unsettled as the fulcrum, or balance point, shifts. You need to realize that any change will create unbalance and affect everyone within your relational system. No one likes feeling out of balance. On the Tilt-A-Whirl at the county fair, it's fun. In your daily life I'm sure you'd rather *not* walk around feeling like you're about to toss your cotton candy.

Yet, those who choose to live differently will move their centers and deal with the nausea until it subsides. Like a child learning to walk, we can all use a balancing hand as we learn new attitudes and behaviors. You can find the names and contact information for support groups, therapists, recovery groups, pastors, rabbis, doctors, and self-help programs at local libraries, churches, hospitals, clinics, community centers, and through the local Department of Community Affairs. Although help, in whatever form you choose, won't give you the ability to walk on new legs overnight, learning to live with a new balance point will take a lot less time if you try it with some help.

To intentionally shift the middle can be scary. It feels as if the earth moves under your feet, and it's not that adolescent-falling-in-love thing. Every synapse in your mind screams, "No. Put the middle back in the middle." "Sorry," you say in a comforting voice. "There is a new middle." Some wait until they just can't hold up both ends of the relationship anymore, and choose to move the middle rather than collapse under the weight.

If learning how to live with the significant idiot in your life is merely a matter of lightening up, you're in pretty good shape. But for many people, learning to relate in new ways and enforcing boundaries is nothing short of terrifying. As a recovering idiot, it blows *my* mind. And my mind isn't the best-manicured garden of sensitivity around. The more I become aware of myself and those around me, the more I realize what a big deal it can be to move the middle.

Ouch

What, give up resentment? Victim-ism? Control-ism? Know-it-all-ism? That smarts. I've never plucked my eyebrows, but I've torn bandages off my hairy legs. Saying "good-bye" to familiar parts of your psyche can hurt like that. Even if they're negative parts, they're *yours*. You know them well.

Giving up behaviors and beliefs that don't work for you is a practical thing to do. But familiarity is usually far more comforting than the unknown, regardless of the promise a positive change offers. It can hurt to give up old, even unsuccessful, habits. The price for replacing old behaviors with new can include the loss of the familiar; chastisement from those who liked the old you better; and friends who accuse you of abandoning them because you will no longer listen to their tales of woe for more than 60 minutes at one sitting.

The hope for a better way of being, with stronger, happier relationships—even with people you already know—can propel you forward in spite of the discomfort. Don't be surprised by mood swings and alternating good days/bad days when working on the new you. Your software suite wasn't written in a day and it can't be *over*written in a day; although it can crash in a nanosecond. Expect error messages. When they appear, reboot. Most of the error messages come from that sneaky inner idiot saying, "Are you sure you want to delete Criticizing 5.0?" Click "Yes." If another window pops up asking, "How will they know when they need to improve?" Type in: "They'll figure it out. And please stop sending error messages when I'm working on myself."

The Helping Hand

"Okay," my Higher Power says. "Take my hand. We'll get through this transition together." I take my HP's hand, and with my first step, my inner voice starts up, "Whoa, Johnny boy. This feels totally weird." (Your inner voice might have a more mature vocabulary than mine, but it will speak up, just the same.) Those inner voices are our inner idiots calling.

Another regular at Idiots Exposed shared how he tried to convince his sponsor early on that he needed to put off doing the next right thing so as not to exacerbate his fear of change. "I'm afraid," he told his sponsor.

His sponsor said, "I know. But do it anyway."

"No," he insisted. "You don't understand. I'm really terrified."

"I understand," the sponsor said calmly. "Do it anyway."

He tried a few more times until he finally got the point and it changed his life. No matter how we feel about doing the next right thing, we need to just do it anyway.

Another IE mentor once told me, "I can't help with how you feel, but I can recommend some things to do." As always, it's the doing, not the thinking, talking, or feeling that changes us. At best, changing ourselves opens up opportunities for others to follow suit. At worst, changing ourselves will have no effect whatsoever on others. But that's not why we changed. We decided to live happier and more fulfilling lives—idiots or no idiots. So, the worst ain't so bad.

Keys to living with an idiot

⇨ **Move the middle.** Learning how to live with an idiot or make any other significant improvement in your life requires change at your very core. Nibbling around the edges won't get it done. Chances are you've been nibbling around the edges of a lot of things for years and, guess what? There has been no appreciable change. What a surprise! The middle can be the fulcrum on which everything balances. It can also be the low point to which everything drains. No matter which purpose the middle serves, it must be moved if true change is going to take place. Imagine a puddle in the laundry room (perish the thought) and the drain is in the high point of the floor. It needs to be moved. Imagine a 10-foot teeter-totter with 3 feet on one side of the fulcrum and 7 feet on the other. It takes *doing* those things you know you can do to move the middle.

⇨ **Adjust your balance.** Shift the load of the entire relationship off your shoulders. Changing to make yourself a complete and authentic person, more capable of holding your space in the universe through any relationship, means shifting your balance point. It might feel like you're in a fun house, walking in rooms *designed* to throw off your sense of balance. But in real life, "fun" is not the word for it. You should expect intentional new behaviors to feel strange. You can balance your new attitudes and behaviors with the progressive elimination of old stuff. If you decide to discontinue sofa-side service to a garden slug, you can do it by reducing one meal a week. Share what's going on. Don't be sneaky. "You're on your own for dinner tonight because I'm going to (fill in the blank)." The fill in the blank could be, "sit in the kitchen, watch *my* channel, and eat *my* dinner." When you take something away, something new needs to be put in its place to bring about the new equilibrium. When you remove something you've relied on emotionally, even if it is not healthy, you need to replace it with something better to maintain balance.

⇨ **Extend a hand.** Someone will take it. If you keep your hands in your pockets, nobody will be able to reach out and help you balance, guide your way, or just let you know you're not alone. Extending beyond yourself can cause unbalance. It seems strange that reaching out for help can cause you to tip, but that's part of reaching out in faith. I hear time after time at Idiots Exposed about how people refused for years to trust enough to reach out. When they finally did, and they felt themselves starting to fall, they suddenly found themselves supported. I relied heavily on intellect to get me through tough times in the past. Truly operating on faith is new to me. I don't mean *having* faith. I mean actually stepping off the cliff and praying I was right to trust. I've done it and I'm still here. With one hand in the God of your understanding's hand, close your eyes and dare to extend your other hand. When someone takes it, look up to see whose hand is in yours. It might be your idiot. Life begins at the edge of your comfort zone. If you don't reach beyond your- self, you can't grow.

Inner Peace

If I want to live in a relationship with trust, I need to be trust*wor- thy,* regardless of what others choose to do. If I want to be worthy of compliments, I need to compliment others. If I want to accept and be accepted by others, I must first accept myself. Then I can accept others. If I want others to forgive me, I must be willing to forgive. If I want to be appreciated, I need to appreciate myself *and* others. If I want to be affirmed, I must be affirming.

All of this is our part, and all we can do is our part. As long as we hold on to bits and pieces of old stuff, refusing to surrender them to our new natures, there won't be a sense of peace. As long as I harbor resentment, I block my own happiness. If I allow idiots to bug me to the point of screaming, who's to blame? Idiot-proofing is the protec- tive coating that comes from doing the things I know to do, and leav- ing the rest to the God of my understanding. Higher Power–assisted steering helps me steer clear of idio-t-syncracies.

Depending on how miserable we've allowed others to make our lives, happy and peaceful moments might seem like the impossible dream. But when they start coming, one at a time, then two back to back, getting a little longer each time, they feel like warm sunshine on a cold winter day. "I know it's cold all around me, with ice and snow everywhere. But that sun feels so go-o-o-o-d. Just right here, right now, it feels great." Knowing the warm, peaceful feeling is out there is great incentive to keep doing things to take care of ourselves, just like we take care of others. No less. More doing, over time, means more peace.

Chapter Summary

Because I view everything and express myself through my frame, changing my frame gives me a whole new perspective. What a great gift from above. I am empowered. I can re-frame my world and rein- vent my relationship to everything in it—even idiots—just by chang- ing my choices. I can redistribute my load and adjust the balance of my life. My significant idiots and others might push back at my new boundaries, but my choices will take root as I start to feel better about myself.

"Get used to it," I tell them with confidence. "This is the new me and I'm not going backwards. If you want to come along for the ride, I'd enjoy the company. If you want to hear how I'm doing it, pull up a chair. From now on, I'm a complimenting, accepting, forgiving, appreciating, and affirming *machine.*"

Privately, we can rehearse loving and accepting our inner idiots. It's a safe arena to practice how we'll handle the clueless creatures that live around us. Close your eyes. Breathe deeply, slowly, and steadily. Look out into your inner space. Can you see your inner idiot standing there? Say, "It's okay. You can come closer." As your inner idiot approaches, smile and open your arms. Give your inner idiot a big hug. "It's okay," you say again, resting your hands on your inner idiot's shoulders. "We're going to get through this—together—and it's going to be great."

I caught Shirley on the way into the meeting Thursday night. She looked relaxed from her head to her toes. I noticed the difference immediately. She was smiling as if she were 20 years younger and 10 pounds lighter. "How was dinner with your son and daughter-in-law, Shirley?"

Her smile grew wider still. "It was a miracle."

"That good?"

"Better."

"Tell me about it."

"I'll give you the *Reader's Digest* version, 'cause I'm going to share the whole thing in group tonight."

"What happened?"

"They changed."

"Really?"

"They were happier and more relaxed than I've seen them in years. Even my husband had a good time."

"You don't say."

"My daughter-in-law called earlier that day and asked me to choose the restaurant, so I thought about it and told her where I wanted to go."

"Great."

"When we met them there, I told her how pretty she looked."

"Wonderful."

"They were the first words out of my mouth."

"What did she say?"

"She thanked me and told me how nice I looked."

"Your son?"

"He gave me a big hug and kiss." Shirley leaned closer to whisper. "He was so excited to see his wife and mother getting along that he couldn't stop smiling. He even hugged his father."

"Get out."

"It's just incredible how...how...," she smiled, looking up toward the sky as if her next words were inscribed somewhere in the clouds.

I opened my eyes wider and waited. It wasn't so long ago that I would have finished her sentence for her. But I really wanted to hear what was going to come out of her mouth.

"...how *good* it feels not to live with all that tension between us all the time."

"Wow," I said. "Shirley, I'm so happy for you."

"All I did was re-frame the relationship in my own mind."

"I think you did more than that."

"That's where it started. Then I thought about the relationship and surrendered the whole thing to my Higher Power. A wee, small voice said, 'You do your part, and I'll do mine.' With that load off my shoulders, I said and did the things I knew would affirm her and let her know that I appreciate her. I did so little and the change was huge."

"Who changed?" I asked, genuinely curious to hear her answer.

"I did for starters," she said with a laugh. "But both she and my son responded. For that I'm truly grateful." She pressed her palms together like a child in prayer.

I nodded my head.

"They didn't have to, you know," she went on.

I nodded my head in agreement.

"After I prayed about the things I was going to start saying to her and the ways I was going to respect her home and her decisions, a peaceful feeling came over me. Even my husband noticed."

"Did he say anything?"

"No," she said with a slightly more impish grin. "He just smiled at me for the first time in years and now he touches my shoulder when he walks by my chair or my arm as he passes me in the kitchen."

I returned her impish grin.

"Opportunity," she said as if the word were written on the side of the church behind me in 3-foot letters.

"Opportunity?" I repeated, tempted to turn around and look, until I noticed her eyes boring into mine with an evangelistic passion.

"Doing the next right thing, and the next right thing, and the next, and the next," she said, "guarantees nothing."

I raised my eyebrows a little.

"I can't *make* another person in a relationship respond in any way other than how they choose. All I can do is my part. I can't guarantee happiness, but I can quit doing the things that block it."

I nod in agreement as she raises her index finger to drive home her point.

"And there are a lot of things I *can* do. I focus on the positive things I can do, whether anybody responds to me or not. Then, by doing them, one after the other, I can create *opportunities* for the relationships I want. That's so exciting. I've always had the power to shut myself off from people or drive wedges into relationships with my words and action. But until now, I never realized I could *open up* all the possibilities for the kind of relationship I really want by choosing other words and actions."

She smiled at me again and blinked both her eyes in excitement. I held my hands shoulder high, palms up, shrugged my shoulders, and shook my head. I was speechless. Shirley had said it all.

To-do list:

- ☑ Decide what you want.
- ☑ Say what you want.
- ☑ Let go of the outcomes.
- ☑ Move the middle.
- ☑ Adjust my balance.
- ☑ Extend a hand.

Index

About the Author

John Hoover, Ph.D., holds a master of arts degree in marriage and family therapy from Azusa Pacific University in addition to his master's and doctorate degrees in human and organization development from the Fielding Institute in Santa Barbara. Dr. John is a popular speaker, organizational leadership/communications consultant, and executive coach. You can learn more about Dr. John at *www.idiotworld.org*.

His books include:

⇨ *Unleashing Leadership: Aligning What People Do Best With What Organizations Need Most* with Angelo Valenti, Ph.D. (Career Press, in press for 2005).

⇨ *How to Work for an Idiot: Survive and Thrive Without Killing Your Boss* (Career Press, 2003).

⇨ *Leadership When the Heat's On*, revised edition with Danny Cox (McGraw-Hill, 2002).

⇨ *Think Out of the Box* for Mike Vance and Diane Deacon (Career Press, 1995).

⇨ *Seize the Day: 7 Steps to Achieving the Extraordinary in an Ordinary World*, revised edition with Danny Cox (Career Press, 2002).

⇨ *An American Quality Legend: How Maytag Saved Our Moms, Vexed the Competition, and Presaged the Quality Revolution* with Robert J. Hoover (McGraw-Hill, 1993).